Famous
AMERICAN
FREEMASONS

Todd E. Creason

To my three girls:
Valerie, Jaclyn & Kathryn

And to the memory of my great friend,
Jack F. Babey

Library of Congress Cataloging in Publication Data

Creason, Todd E. (1967-)

Great American Freemasons / Todd E. Creason.

p. cm.
Includes bibliographical references.
ISBN 978-1-4357-0345-2
1. Freemasons—History. 2. Freemasonry—United States—History.

Copyright © 2007 by Todd E. Creason

All rights reserved. No part of this book may be reproduced or transmitted in any form or by any means, electronic or mechanical, including photocopying, recording, or by any information storage and retrieval system, without the written permission of the Author.

Published by Lulu.com

Printed in the United States of America

Acknowledgements

Without question, writing a book is not a single effort. There were a lot of people who contributed, whether they knew it or not. I'd like to take this opportunity to thank some of them.

To my editor and mother, Jane Creason, who spent countless hours correcting my grammar and punctuation, making suggestions, and checking my facts. Much of the credit for how this turned out can be attributed to her excellent editing skills which have been honed to perfection over decades of teaching English and rhetoric, and grading thousands and thousands of poorly written papers—in other words, she was uniquely qualified to edit my prose. Without her contribution and feedback, this book would have been a lot more challenging to read to say the very least. I have often wondered over the last few months, how I might fair in one of her college rhetoric classes—and what kind of grade she might give this book. Perhaps there are some questions best left unanswered.

To my wife, Valerie, who has been listening to my impromptu lectures on American history for over a decade now, usually, she remarks, when we are in the car and she can't get away. When I finally decided to write this book, she listened to my early ideas and helped me put them together into this form. She also gave me the freedom to write, taking on a much larger share of the responsibilities of home life. I had no idea this was going to be such a massive project when I started. And did I mention we had a baby girl, Kathryn Marie, during the period I was researching and writing this book? Thank you, Valerie.

To my friends at Ogden Lodge No. 754 in Ogden, Illinois, I'd like to give special thanks for accepting me and making me one of their brothers. I have enjoyed few things as much as the time I've spent with these men. In particular, I'd like to give special thanks to Brother Stephen "Hoop" Hooper who was instrumental in my becoming a Mason. I'd also like to thank Carl W. Lewis, who selflessly spent many evenings helping me to become a Master Mason, and Brother Denver Phelps, a true patriot who shares the same deep love of history and tradition that I do.

To the members of the Scottish Rite Valley of Danville, I give special thanks for encouraging me to get involved after I joined in Spring 2006. I dedicate Chapter 15 to the directors and cast of the 26th Degree for giving me my first opportunity to participate in a Scottish Rite degree. The original idea for writing a book came from that experience. Hopefully, I'm a better writer than I am an actor . . . and I can hear a few of them saying "well, you wouldn't have to be a very good writer . . . "

To my daughter Jaclyn Creason, who, with the help of her friend Bud Jenkins, helped me decide which Americans to profile in this book. We sat down one evening and went through a very long list of names of Freemasons I had assembled as possible candidates for inclusion in my book. It may seem odd that a couple teenagers helped me as much as they did, but they actually helped me in two ways—knowing which famous Americans they had learned about in school was just as important for me to know in compiling the final list as knowing which individuals they had not learned anything about—and should have.

To my friend Jack Babey, one of the best friends I've ever had. He was fascinated by the topic of Freemasonry, and when I had the idea of writing a book on the subject, he had a lot of very good ideas, many of which I have used. Jack passed away in November of 2006, and there is seldom a day I don't think about him.

★ ACKNOWLEDGEMENTS ★

To Billie Scales, who rarely failed to asked me on a daily basis how this book was coming along. Her persistent inquires very often drove me to continue working on it, even during some of the more difficult phases of the project. You don't have to ask anymore, Billie. It's done.

And to a group of my oldest friends affectionately known as "The Board" I give special thanks for their kind remarks and encouragement. They read excerpts of this book from the beginning, and helped convince me that what I was writing was actually interesting. In fact, one of these old friends is a school teacher and used excerpts from one of my chapters in her lesson plans. I am truly blessed by the friends I have made in life.

And finally, my great thanks to my father, Don Creason, who first inspired my interest in history through his insatiable appetite for collecting antiques. I learned a lot about antiques from him growing up, and it was only natural as a result I developed a curiosity about the past. He contributed to the book in a big way also. While writing this, he saved the day by finding a one hundred and seven year old book documenting the issues and participants in the Presidential election of 1900. It was an invaluable research source in two of the chapters in this book.

Thank you, one and all, for your encouragement and assistance in writing this book. Without your involvement, I never would have had the idea to begin with, and I could never have finished it alone.

Todd E. Creason
Thanksgiving Day, 2007

Contents

Acknowledgements   3

Introduction   11

AMERICAN PATRIOTS
1. The General   25
2. The Sage   33
3. The Friend   41
4. The Warrior   49
5. The Rider   57

AMERICAN PRESIDENTS
6. The Era of Good Feelings   67
7. Old Hickory   77
8. The First Modern President   86
9. The Rough Rider   94
10. The New Dealer   102
11. Where the Buck Stops   111
12. The Healer   119

MILITARY MEN
13. The Stand   129
14. The Charger   137
15. Friendship and War   146
16. The Raider   155
17. The Hero   164

AMERICAN ENTERTAINERS
18. The Musician   175
19. The Writer   183

20.	The Raconteur	191
21.	The Cowboy Philosopher	199
22.	The Singer	206
23.	The American	214

AMERICAN LEGENDS

24.	The Explorers	225
25.	The Equalizer	232
26.	The Empresario	240
27.	The Old Scout	249
28.	The Aviator	258
	Conclusion	265
	Bibliography	*273*

Famous AMERICAN FREEMASONS

"From the mountains, to the prairies,
To the oceans white with foam,
God bless America,
My home, sweet home."

—*Irving Berlin*
Munn Lodge No. 190, NY

Introduction

This is not a book about Freemasonry. This is a book about Freemasons. There are no Masonic secrets revealed here. There are no ancient mysteries uncovered or myths debunked. There are books like that if that is what you are interested in, but this is not one of them. This is a book about Americans—great Americans who also happened to be Freemasons. And this is also a story of American history and American culture—told through the lives and accomplishments of some of those men who molded our country, each in his own unique way.

Writing this book was a labor of love—and a long time in coming. I have been studying American history for most of my adult life. I am neither a historian nor a Masonic scholar. I am just an American who has always been interested in the story of America and in the men who created it. America's emergence as a nation is a fascinating story. Those of you who are familiar with it will understand that it is a miraculous story—miraculous because America was first able to secure her freedom from England and then survive the many adversities that followed—civil war, economic upheavals, assassinations, World Wars, civil rights, terrorism, corruption.

There are few subjects more interesting or more important than history, but, as a whole, Americans know very little about their own past. There are few topics more neglected in public schools than American history. Fortunately, things are beginning to change as more Americans are taking an interest in history. Thanks to the efforts of modern writers like James

Flexner, Joseph Ellis, David McCullough, H. W. Brands, and William J. Bennett, American history is being presented in a style that appeals to the general reader. As a result, history is beginning to come alive in the minds of Americans. Instead of seeing history as a collection of dull dates forced upon them in school or some verdigris-encrusted monument on an old battlefield or a crumbling statue collecting pigeons in front of the courthouse, Americans are able to see their history in color. They are rediscovering the flesh and bone characters and the events behind the marble and sandstone monuments. Television has contributed in a positive way to this resurgence of interest in American history as well. Television channels such as PBS, History Channel, History International, and Discovery have done an excellent job of producing interesting and accurate programming that brings history into the living rooms of millions of Americans.

When studying American history, I found one interesting side note over and over again—references to Freemasons and Freemasonry. I have also done a lot of reading about Freemasonry. What has fascinated me the most is the idea that there is still today an institution which has remained largely unchanged by the passage of centuries—yet nobody really seems to know for certain where it came from. Even more interesting is that the fraternity holds true not only to following the ritual traditions but also to teaching the same set of principles and moral values that its members have held to be honorable and virtuous since the fraternity began.

Masonry has always been shrouded in myth and mystery, possibly because it has been around so many years, but more probably because of the inherent secrecy of the organization. Freemasonry has been fodder for conspiracy theorists going back to the founding of the Grand Lodge of England in 1717. With the founding of that lodge, Freemasonry went from being a society that met clandestinely in secret locations with members known only by other members of the society to being a publicly known fraternity whose membership is known to all.

★ INTRODUCTION ★

But Masons still guard their secrets. The rituals for opening and closing the lodge and for the initiation of new members are still considered Masonic secrets. This sustained secrecy continues to generate myths about the society.

Among the most interesting of these myths are the ones about Freemasonry and its involvement in the American Revolution and later in the founding of the United States of America. One of the most prevalent myths is that Freemasons planned and organized the events that led up to the Revoltionary War—that America was founded by Freemasons. In fact, according to these myths, America was a nation founded on the principles of Masonry.

Masons enjoy being surrounded by myths about their involvement in the creation of this great nation as much as the conspiracy theorists enjoy creating them. To this day, Masons do not deny these claims—nor do they admit to them. In fact, Masons throughout history have had little to say about any of the outrageous myths about them, and this is much of the reason these myths exist at all. Modern day Masons are proud of the fact so many of their brethren were involved in the events that led to the founding of the United States of America. This is not a myth, this is the truth.

Masonry was wide spread at the time of the Revolutionary War, but its involvement in it was not nearly as great as these later myths would claim. But, as with all good stories, there is just enough to make these myths seem plausible. The fact is many of our founding fathers were Freemasons since Freemasonry was so prevalent in America at the time, especially among influential men. Conspiracy theorists claim the proof of Freemasonry's involvement in the events which led up to the Revolution and the founding of the United States can be found in many places. They often cite the number of Freemasons involved in the Revolution. But this is where fact and fiction divide.

One of the most common misconceptions is that the majority of the fifty-six signers of the Declaration of Independence were Freemasons. Conspiracy writers often cite that somewhere between fifty-one and fifty-five were Freemasons. In fact, of the fifty-six signers, only nine were Masons: William Ellery, Benjamin Franklin, John Hancock, Joseph Hewes, William Hooper, Robert Treat Paine, Richard Stockton, George Walton, and William Whipple. That means that only sixteen percent of the signers of the Declaration of Independence were Masons—hardly a majority.

It is also commonly held that upwards of fifty of the fifty-five members of the Constitutional Convention held in Philadelphia in the spring of 1787 were Freemasons. But the truth is only eighteen of those delegates were Masons: Gunning Bedford, John Blair, David Brearly, Jacob Broom, Daniel Carroll, Jonathan Dayton, John Dickinson, Oliver Ellsworth, Benjamin Franklin, Nicholas Gilman, William Houston, Rufus King, James McClurg, James McHenry, William Patterson, William Pierce, Edmund Randolph, and George Washington. Of the thirty-nine delegates that signed of the Constitution, only thirteen were Masons.

Another myth is that all of Washington's generals were Freemasons. In fact, it has been said that Washington trusted only Masons in leadership roles, which is why, according to these sources, Washington employed only Masons as generals. This myth may have been propagated in part by actual statements made by one of Washington's most famous generals, Marquis de Lafayette, who indicated that once he became a Mason, George Washington's trust in him was strengthened, and shortly thereafter, Washington gave him an important command. The fact is, however, that Washington had sixty-one general officers who served him in the Continental Army—nineteen major generals and forty-two brigadier generals—and only thirty-four of them were Masons. If Washington trusted only the generals who were Freemasons, we can only imagine his surprise and disappointment when one of his trusted Masonic brothers and generals turned traitor to the American cause—Benedict Arnold. American Masons do not have much

★ INTRODUCTION ★

to say about General Arnold. Americans think about as much of Benedict Arnold—the treacherous malcontented traitor—as our British brothers think about their Scottish-born compatriot—and blood-thirsty pirate—John Paul Jones.

In truth, there are without question some interesting correlations between Masonry and the way our early government was set up and with some of the tenets our founding fathers considered important. For instance, Masonic lodge officers have always been elected by the members of the lodge. Once the officers are elected, the primary officer, the Master of the Lodge, appoints other members to the remaining posts in the lodge—not unlike how elections and appointments in government are done today. The basic idea is if the man elected is trusted, the decisions he will make in appointing the remaining positions in the lodge are also trusted. This concept may not seem unusual in today's world, but in the 1700s, this enlightened approach was unique. At the time of the Revolutionary War, there were no public elections and no elected officials. The king of England inherited the throne of power through his bloodline. Governors of territories were appointed by the king, and every important leadership role was either appointed by the king or by the king's governors. The common masses had no choice of who was selected to govern them. They paid taxes as their king and their governors dictated, having little recourse if they disagreed. The concept of the common masses deciding who represented them in positions of power was unknown. Of course, there were some ways for feisty colonial Americans to show their disapproval—like throwing a boatload of goods into a harbor and deciding to become a nation of coffee drinkers.

Another interesting correlation is Masonry's views about religion. Masonic lodges are religious but non-sectarian. They support no single religious belief, only a belief in God. All Masons must profess a belief in God before they are accepted into the lodge. There are no atheists amongst Masons. But beyond professing a belief in God, each man's faith and beliefs are his own—he is never asked what those beliefs are. Since Masonry is about bringing people together, discussions about religion are not permitted within the walls of a Masonic lodge.

Masons come from many religious backgrounds and beliefs. In America, the King James Bible is most commonly found on the altar. In other parts of the world, one might find displayed on the altar the Tanach, the Koran, or the Proverbs of Confucius out of respect for prevalent religious beliefs in that part of the world. In some lodges in Israel, it would not be uncommon to find three sacred texts opened indiscriminately on the altar—the Bible, the Tanach, and the Koran.

In Masonic lodges, prayers and references to God are also non-sectarian in order to respect the variety of religious beliefs that may be represented in the lodge. Terms for the deity vary, but in America, the most common reference to God is "Grand Architect of the Universe," which is compatible with most of the religious beliefs prevalent in American lodges.

Freedom of religion was very important to the founding fathers as well. It was the first civil right granted in the First Amendment: "Congress shall make no law respecting an establishment of religion, or prohibiting the free exercise thereof . . ."

Another connection with the early establishment of America is the Masonic ideal of equality. Every Mason is a brother and an equal, whether he is the Master of the Lodge, the Grand Master of the Grand Lodge of the state, or the newest member of the fraternity. There is no hierarchy in the fraternity. There are those who do more, there are those who take on the responsibility for leading the fraternity, there are those who attain titles because of their willingness to take on these roles, but Masons are all equal—there is no degree higher than the Master Mason, the 3° of Masonry. Many Masonic conspiracy theorists believe that a 32° degree Mason is somehow higher in rank. Those additional degrees, however, only represent an individual brother's desire to learn more about Masonry and in no way determine rank or privilege. The 33° degree is an honorary degree bestowed by the Scottish Rite of

Freemasonry to a brother who has contributed greatly to the fraternity.

Equality was also a very powerful idea in the founding of the nation—the idea that no office, no power, no position granted by the electorate outweigh the rights of the individual. This concept was powerfully and perfectly proclaimed in the Declaration of Independence: "We hold these truths to be self-evident: That all men are created equal; that they are endowed by their Creator with certain unalienable rights; that among these are life, liberty and the pursuit of happiness . . ."

Whether these ideas were borrowed from Masonry or whether they were enacted because they were seen as the right way of doing things may never be known for certain. Masonry has a long history of bringing together people of many different backgrounds and beliefs. The two topics that early Freemasons saw as ones which created division were religion and politics, so these topics, centuries ago, were determined to be unsuitable for discussion in the fraternity. Masonry has never been, nor is it ever likely to be, a political, religious, or militant organization.

Nearly every reliable source indicates it is unlikely that the ideas for Revolution were hatched out in the politically and religiously neutral Masonic lodges. There is an excellent story, cited in *The Complete Idiot's Guide to Freemasonry* by S. Brent Morris PhD., 33°, which epitomizes the attitude of Freemasons during that time.

During the Revolutionary War, Unity Lodge No. 18 was a military lodge attached to the British Army's Seventeenth Regiment of Foot; it was chartered by the Grand Lodge of Pennsylvania which was then held by British loyalists. A military lodge has a charter granted to a unit, not to a single location. It is a traveling lodge that moves with the unit during its military operations. There were military lodges on both sides of the Revolutionary War. At the Battle of Stony Point, New York, during the fighting against American forces, the British lodge's charter and regalia fell into the hands of General Samuel H. Parsons of the Continental Army. But Parsons, who belonged to American Unity Lodge, saw fit, even during war time, to return the property to the British lodge with a note:

West Jersey Highlands, July 23, 1779

Brethren: When the ambition of monarchs or jarring interest of contending states, call forth their subjects to war, . . . and however our political sentiments may impel us in the public dispute, we are still Brethren, and (our professional duty apart) ought to promote the happiness and advance the weal of each other. Accept therefore, at the hands of a Brother, the Constitution of the Lodge Unity No. 18, to be held in the 17th British Regiment which your late misfortunes have put in my power to restore to you.

Samuel H. Parsons.

Unity Lodge No. 18 again lost its charter in 1786. To obtain another charter, members turned to their former enemies, who had regained control of the Grand Lodge of Pennsylvania. Unity Lodge No. 18 offered to pay all back dues, and the Grand Lodge of Pennsylvania welcomed them back, allowing them to pay whatever dues they thought they owed on the "honor system."

It is a great story that Freemasonry influenced the events of the Revolutionary War and the founding of the United States—but it is just that, a story. What cannot be disputed is that some great men who also happened to be Freemasons were involved. Without those men, some of whom played central roles in the founding of America, the goals to secure freedom from Britain would have most assuredly failed. The ideas of freedom and basic human rights were new ideas—ideas that incited the colonists into armed conflict and led to

★ INTRODUCTION ★

the Declaration of Independence, the Revolutionary War, and finally, the Constitution.

After I began researching the subject of Masonry, I began to notice the signs and symbols of the fraternity everywhere I went. I noticed the symbols on cars passing me on the interstate. I saw the symbols on buildings. I saw the symbols on cemetery stones. And one evening, when I saw a Masonic symbol on a ring worn by a friend of mine, I asked him about it. After several long conversations on the subject, I joined them.

In the years since I became a Mason, I have developed a great affection for Masonry and greater still for the men I have had the privilege of knowing. I have met men from many walks of life with a variety of religious beliefs, ethnic persuasions, and economic and educational backgrounds. These men come together peacefully and voluntarily; they perform their work and accomplish many remarkable things together, not because they feel they must but because they want to. Their differences are many, but they all share a common bond—they are Masons. Their strength is in their ability to build on their commonalities instead of letting their differences divide them.

In my research about Freemasonry and later in my experiences within the fraternity, I have come to realize that there are a lot of words that no longer carry the strength they once did in American culture—words like honor, character, virtue, responsibility, justice, duty, freedom, equality, and tolerance. But there is a place where, in the hearts and minds of its members, these words and ideas still carry the same weight and still hold the same meanings that they have had for centuries. There is a place where men still strive towards their own improvement through their entire lives towards these ideals, and, in the process, they make themselves better men, stronger citizens, more involved community leaders, and better husbands and fathers.

I considered writing a book on Masonry, but the libraries and bookstores are crowded with such books, written by better authorities than I am. In my research, I found a lot of myths and misconceptions about Freemasonry, along with outright criticism of the organization. I considered writing a book to debunk some of those myths and misconceptions, but those books also exist.

I finally found my book topic after I joined the Scottish Rite and became a 32° Mason. The degrees in the Scottish Rite are performed as stage plays, each allegory teaching a particular moral, virtue, or tenet deemed important for Masons to master. I was invited to play a small part in one of the allegories. This degree was a period piece set against the backdrop of the Battle of Gettysburg during the Civil War. The characters in the allegory were real participants in the Battle of Gettysburg—names from American history that I knew well. While I knew the characters and the events, what I did not know from my previous studies was that all the men involved in that historical event were Masons. I began to wonder about famous American Freemasons and what their unique contributions to our history and culture have been.

This book is a partial answer to that question. It would have been difficult to include all the famous Masons I found in my research since I found literally hundreds. William Denslow's 1957 book, which includes an introduction written by Harry S. Truman, is entitled *10,000 Famous Freemasons*. It profiles a large number of the fraternity's most illustrious and accomplished members, and there are more famous Masons who could be added to that impressive list since Denslow's book was published fifty years ago.

I determined the best way for me to describe Freemasonry was not to tell the history of Masonry or to explain the principles or even to debunk the myths. Instead, the best way was to describe some of the men who have been involved. I decided to let Freemasonry be judged by the company it keeps.

My hope is that you will learn something about the kinds of men who have been involved in the world's oldest fraternal organization. Even more, I hope that you will learn

★ INTRODUCTION ★

something about this great country of ours that will lead you to further exploration of American history. Hopefully, you will continue this journey through the vast tapestry of remarkable events and people that populate our past. You will find here only a very few—patriots, Presidents, military leaders, entertainers, and those who can only be described as American legends. For every one I have included in this book, there are many more waiting for you to discover, and, in the process, you will learn more about our country—and the principles and ideals upon which it was founded.

You may even find within yourself some small spark of pride, some glimmer of patriotism that seems to be lacking in today's world. If you do, I have fulfilled my original intent.

AMERICAN PATRIOTS

"We must, indeed, all hang together or, most assuredly, we shall all hang separately."

—*Benjamin Franklin*
St. John's Lodge, PA

ONE

The General

"A government is like fire, a handy servant, but a dangerous master."

His Indian name was Conotocarius, the same name that had been given to his great-grandfather over a century before. He had a great love of the outdoors, of exploration, and of adventure. His first job was surveying the lands owned by the wealthy Fairfax family—lands that extended west of the Blue Ridge Mountains and into the wilderness of the Shenandoah Valley region. On one of his first grand adventures as a surveyor at the age of sixteen, Conotocarius found himself lost for awhile in the Blue Ridge Mountains. He encountered a rattlesnake and swam his horses across rivers and streams bursting with water from the winter thaw. But despite the hardships of that first journey, he was not deterred; in fact, the journey invigorated him. On that same trip, he encountered a group of Indians, one of whom carried a scalp with him. When encouraged with rum, the Indians performed a rarely seen dance for Conotocarius—the war dance.

Little did that group of Indians know that Conotocarius would go on to become one of the greatest warriors and chiefs in the history of the world, but not a chief or warrior of the Indian nation. Conotocarius, which meant "town taker," was aptly named. He would become famous for taking towns—Boston, Lexington, Yorktown, and New York. Conotocarius is better known in American history as General George Washington.

George Washington towered above the Second Continental Congress on June 16, 1775. He was a giant of a man for his time, standing over six feet tall with broad shoulders and massive hands. He was dressed in his blue uniform with buff trim, which he had taken to wearing to each session of the Second Continental Congress. Benjamin Rush said of him, "He has so much martial dignity in his deportment that you would distinguish him to be a general and a soldier from among ten thousand people."

Washington had not attended the vote the day before, but he now stood before the assembly and reluctantly accepted the commission for which the body had nominated him—commander in chief of the Continental Army. He had seemed reluctant to accept the nomination in both his speech and in his correspondence home. In fact, in a letter to his wife, Martha, and to his brother, he stated he had not sought the nomination and had done all in his power to stop it. In reality, however, as a leading candidate for the nomination, he had done little to discourage it.

This ambiguity was a pattern Washington would repeat when asked to chair the Constitutional Convention and when he accepted the Presidency of the United States. It was as if he were trying to convince himself that his success was not a result of his own ambition or his own doing but that it was thrust upon him from outside sources. It was fairly obvious, however, in June, 1775, that his uniform was advertising his willingness to serve in the capacity of commander in chief.

★ THE GENERAL ★

His brief acceptance speech made two main points. First, he explained that he did not feel qualified for the position: "But lest some unlucky event should happen unfavorable to my reputation, I beg it may be remembered by every Gentleman in the room, that I this day declare with the utmost sincerity, I do not think myself equal to the Command I (am) honored with." Second, he wished to serve without pay.

In just a few words, George Washington became the military leader of the American Revolution and a traitor to the British Empire to which he had sworn allegiance. He stood before Congress not only as the military leader of the American Revolution but also as the only member of the Continental Army. Since Congress had elected their general before there even was an army, it was up to Washington to make that army a reality.

Nobody understood the odds of winning against the British better than Washington, but he was not convinced it would come to open warfare. He believed that King George III would be impressed with the American resistance and would order Parliament and his ministry to work towards an acceptable compromise with the Americans. In a letter to his wife, shortly after he was commissioned as commander in chief, Washington wrote that he expected to be home by autumn. Washington had no idea that when he left in 1775 for Philadelphia that, with the exception of one stopover in 1781, he would not return to Mount Vernon until 1783.

As the new commander in chief in 1775, Washington knew if the situation deteriorated into armed conflicted, even raising an army would be a nearly insurmountable task. Then taking that army up against one of the largest, best-trained, most-experienced forces in the world would leave little chance for victory. But Washington knew, as did the rest of the Congress, that doing just that was necessary.

No one was more pleased with the vote than John Adams, who had lobbied hard for the nomination of Washington. He felt Washington was the best candidate; in fact, he felt

Washington was the only candidate who should serve in that capacity. However, even Adams had some misgivings about the chain of events that Congress had initiated that day. Specifically, he was concerned about Washington. Adams knew that a man like Washington, despite his seeming reluctance, was ambitious. Adams recognized the danger of setting up a man to be the symbol of the Revolution, especially if he were as ambitious as Adams believed Washington to be. In his reading of history, Adams knew that strong, courageous men such as Washington often sought as much power as they could attain. If Washington were successful, he would become the kind of hero people would worship and revere with such zest that he could assume any power he wished to have. He might even become "king" of the new republic—the very thing the Revolution was fighting against.

Washington's accomplishments during the years that followed are well known, his tactics legendary. He became the greatest hero of the most unlikely victory in the history of the world. Even though he won only three of the nine battles he fought in the Revolutionary War, those victories were enough to defeat the British. With the British surrender at Yorktown on October 17, 1781, a new nation was born. Washington became its iconic symbol, shrouded more in myth and legend than in fact. He, as "Father of Our Country," came to represent what could be accomplished through strength of character, determination, and persistence.

Showing the same reluctance he had shown when taking command of the Continental Army, Washington went on to serve two terms as President of the United States. By the time his second term in office was nearing completion, he had helped to establish the country's financial system and had all but eliminated the Indian threat east of the Mississippi River. In addition, the Jay's Treaty and the Pinckney Treaty with Spain had expanded the new nation's territory and removed some serious diplomatic difficulties. Even though there were fundamental differences between the members of the Democratic Republican Party and the members of the Hamiltonian Federalist Party by the time Washington's second term neared completion, the two parties were at least united in their acceptance of the new federal government, although Washington had some concerns about the inability of the two parties to agree on very much else. Then, probably to John Adams' relief, Washington retired after his second term ended in 1797, setting a precedent of two terms.

Washington delivered a masterly Farewell Address that made three very important points. His first point warned about political factionalism. The two political parties which had formed in the 1790s, had begun feuding almost immediately. Washington urged Americans to unite for the good of the whole country. His second point cautioned against making foreign alliances, specifically about getting involved in the war between France and Britain. Both parties were leaning towards stronger foreign ties: the Federalists with the British and the Democratic Republicans with the French. His final point called for maintaining political prosperity through morality and religion. Washington's Farewell Address quickly became the political basis for the formation of the new nation. As the symbol of American republicanism, it was adopted as the nation's political philosophy.

Washington returned to Mount Vernon, promising never to go more than ten miles from his beloved plantation again. But he broke his promise. Even after his retirement, Washington returned to Philadelphia and to military service at his country's call to assist in raising another army, this time against the French. Washington's position was intended more to scare the French—letting them know the old general of the Revolution was still around—than to lead another army into armed conflict.

Back home at Mount Vernon, George Washington was making plans for some improvements to the estate. On the morning of December 13, 1799, he worked outside in the cold and the rain with his compass, marking the ground where the improvements would take place. When he returned to the house, he was seized with chills and nausea and finally went to bed. By morning, his condition had worsened, and a doctor was sent for. Medical practice was crude in early American history. According to common practice, Washington was bled several times. After that, his strength began to fail. He died the evening of December 14, 1799, at the age of sixty-seven. It is believed he was most likely suffering from a form of laryngitis, but experts today believe he probably died from blood loss because of the more than two and a half quarts of blood his physician had bled from him in just over thirteen hours.

The reverence with which Americans consider Washington is unparalleled. His face appears on United States money, has been made into hundreds of statues and busts, and is carved on Mount Rushmore. His famous portrait hangs in classrooms and courthouses around the nation. His name has been used to name the nation's capital, one state, and hundreds of public schools, universities, city streets, lakes, rivers, and monuments. And his name is forever linked in Americans' minds with famous places and heroic battles in our distant past: Bunker Hill, Yorktown, and Valley Forge. George Washington so believed in the principles of his new nation and government that he refused to allow himself to dominate it. He helped bring this nation into existence by defeating the British and helped guide its early beginnings as the first President. Then he wisely stepped back, allowing the government to grow from the seeds he had planted.

Brother George Washington was raised a Master Mason at a young age on August 4, 1753, at Fredericksburg Lodge, Virginia (now known as Fredericksburg Lodge No. 4). While he was not active in his lodge—in fact, it is believed he did not attend any meetings between 1755 and 1777—he did comment favorably about the fraternity on numerous occasions, and he performed several Masonic functions. In 1791, Brother Washington described

Masonry as being "founded in justice and benevolence." He believed "the grand object of Masonry is to promote the happiness of the human race."

On April 30, 1789, Washington was inaugurated the first President of the United States in New York. When the ceremony commenced, it was discovered that no Holy Bible had been provided to swear in the new President. Jacob Morton, who had been the marshal of the parade and was also the Master of the St. John's Lodge, remarked that he could get the altar Bible used at the St. John's Lodge nearby. He was encouraged to do so, and the Bible was retrieved. Washington was sworn in on that Bible by the Honorable Robert R. Livingston, Chancellor of the State of New York and Most Worshipful Grand Master of Free and Accepted Masons of the State of New York. Once Washington had finished his oath, he leaned over and kissed the Bible.

The Washington Bible has been used to inaugurate four additional Presidents: Harding in 1921, Eisenhower in 1953, Carter in 1977, and George H.W. Bush in 1989. It was intended to be used to inaugurate George W. Bush in 2001, but damp weather prevented its use. The Washington Bible has also been used in numerous public occasions including Washington's funeral procession in New York, the dedication of the Washington monument in 1885, and the rededication of the monument in 1998. The Bible is still in active use by the St. John's Lodge. When not in use or on tour, it is on display at Federal Hall in New York, the very place where George Washington swore his allegiance to the Constitution of the United States and became the "Father of His Country."

In 1793, President Washington, wearing Masonic regalia, led a large procession of Brother Freemasons, military units, government officials, citizens, and stonemasons to the top of Capitol Hill, where he performed the Masonic ceremony of laying the cornerstone of the United States Capitol Building. The symbolic ceremony involved trying the cornerstone by the plumb, the level, and the square, and then blessing it with the corn of plenty, the wine of happiness, and the oil of joy. Using a symbolic trowel, he spread the symbolic cement which was meant to unite the individual stones of the building into one solid mass and to bring all Americans together as one people. The public cornerstone ritual is still practiced by Freemasons today.

Another story is that several State Grand Masters approached Washington about forming a Grand Lodge of the United States, much like the Grand Lodge of England. They asked him to serve as Grand Master of this United States Grand Lodge. Washington declined the offer. To this day, each state in the Union governs its own lodges independently with no national Grand Lodge.

At the age of 62, George Washington, wearing Masonic regalia and the Past Master's Jewel, sat for a portrait painted by artist William Joseph Williams. It is one of several portraits of George Washington as a Freemason.

As revered as Washington is by his country, he is revered to this day even more by his Masonic brethren. One uniquely American Masonic tradition is attributed to George Washington. Legend has it that George Washington first presented an America flag to a Masonic Lodge during the Revolutionary War. The American flag has been displayed in American lodges ever since, and every Masonic meeting in the United States is opened with the Pledge of Allegiance

TWO

The Sage

"The Constitution only guarantees the American people the right to pursue happiness. You have to catch it yourself."

The young man was robust and energetic. He was in the physical condition of a trained athlete. He loved to exercise and stayed in shape by running up and down the stairs of the print shop where he was employed with a double load of lead trays. He also enjoyed a peculiar form of exercise—swimming. In London, he was often found entertaining his friends by performing extraordinary feats in the Thames River—swimming more than two miles not only above the water but also underneath it. He even experimented with tying fins onto his hands and feet much like modern scuba divers. This was during a time when swimming was considered dangerous. There was always the risk of drowning. In addition, many people believed, as they still do today, that spending time wet and cold could lead to illness. During that time, even a minor illness could become life threatening.

Long before anybody understood anything about germs and bacteria, this young man, however, had come to the conclusion that people more often became ill after having contact with other people. He also observed that a lack of exercise and too many excesses seemed to make people even more susceptible to illness. He knew he could spend a couple of hours swimming in the cold water with no ill effects. In fact, on a trip back to Philadelphia from London, he jumped off the ship and swam laps around it to the amazement of the passengers and crew—until the appearance of sharks curtailed his exploits in the water.

Decades later, the image of this man—older, more rotund, bespectacled, and balding—would be known world-wide as it still is today. He is one of America's most prolific philosophers, raconteurs, and thinkers, as well as one of our most beloved founding fathers—Benjamin Franklin.

It is difficult to believe that one man in the span of eighty-four years could accomplish so many things, be so many things, and represent so many things to so many people. Benjamin Franklin, because of his extensive contributions to the causes of independence for the United States, has been called by many historians "The First American." But Franklin was also a writer, a publisher, a philosopher, a scientist, a diplomat, an inventor, and a leading character in the era of enlightenment during the 1700s. The study of science was in its infancy, and the forces that govern the natural world were beginning to be understood. His scientific curiosity, his own philosophy about how people should live, and his tireless pursuit of understanding make him stand out as one of the world's most prolific philosophers and one of America's greatest minds. His influences can be felt in many of the ideals and principles which were captured in those early documents he helped write and which defined America as a nation—the Declaration of Independence and the United States Constitution.

When Benjamin Franklin was young, his father, Josiah, wanted him to make a career in the church, but Benjamin was not interested in organized religion. Instead, he began working for his brother as an apprentice in his print shop. Young

★ THE SAGE ★

Franklin was rather upset when his brother James, who created America's first truly independent newspaper in the colonies, the *New England Courant*, refused to allow him to write for the paper. Benjamin decided to have the best of his brother by writing a series of letters to the paper posing as a middle-aged widow, Silence Dogood. When James published the letters, not realizing Ben had actually penned them, they became a topic of conversation around town. James was very unhappy when he discovered Ben was the author of the letters.

Leaving his apprenticeship without permission, Franklin ran away to Philadelphia, a fugitive. He found employment in several print shops, but he did not care for the prospects he found there. Later, he made a trip to London to buy equipment for a new paper in the colonies. The employer that sent him turned out to be something of a con man, and Franklin found himself stranded in London with no way home. He took a job in a print shop. Later, with the help of a merchant named Thomas Denham, he finally made his way back to Philadelphia, where he worked for Denham as a shopkeeper.

When Denham died, Franklin returned to his original career in printing. He set up a printing house and his own newspaper, *The Pennsylvania Gazette*. Within a few years, after achieving some success and recognition as the editor of his own paper, he began to issue *Poor Richard's Almanac*, which contained folksy wisdom and humor, both original to Franklin and borrowed. Many of the adages attributed to Ben Franklin, such as "a penny saved is a penny earned," actually come from the pages of *Poor Richard's Almanac*.

As his success as a printer took off, Franklin involved himself in planning a number of civic projects. One such project was to pave, clean, and light Philadelphia's streets. He also launched the Library Company in 1731, the first subscription library. During this time, books were hard to come by and expensive. Franklin recognized that by pooling resources, subscribers of the Library Company could afford to buy books from England and share them. Subscribers would have to sign out the books and agree to pay for them if they were lost or not returned—almost exactly the same way lending libraries work today. He also helped to establish the American Philosophical Society, one of the first learned societies in America. Recognizing the need for better treatment for the sick, Franklin brought together a group who formed the Pennsylvania Hospital in 1751. The Library Company, the Philosophical Society, and the Pennsylvania Hospital are still in existence today.

Most people probably don't know that his famous saying "An ounce of prevention is worth a pound of cure" was actually fire-fighting advice. In 1736, Franklin organized Philadelphia's Union Fire Company. Also recognizing that people who lost their homes often never financially recovered, Franklin helped to found the Philadelphia Contribution for Insurance Against Loss by Fire. Those who purchased insurance policies for their properties were not wiped out financially in the event of a fire.

Franklin was doing well as a printer and civic leader. By 1749, he retired from business in order to focus on science, experiments, and the inventions for which he later became famous. But Franklin was already an accomplished inventor, having invented the Franklin stove. His revolutionary design burned fuel and warmed homes more efficiently. Since he invented the stove for the general good and improvement of society, he refused to profit from it by taking out a patent.

In the early 1750s, he turned to the study of electricity. His observations, including his kite experiment which verified the nature of electricity and lightning, brought Franklin international fame.

From an early age, Franklin seemed to have established his own beliefs about religion based on his own observations. He loved science and conducted experiments on everything from electricity to the movements of water. During this period of Enlightenment, man was just beginning to understand that there were natural rules that applied to all things natural. Franklin made scientific tests and inquiries into these natural subjects of interest using his rational mind and logic to try to understand the forces governing the nature of what he was studying. Sometimes his observations contradicted what was believed at the time, like his observations about the nature of electricity and about colds and other illnesses coming from person-to-person contact. Franklin seemed to apply this same disregard for what was already known and accepted to religion, modeling his own beliefs on his observations and logic. He was a self-proclaimed deist. He believed there was a big difference between morality and religion. Morality was more dependent on virtue and actions rather than on strict observance of religious doctrines and orthodoxy. In other words, he believed it was more important what an individual did every day than where he attended church on Sunday and what dogma or orthodoxy he practiced in daily life. Franklin believed that most religious orthodoxy was an invention of man, not God. As one might expect, Franklin drew some criticism for his repeated attacks on organized religion. However, even though he criticized religion, Franklin did believe in one God, and he did not believe religion was bad; in fact, he thought the weaker the church, the weaker the society. He simply did not believe there was any right way or a wrong way to believe, so long as the meaning was virtuous. According to historian David Morgan, Benjamin Franklin was the "champion of generic religion."

As a result of his own religious beliefs, Franklin contended that every man had the right to believe whatever it was he wished to believe. Franklin believed that religion was a personal choice. The freedom of religion was one of the first basic premises in the Constitution of the United States of America. Another one of Franklin's beliefs about freedom was the absolute necessity that church and state be separate. Laws should be based on morality, logic, and rational thought, not on any one religious belief.

When Thomas Jefferson finished penning the Declaration of Independence, Benjamin Franklin was asked to review it and to suggest any changes he deemed important. His changes were minimal, but one he made demonstrated his core beliefs about church and state. Thomas Jefferson had written, "We hold these truths to be undeniable and sacred." Franklin changed it to, "We hold these truths to be self-evident." Jefferson's term "sacred" seemed to suggest that man's equality was a right endowed upon them by their creator—a religious belief. Franklin's change made it a statement of rationality and logic.

Franklin was one of America's first examples of the successful application of the American dream. He was a tradesman who, through his own wit and self-determination, became a founding father of the United States. He stood before kings but was respected and admired by his peers as well. He was a man whose accomplishments in multiple fields are unrivaled to this day. Most men would feel successful if they had accomplished even part of what he accomplished, such as the experiments with electricity or the invention of the bifocal spectacles. But Franklin saw many of these accomplishments as mere trifles—the result of some passing interests or the solution to a particular problem. Franklin enjoyed the acclaim some of his discoveries brought him, but acclaim was not his motive—knowledge was his only goal.

Franklin saw himself as a man born ahead of his time. His only regret was having been born just prior to what he believed was going to be an amazing age of discovery. He stated that he would miss "the Happiness of knowing what will be known 100 Years hence." He believed that just ahead, there would be "Discoveries made of which we have at present no Conception."

One of Franklin's last accomplishments was writing an anti-slavery treatise in 1789. He died on April 17, 1790, at the age of eighty-four. More than twenty thousand people attended the funeral. His great electric personality was gone, but his light continues to shine on. As Franklin once said, "If you would not be forgotten, as soon as you are dead and rotten, either write things worth reading, or do things worth writing."

★ THE SAGE ★

Benjamin Franklin very much wanted to join the Freemasons, but at first he had a difficult time getting invited to join. Much like Franklin, the Freemasons were dedicated to civic works and fellowship. They held a nonsectarian policy about religious toleration which mirrored his beliefs. Franklin also saw membership as a step on the social ladder. In hopes of currying favor with the Freemasons, he began to publish small, favorable pieces about the Freemasons in his newspaper. When that did not work, he tried a different tactic. In December of 1730, he published a long article in his paper claiming to have uncovered some of the secrets of the Freemasons. He claimed one of these secrets was that many of the so-called "secrets" were actually hoaxes. Within a couple of weeks, Benjamin Franklin was initiated into the St. John's Lodge. Shortly after his initiation, his newspaper printed a retraction of the article and put in its place a glowing piece about the positive influences of Freemasonry.

Brother Benjamin Franklin became a Master Mason at St. John's Lodge in Philadelphia in 1731. He was a very active Freemason his entire life, eventually becoming Master of his Lodge and later, in 1734, the Grand Master of the Grand Lodge of Pennsylvania. In 1749, he was appointed Provincial Grand Master of Massachusetts. He also visited the Grand Lodge in England and was accepted as a member of the influential Lodge of the Nine Sisters (or Nine Muses) in Paris, where he assisted with the initiation of Voltaire as a Master Mason and helped in the election of such influential members as John Paul Jones. It seems unusual that a man such as Benjamin Franklin would join Freemasonry. He was an innovator, an inventor—someone who was always at the forefront of new ideas and new philosophies, yet the organization he joined, and so faithfully served, was an organization all about tradition and ancient ritual.

Perhaps Franklin saw Freemasonry as a model of what a proper governing body should be; in fact, inferences about Freemasonry and the development of the ideals in the United

States have been made before. Lodges have always elected their own leaders and practiced tolerance of all religious beliefs. Whatever it was that Franklin admired in the organization, he never tried to change it. In fact, Franklin worked hard to preserve it by helping to create the by-laws of the St. John's Lodge in Philadelphia and by printing the American Constitutions for Freemasonry.

The epitaph he wrote for himself only very slightly disguises the Masonic theme of immortality which our legend attests and that he believed:

> The Body of
> B. Franklin,
> Printer;
> Like the Cover of an old Book,
> Its contents torn out,
> And stript of its Lettering and Gilding,
> Lies here, Food for Worms.
> But the Work, shall not be wholly lost,
> For it will, as he believed, appear once more,
> In a new & more perfect Edition,
> Corrected and amended
> By the Author.

THREE

The Friend

*"Humanity has won its battle.
Liberty now has a country."*

The young man entered the French army at the age of fourteen. At nineteen, he was a captain of dragoons when the American colonies proclaimed their independence from Britain in 1776. The King of France was willing to turn a blind eye toward a few French soldiers who wanted to fight in the American cause, in the hope that such assistance might garner France some trade considerations with the newly forming nation. The young man was immediately enamored with the idea of helping the colonists in their brave struggle for independence. He later wrote in his memoirs, "My heart was enrolled in it."

His friends and family tried to discourage him from getting involved in the conflict. While the King of France was quietly not opposed to the American cause, he was caught in the center—quietly supporting the American cause, but at the same time under pressure from the British not to become involved in the conflict. The French did not want to incite a war with Britain by openly helping the Americans.

The young man was able to arrange service in the Continental army. Through an American agent in Paris, he was to enter the American service as a major general, which was quite impressive for a nineteen-year-old boy who had little formal military training and had no experience in war. He had never faced a cannon or a musket fired in anger on a battlefield.

But about the time he received his commission from the American agent, news arrived of grave disasters in the American cause. After forcing General George Washington into retreat, British General Howe had occupied New York City. General Washington's loss of New York and his indecisiveness caused the French to be concerned about his military ability. The young man's friends and family again advised him to give up on the insane notion of fighting for the colonies since that fight was apparently a lost cause. Even the American envoys, including Benjamin Franklin, who were in France to solicit assistance from France's king, discouraged him from going to America. The American envoys were concerned that the loss of French soldiers on American soil, especially the loss of such prestigious young French aristocrats, could damage the tenuous bonds they were trying to forge in France.

The young man was afraid that if he persisted with his public plans, he would be stopped either by his family or by the king himself. However, instead of giving up the idea, he kept his plans quiet. Without informing his family and under a cloak of secrecy, he purchased a ship, the *Victoire,* and hired a crew to take him and several other French volunteers to America to fight in the colonist's war for independence. But by the time the ship was ready to sail, news of his plan had leaked out.

The king, pressured by the British ambassador at Versailles, issued orders—a *lettre de cachet*—to have the ship *Victoire* seized and the young man arrested. However, the man was able to escape from custody. Then disguised as a courier,

★ THE FRIEND ★

he made his way back to the ship. Before a second *lettre de cachet* could stop him, he reached the ship and set sail for America.

He told his closest friend among the group, Johann de Kalb, "I am an outlaw. I prefer to fight for the liberty of America rather than lose my own liberty and languish in a French prison. So, my friend, we shall be comrades in arms after all."

Although two British ships were sent in pursuit, the men escaped. They were criminals—they had violated the king's direct order and thus would face permanent exile from France if captured. The volunteers on the ship *Victoire* hoped they would find a home in America. After a difficult two-month journey, they landed safely on June 13, 1777, on North Island near Georgetown, South Carolina.

From there, the young man made his way to Philadelphia, then the colonial seat of government, to present himself to the Continental Congress for service at the rank of major general as promised by his American agent. At that time Congress could hardly know that this nineteen-year-old young man—this criminal and exile from France—would become one of the best-known heroes of the American Revolution. Two hundred years later, he was still so beloved by the American people that he was made an honorary citizen of the United States of America by Congress—one of only six individuals in American history to be honored in that way.

This young man was none other than the French aristocrat and military captain, Marie Joseph Paul Yves Roch Gilbert du Motier—also known as the Marquis de La Fayette (or Lafayette as he preferred to be called).

The Marquis de La Fayette was born on September 6, 1757, at the Château de Chavaniac in the Auvergne region of France into the wealthy French aristocratic family of La Fayette. Lafayette was educated at the Lycée Louis-le-Grand. At sixteen, he married Marie Adrienne Francoise de Noailles, daughter of the Duc d'Ayen of the aristocratic family of the de Noailles. As his father and grandfather had before him, Lafayette entered the royal guards prior to enlisting in the American Continental Army in 1777. Little did Lafayette know when he landed in America that he had little to worry about concerning exile from or imprisonment in France. As soon as news of his escape to America became known to the French court, he became a hero to the French people. The king was quietly pleased. The only person in the French court who was still angered at Lafayette's actions was the Duc d'Ayen, his father-in-law.

When Lafayette's party of fifteen Frenchmen and one German presented themselves to the Continental Congress on July 27, 1777, they expected to be immediately assigned to military service and promptly reimbursed for their travel expenses since each of them carried commissions issued by the American agent in France, Silas Dean. However, Dean had greatly exceeded his authority. Not only did the Continental Congress lack the funds to pay them, but General Washington was discovering that many of these European adventurers who were volunteering to fight in the American cause were more trouble than they were worth. The members of the Foreign Relations Committee who interviewed Lafayette discovered he lacked any combat experience, and at nineteen, he was the age of most American lieutenants. The notion of making him a major general was absurd. Lafayette was thanked for his offer to aid them, then encouraged to return to France.

Lafayette, believing he would be at the very least imprisoned in France, had no interest in returning. He wrote a brief letter to the Continental Congress from his room at a local inn, stating, "After the sacrifices that I have made in this cause, I have the right to ask two favors at your hands: the one is, to serve without pay, at my own expense; and the other, that I be allowed to serve at first as a volunteer in the ranks."

General George Washington was expected the following day in Philadelphia. The Continental Congress left the decision to him. Washington already knew of Lafayette. Benjamin Franklin had written him from France, shortly after Lafayette

★ THE FRIEND ★

escaped to America, asking Washington to look after "the boy" both in financial terms and otherwise. When Washington met with Lafayette for over an hour, it is said they took to each other almost immediately. Washington, known as an excellent judge of character, saw that Lafayette was a natural leader of men. At Washington's request, the Congress confirmed Lafayette's appointment as a major general. To ease his disgruntled senior officers, Washington informed his staff that Lafayette's rank, for all practical purposes, was strictly an honorary appointment.

Very soon, Lafayette distinguished himself with the senior members of Washington's staff, who had been prepared to snub the French "major general." He suffered the same hardships, he was modest, he never mentioned his great wealth, and he took great care never to criticize or insult his American comrades. When he was asked his opinion, he invariably replied, "I am here to learn, not to preach or teach."

Lafayette became close friends with Colonel Alexander Hamilton, aide-de-camp to Washington, and Colonel Henry Knox among others. But no friendship was stronger than the bond he formed with General George Washington. It was said they established such a rapport with one another they could sometimes communicate with just a glance. Lafayette, in later years, would refer to Washington as "my father." Washington, indeed, treated Lafayette as a son.

Lafayette's first engagement with the British was on September 11, 1777, at the Battle of Brandywine. British General Howe had left his New York headquarters, sailing with 15,000 men to Chesapeake Bay. He was opposed by Washington's force of 11,000, but Howe was able to flank Washington and cross Brandywine Creek. The only thing keeping the British from accessing the road to Philadelphia was the center of Washington's line—and that line was beginning to falter.

Wearing his blue-and-buff uniform, Lafayette, who had no command, busied himself by moving up and down the center of the American line at the climax of the battle, trying to encourage the defenders. As the American center started to falter, Lafayette galloped up to within a few yards of the British position, rallying the American defenders into holding the center of the line. His brilliant gold epaulettes on the shoulders of his uniform not only buoyed the morale of the American defenders but also attracted the attention of British sharpshooters. One bullet passed through his hat and another through his coat without touching him; however, later his luck failed. He was hit in the leg and forced to leave the field. Even so, his example of bravery had inspired the American soldiers and may have been more responsible for the stiffening of the center line than any other factor.

When news of his exploits at the Battle of Brandywine reached Paris, it created a sensation, and Lafayette was hailed a hero. Benjamin Franklin commented that Lafayette's conduct doubled the popularity of the American cause in Paris. By January, 1778, the Prime Minister of France notified Benjamin Franklin and the other members of the American mission that King Louis XVI of France recognized the independence of the United States, due in part to the exploits of Lafayette and the American victory at Saratoga. The following month, King Louis XVI dispatched a fleet of French ships to provide direct military aid to the American cause. In addition, he ordered supplies and munitions be delivered to the American Continental Army.

Lafayette went on to distinguish himself in several campaigns, including the Battle of Monmouth and most notably the siege of Yorktown. There is no question that his contributions in battle helped to win several key victories and that news of his exploits back in France helped bring the aid of the French into the American Revolutionary War—without which it is unlikely the American Revolution would have resulted in victory over the British.

Lafayette's story, however, does not end with the American Revolution. He went on to become a national hero during the French Revolution as Commander of the French National Guard. Lafayette had the difficult task of protecting the king

★ THE FRIEND ★

and queen while at the same time advancing the cause of French freedom.

Lafayette's friendship continued with George Washington. He visited Washington at Mount Vernon after the war, and named his son George Washington de Lafayette, in honor of his great friend.

What Lafayette may have originally seen as a grand adventure of youth—journeying to American to fight in the American Revolution—turned into a lifelong belief in life, liberty, equality, and freedom. Those ideals were much more to Lafayette than just words. He believed them with the same intensity as did the American patriots he joined, and he fought for those same ideals for the remainder of his life. Lafayette said, "When a government violates the people's rights, insurrection is, for the people and for each portion of the people, the most sacred of the rights and the most indispensible of duties."

Lafayette was one of our greatest American patriots—he just happened to be French.

It has been disputed for two centuries where Lafayette became a Mason. There are no definitive records showing exactly when and where Lafayette was initiated. Lafayette was a hero of both the American Revolutionary War and later two French revolutions. Freemasons from both countries are anxious to claim him as their own. French Masonic scholars believe he was made a Mason in France prior to coming to American and enlisting in the Continental army. However, the most widely accepted and best supported belief is that Lafayette was made a Mason after coming to America, most likely after meeting George Washington. This version is supported by Lafayette's own writings. American Masonic scholars place the time of the initiation during the winter of 1777-78 when Washington's army was wintering over at Valley Forge. It is believed that General George Washington himself may have acted as Master of the Lodge during Lafayette's initiation ceremony.

47

Dr. George W. Chaytor was a noted Masonic scholar and past master. Addressing the Lafayette Lodge No. 14 in Wilmington, Delaware, on January 18, 1875, on the occasion of the lodge's fiftieth anniversary of its constitution, he made the following statement on the subject of Lafayette's admission into the Masonic order:

> He [Lafayette] was not a Mason when he landed in America, nor was he a Mason at the Battle of Brandywine. The Army under Washington, in December, 1777, retired to Valley Forge, where they wintered. Connected with the Army was a Lodge. It was at Valley Forge that he was made a Mason. On this point there should be no second opinion—for surely Lafayette knew best where he was made a Mason.

Lafayette's own remarks do support the fact he was made a Mason in America, after having met General George Washington. Lafayette said, "After I was made a Mason, General Washington seemed to have received a new light—I never had, from that moment, any cause to doubt his entire confidence. It was not long before I had a separate command of great importance."

FOUR

The Warrior

"It seems to be a law of nature, inflexible and inexorable, that those who will not risk cannot win."

In July, 1905, an unusual procession made its way down the avenues of Paris, France. A casket, draped in an American flag, was being led by a squadron of French Cuirassiers in shining helmets, followed by a column of five hundred United States Navy blue-jackets. The casket wound its way through the streets, stopping at Les Invalides before the tomb of Napoleon, where speeches about this most accomplished man were made by diplomats and statesmen. The casket continued on to Cherbourg, France, where a squad of four U.S. Navy cruisers waited to take the casket westward across the Atlantic and back to the States. The cruisers—the *Brooklyn*, the *Tacoma*, the *Galveston*, and the *Chattanooga*—were met by seven battleships, and the flotilla slowly made its way through the Virginia capes and up the Chesapeake Bay to the U.S. Naval Academy at Annapolis, Maryland. Hundreds of midshipman stood at attention as the casket passed by. The Academy band played Chopin's Funeral March as cannons fired a continuous salute to one of America's own sons who had returned home.

The President of the United States, Teddy Roosevelt, spoke at the service, commanding every officer in the Navy to know this man's deeds. To this day, all midshipmen at Annapolis are required to memorize this man's pronouncements on the correct training and proper manners for an officer and a gentleman. Finally, at the end of his long journey from France, this man was laid to rest in a marble sarcophagus, modeled after Napoleon's own crypt. The inscription on the tomb reads, "He gave our Navy its earliest traditions of heroism and victory."

Not a bad ending for a notorious pirate who by 1905 had been dead for 113 years. The location of his original gravesite, long forgotten and paved over, had been found only by extraordinary effort, and his body exhumed for a burial more befitting a man of his accomplishments. But this was no ordinary pirate. This was one of the Revolutionary War's greatest heroes—John Paul Jones.

John Paul Jones (born John Paul) was born in 1747 in Kirkcudbright, Scotland. His father was a gardener at the Arbigland estate, and his mother was a member of the MacDuff clan. John Paul began his career at the age of thirteen on the ship *Friendship*. He made numerous trips to Fredericksburg, Virginia, where he most likely visited his brother who had settled nearby. In his youth, he served on several other ships, including the *King George* as the third mate and the slavery ship *Two Friends* as the first mate.

While sailing on the *Two Friends*, John Paul began to form strong opinions about the institution of slavery. He left his well-paying job aboard that ship while she was docked in Jamaica. After he made his way back to Scotland, he eventually obtained another position aboard the brig *John*. It was on his first journey aboard *John* in 1768 that his career took a gigantic leap. When both the captain and the mate died suddenly of yellow fever, John Paul managed to navigate the ship

★ THE WARRIOR ★

back to Scotland. The grateful owners rewarded him lavishly with ten percent of the cargo along with making him master of the ship and giving him command of the ship's crew.

John Paul made two trips to the West Indies, but on the second trip in 1770, he found it necessary to flog one of the crew. The experienced crewman later died, leading to accusations that John Paul's discipline was "unnecessarily cruel." On his return, John Paul was arrested on charges of unnecessary brutality but allowed to post bail. Later, he returned to the Caribbean to obtain evidence that the sailor had been in good health when he came aboard and that he had actually died of an unrelated fever on the voyage. The suit was dismissed by the Admiralty, but the embarrassment and rumors about John Paul caused him to leave Scotland and to take a job on a London-registered ship to Tobago.

The incident of the flogging haunted him. The increasing scrutiny of his questionable past led him to leave his position and wealth in Scotland and to move to Fredericksburg, Virginia. When John Paul's brother died in 1773, John Paul took charge of the estate. About this same time, he began using "Jones" as his last name, presumably to put some distance between himself and his questioned reputation.

In 1775, with rumblings of an American revolution in the air, John Paul Jones headed for Philadelphia, where he volunteered for the newly forming Continental Navy. With the help of his friend Richard Henry Lee and some influential members of the Continental Congress, Jones received a commission aboard the 30-gun frigate the *USS Alfred*, becoming the first man to be assigned the rank of first lieutenant of the new Continental Navy. His job was to sail from the Delaware River and to patrol for and attack British merchant vessels in New Providence. The *Alfred* was one of six vessels commanded by Commodore Esek Hopkins. It was aboard the *Alfred* that John Paul Jones was given the honor of hoisting the first United States ensign over a naval vessel. America was declaring her independence and defiantly waving her colors for the first time.

John Paul Jones went on to command a smaller 12-gun ship, the *Providence.* During a six-week period, Jones captured sixteen prizes and brought havoc to the coast of Nova Scotia. His next command, aboard the *Alfred* again, was the result of his own plan to attack the British coal fleet and to rescue American prisoners being held at Isle Royale. That mission too was successful. As a bonus, Jones captured the British ship the *Mellish,* which was loaded with vital winter uniforms and supplies for the British troops in Canada. The loss of these supplies significantly contributed to the success of the Continental Army at the Battle of Trenton, not only because the British did not have the supplies for winter but also because George Washington's Continental Army desperately needed them. The British troops defeated by Washington's Continental Army on Christmas and New Year's at Princeton and Trenton must have been quite surprised to see the soldiers who defeated them wearing their missing British uniforms—compliments of John Paul Jones.

Despite his accomplishments, John Paul Jones was given command of a smaller 18-gun frigate ship, the *Ranger.* This lesser command was primarily due to his conflicts with Commodore Hopkins. Jones believed Hopkins was demeaning his accomplishments and standing in his way of advancement. In November, 1777, Jones set sail for France with orders to assist the American cause however possible. When he met with American commissioners, including Benjamin Franklin and John Adams, he was assured the command of the new ship *L'Indien* being built for America in Amsterdam. However, the British were able to wrestle the ship from American hands and ensure its sale to the French, who were not yet in alliance with American, thus leaving Jones without a command. It was during this time in France that Jones became close friends with Benjamin Franklin, whom he came to greatly admire.

In February, 1778, France signed a Treaty of Alliance with America. Several days later, the frigate *Ranger*, with John Paul Jones in command, was the first American Navy vessel to

★ THE WARRIOR ★

be saluted by the French with a nine-gun salvo fired from Admiral Piquet's flagship. It was the first time a foreign power had given recognition to America as an independent nation.

In April, 1778, Jones set sail from France to the coast of England, but bad weather diverted him to Ireland, where he chanced to encounter the 20-gun Royal Navy sloop, the *HMS Drake*. There are conflicting accounts and great controversy about what happened aboard the *Ranger* during the first attack against the *HMS Drake*. It was, however, unsuccessful. The second attack was also unsuccessful. Rumors of mutiny and resistance on the part of the *Ranger* crew abounded. Jones claimed a drunken sailor dropped anchor at the wrong time, thwarting the attack.

Jones headed to Whitehaven after the unsuccessful second attack. Once again rumors and inconsistencies abound about the events there. He allegedly set the town ablaze, but it is difficult to ascertain if any real damage was actually done. Jones headed to the St. Mary's Isle with a plan to capture the Earl of Selkirk and then use him to free American sailors pressed into service in the Royal Navy. The plan failed because the Earl of Selkirk was not there. Neither the Whitehaven attack nor the plan to assault St. Mary's Isle had much to offer in strategic advantage.

Despite his failures in Whitehaven and St. Mary's Isle and the rumors of growing unrest among his crew, even a possible mutiny lead by First Lieutenant Thomas Simpson, John Paul Jones was determined, against overwhelming odds, to turn the fiasco into an American victory. John Paul Jones was determined to return to the *HMS Drake* still anchored in Carrickfergus and take her as a prize. This time the two ships engaged each other in a furious hour-long battle, which cost the British captain not only his ship but also his life. Jones was successful, and the *HMS Drake* was taken.

Jones' First Lieutenant Simpson took command of the *Drake* for the return trip to Brest. Jones diverted to chase another prize on the voyage home, causing another conflict with Simpson. When both ships arrived back in port in Brest, Jones immediately called for the court marital of Simpson and kept Simpson detained on the ship. Simpson was later released from the charges, partly due to the influence of John Adams, who was still serving as the commissioner to France. Adams later implied in his memoirs that the facts in the case seemed to support Simpson and that Jones wished to take full credit for the victory of the *HMS Drake*.

Regardless of the controversy surrounding Jones' mission to Ireland and the capture of the *HMS Drake,* the battle was a very important victory for the Revolution. Jones was the first commander in American history to win a military victory, proving that the British were far from invincible. Victory over such long odds was an important symbol to the American cause and steeled the resolve of the young nation.

Even after such a huge victory, John Paul Jones was not done. In fact, his greatest achievement yet was just over the horizon.

In 1779, John Paul Jones took command of a rebuilt merchant ship, the 44-gun *USS Bonhomme Richard*. Along with the 32-gun *Pallas*, the 32-gun *Alliance*, and the 12-gun ships *Vengeance* and *Le Cerf*, Jones began patrolling for prizes off the coast of England. On September 23, 1779, Jones' five ship squadron encountered a large convey of forty-four merchant ships. Jones realized he was looking at the Baltic Fleet, the main supplier of naval stores for the British in America. It was the fleet he had been waiting for. In fact, he had proposed a plan to intercept the vital supply line months before. Jones immediately set out to intercept the fleet, but he realized they were well defended by the large 44-gun *Serapis* and the 22-gun *Countess of Scarborough*. The *Bonhomme Richard,* the *Alliance,* and the *Pallas* engaged the British warships while the smaller ships pursued the Baltic Fleet as they tried to make a run back to the safety of the coast under the protective guns of the fort at Scarborough.

★ THE WARRIOR ★

The *Alliance* set out to attack the smaller of the two ships, the *Countess of Scarborough,* while Jones assaulted the *Serapis* with the help of the *Pallas.* In preparation for the attack, Jones sent midshipmen up into the rigging armed with swivel guns and small explosive charges. Twice, the huge *Serapis* raked the *Bonhomme Richard* with devastating effect, cutting her main mast and holing her below the water line.

The *Bonhomme Richard* was burning almost as fast as she was sinking. During the battle, the *Bonhomme Richard's* ensign was shot away. Thinking Jones was yielding, the British captain called over to Jones and asked if he had struck his colors in order to surrender. Jones purportedly shouted back, "I have not yet begun to fight."

Jones rammed the *Serapis* with his dying *Bonhomme Richard.* His men threw grapple hooks into the rigging of the *Serapis*, tying the two ships together. The midshipmen above began raking the deck with fire and tossing explosives down onto the *Serapis* and into her open top hatches while the cannons focused on cutting her main mast. A huge explosion rocked the *Serapis* when the explosives being rained down from the rigging above ignited unexploded powder cartridges below the decks. Jones' men flooded onto the deck, and the *Serapis* was captured.

Jones wanted to save the *Bonhomme Richard*, but she was too badly damaged. Knowing the ship was doomed, he cut her loose from the *Serapis* to prevent her from sinking the prize. The crew made every effort to patch the ship and to toss off extra weight to keep her afloat, but the damage was too extensive. A short time later, the *Bonhomme Richard* sank.

Meanwhile, the *Pallas* captured the *Countess of Scarborough*, thus securing John Paul Jones' legend forever. At the same time he was being reviled in Britain as a notorious pirate, he was being honored by France and America as one of the greatest captains in naval history. His daring and tenaciousness as a privateer firmed the resolve of the new American nation to build a great American naval fleet. The damage he did to shipping was instrumental in helping America win the American Revolutionary War against Britain. His victories buoyed the American cause and showed that even the great British Empire was not impervious to defeat.

Brother John Paul Jones was made a Master Mason in 1770 at St. Bernards Lodge No. 122, Kirkudbright, Scotland. He found lodges of Freemasons wherever he traveled on his journeys. Brother John Paul Jones was accepted and inducted into the most prestigious lodge of Freemasons in Europe at the time, the Lodge of the Nine Sisters, whose members included Voltaire and his friend Benjamin Franklin.

FIVE

The Rider

"The regulars are out!"

Being a dentist in the 1760s was more about being a mechanic who fixed the damage nature had already done than about preventing the disease and decay that destroyed the teeth to begin with. What caused tooth decay was still a mystery to dentistry at that time, but decay was an epidemic problem in Colonial America. Surgeon dentists pulled teeth, often a harrowing experience that could lead to fractured jaws and serious infections. But one young Boston dentist did not pull bad teeth; he only cleaned and replaced them. And he was good at it. Replacement involved bridging the gaps of missing teeth by tying teeth crafted from hippopotamus tusk or the teeth of sheep to existing teeth with thin wire made of silver or gold or sometimes silk thread. This procedure when performed by other dentists was mostly cosmetic, but the young Boston dentist claimed in his advertisements in local papers that these replacements not only looked as natural as real teeth but also enabled his customers to speak and chew normally.

The young dentist had a good trade in dentistry, claiming to have replaced in excess of a hundred teeth. He even sold a "dentifrice" used to clean teeth, although it is hard to say what that substance might have been. Cleaning potions of that time were made from many different abrasive substances including crushed pottery and gun powder. Some dentifrice pastes even used sugars and bread crumbs to polish teeth. The young dentist was also a pioneer in forensic dentistry, if only by accident. He was able to identify the body of a man by identifying his own handiwork in replacing the dead man's missing teeth. Even if he was successful at dentistry, it was only a related sideline to his main occupation as a silversmith.

However, history has focused very little on either occupation. Instead, what is most important is what he did one night in 1775 to warn the citizens and the militia of the approach of the enemy. The revolutionaries all knew the British would come eventually—just not when or how they would arrive. Fortunately, the local silversmith and dentist, Paul Revere, was able to get the word out—although perhaps not exactly the way people have learned about it in school.

The story of the midnight ride which most Americans have learned is that on the evening of April 18, 1775, Paul Revere saw two lanterns shining from the bell tower of the Old North Church, a prearranged signal of "one if by land, two if by sea." The signal meant the British were coming across the Charles River from Boston to Lexington. Jumping on his horse, Paul Revere began to raise the alarm. He rode through the streets and countryside to warn the citizens and the local militia, shouting "The British are coming! The British are coming!" As a result, the attack of the British force was thwarted.

Much of the credit for this version of the story can be attributed to a famous poem "Paul Revere's Ride," written by Henry Wadsworth Longfellow decades after Paul Revere's

★ THE RIDER ★

death. It was memorized by generations of schoolchildren. It begins:

> Listen, my children, and you shall hear
> Of the midnight ride of Paul Revere,
> On the eighteenth of April, in Seventy-Five;
> Hardly a man is now alive
> Who remembers that famous day and year

Much like the story of George Washington chopping down the cherry tree in his childhood, this story of Paul Revere's ride is more an American legend than it is based in actual fact. The midnight ride of Paul Revere did happen, just not exactly as most students have learned it. In fact, it was such a minor event at the time that little was made of it during Paul Revere's own lifetime. Instead, Revere was better known for other things he accomplished prior to, during, and after the Revolutionary War. His participation in the ride was just a small historical footnote.

The first inaccuracy of the legend is that the lantern signal from the Old North Church was a signal to Paul Revere when in fact it was a signal from Paul Revere to get the message across the river to Charleston. The plan was put into place in advance. When the information about how the British would attack became known, Paul Revere instructed Robert Newman, the sexton of the Old North Church, to put up one lantern if the British were coming across the land and two if they started across the river toward Lexington. Paul Revere planned to ride to warn the other patriots, but this signal was a back-up plan so the patriots in Charleston would get the message the British were on the move and preparing for an attack, in case Paul Revere was captured in his ride.

The British regulars had been posted in Boston since the ports had been closed due to the events of the Boston Tea Party. Paul Revere and a group of patriots known as the Sons of Liberty had kept them under close watch. There had been rumors for some time that the British were planning to move against the patriots, in particular, to arrest John Hancock and Samuel Adams and to seize a weapons store the Sons of Liberty had amassed in Concord.

When the British began to move across the river about 11 P.M. the night of April 18, 1775, the signal was given. There were actually two midnight riders who warned of the British approach. Paul Revere was instructed to cross the Charles River to Charleston, where he could begin his ride to Lexington, while another patriot, William Dawes, took a longer land route around the Boston Neck towards Lexington.

Revere and Dawes alerted patriots along their way, but it is unlikely that, with the countryside full of British patrols, Revere rode through the streets of Charleston and the countryside on his way to Lexington shouting, "The British are coming!" This was a mission that depended on secrecy. In his own account, Revere recalled that he told his fellow patriots along the way that "the regulars are coming out." Another reason shouting "The British are coming!" would have jeopardized the mission was that many of the citizens still considered themselves loyal British citizens, and there was every possibility they would have alerted the British.

Revere made it to Lexington in an hour, arriving there close to midnight. Dawes arrived only thirty minutes later. When Samuel Adams and John Hancock, who were staying at the Hancock-Clarke House in Lexington, received the news, they began to determine a course of action. Revere and Dawes decided to ride ahead to Concord where the militia arsenal was hidden. They were joined by Dr. Samuel Prescott, who happened to be visiting Lexington. It is fortunate Prescott joined them because he was the only one who made it to Concord to give the alarm.

The three riders were stopped and detained by a British road block just outside Concord. Breaking free, Prescott jumped his horse over a wall and escaped into the woods. Dawes also broke free of the British and escaped, but he later fell off his horse and was unable to complete the ride. Revere was detained, his horse was confiscated, and he was escorted at gunpoint back toward Lexington. As morning broke and shots were heard coming from Lexington, Revere's guards left him in the countryside and raced towards Lexington. Revere made his way back to Lexington on foot, arriving in time to see the beginning of the battle on Lexington Green.

Prescott was able to raise the alarm in Concord. The militia was ready for the British when they arrived and successfully repelled them at Concord. In addition, the British were harassed by guerilla fire on the roads, forcing them into a full retreat back to Boston.

Prior to the Revolutionary War, Paul Revere had become involved with numerous political agitators, most namely Dr. Joseph Warren. Revere had participated in the activities of such groups as the Sons of Liberty—the group credited with activities such as the Boston Tea Party. Revere began to work as a rider, often going to New York and Philadelphia, to spread news of the political unrest in Boston. During the war, he served as a major in the Massachusetts militia and later as a lieutenant colonel stationed at Castle William to defend Boston harbor. Revere eventually assumed the command of Castle William. Later, he was dismissed after the disastrous events of the Penobscot expedition, but a formal court-martial exonerated him of the charges of disobeying orders.

Revere was a gifted craftsman in silver. Some of his pieces are on display in museums such as the Boston Museum of Fine Art. Among other things, he crafted plates and tea services and engraved plates for printing presses. One of Revere's most famous engravings depicted the events of the Boston Massacre.

After the Revolutionary War, a great economic depression followed, and the silver trade was difficult. Revere opened a general store that offered hardware and home goods. He became interested in working with metals other than gold and silver. By 1788, he had opened a foundry for iron and brass in

Boston's North End, hoping to take advantage of the growing market for church bells. His foundry, which cast the first bell in Boston, went on to cast nine hundred more.

But much of his trade was in casting bolts and fittings for a growing shipbuilding trade in Boston. By 1801, Revere was a pioneer in copper plating, opening the first copper mill in North America just south of Boston. Copper from Revere's mills plated the dome of the Massachusetts State House. He also produced the sheeting used to cover the hull of the *USS Constitution* (known in another American legend as *Old Iron Sides*). Most of the ships from that era are long gone, but because of the Revere copper sheeting which has protected the ship from the corrosive effects of the sea, the *USS Constitution* has survived to this day. In fact, the *USS Constitution*, the oldest ship still actively commissioned by the United States Navy, is still guarding Boston Harbor as she has been for more than two hundred years.

Whether based in legend or fact, there can be no denying that Paul Revere was a great American patriot, one of the men instrumental in the events that led up to the American revolt against the British. It is because of men like Paul Revere that America became an independent nation. As important as he was as a patriot, a founding father, and a member of the Sons of Liberty, his role after the Revolutionary War as one of America's first entrepreneurs was perhaps even more important. Like many of the other founding fathers—Benjamin Franklin, George Washington, and Thomas Jefferson—he demonstrated that the new nation did not have to be dependent on others to make its own way in the world. Americans were able to produce everything needed for survival without being dependent on outside help. Paul Revere and many other patriots recognized that the island nation of England needed America much more than America needed England.

Brother Paul Revere was a member of St. Andrew's Lodge, Boston, Massachusetts. The lodge had been organized in 1756, but it had not received its charter from the Grand Lodge of Scotland. Revere was initiated into the lodge as an apprentice on September 4, 1760, the very day the St. Andrew's Lodge received its charter from the Grand Lodge of Scotland. The membership of the lodge was not based on wealth or prestige but entirely upon character. The lodge was silent, but it held great influence in Boston. It promoted the brotherhood of man. It is a common legend that some of the members of St. Andrew's Lodge may have even influenced the events leading to the American Revolution.

The St. Andrew's Lodge at that time had bought the old Green Dragon Tavern, a large brick structure on Union Street, in which to hold lodge meetings. It was known that other lodges and some radical groups were also meeting there under the well-established secrecy of the Masons. Though controversial among historians, some believe that many of the revolutionary ideas may have been hatched at the St. John's Lodge under the verdigris encrusted copper dragon that decorated the entrance of the tavern.

In all likelihood, the mission to fill Boston Harbor with English tea was planned at the Green Dragon. The only question is whether it was planned by the Masons or one of the revolutionary groups meeting there. The lodge is known to have met the evening the tea ships arrived from England; however, the official record of the lodge indicates the lodge was adjourned because of too few members to meet. It is also known to have met the night of the Boston Tea Party, but the record indicates the same thing for that night as well—adjournment because of too few members to meet. It is more likely that one of the groups, such as the Sons of Liberty, planned the Boston Tea Party. Several members of St. John's Lodge, like Paul Revere, also belong to the Sons of Liberty. But there is little evidence that connects the Masonic lodge with the revolutionary groups that were known to be involved with the Boston

Tea Party, primarily the Sons of Liberty—other than sharing the building. It makes for an interesting story nonetheless.

Revere later served as Grand Master of Massachusetts from 1794-1797. He was an active Mason for the remainder of his life.

THE PRESIDENTS

"I do not look upon these United States as a finished product. We are still in the making."

—*Franklin D. Roosevelt,*
Holland Lodge No. 8, NY

SIX

The Era of Good Feelings

"A little flattery will support a man through great fatigue."

The two secretaries did not get along. Their disagreements were publicly known. The secretary of war, John Armstrong, was an arrogant, abrasive man, who openly showed his dislike of the secretary of state, who though usually a very tolerant and patient man, fought against Armstrong. He believed Armstrong was not the right person for the job of secretary of war; in fact, he believed he should have been assigned to the position.

The British were massing forces in the West Indies, and there were reports of troops massing in European ports as well. The secretary of state believed that there was a plan for the British to attack the capital city of Washington, D. C. He strongly urged the formation of an intelligence service to track enemy movements and to give advanced warning of an invasion force. But Secretary of War Armstrong, in his typical demeaning and condescending way towards the secretary of state, dismissed the idea of an attack on the capital as a fable, saying he had confidence in the military force employed. Some critics claim that Armstrong may not have taken any action on the secretary of state's recommendation out of stubbornness, not wanting to concede that the secretary of state might have a point. For whatever reason, Armstrong's opinion never changed—even when a British squadron appeared at the mouth of the Potomac.

Secretary of War Armstrong quickly moved to fortify Fort Washington with six hundred regulars. The secretary of state rounded up a handful of "gentleman volunteers" and offered to help capture the enemy that had been located on Blackstone's Island. He even offered to lead the expedition. The secretary of war quickly vetoed the secretary of state's plan and then admonished him, stating that the responsibility lay with the militia. The British withdrew from Blackstone's Island, but raids along the Chesapeake River continued with little or no action taken by Armstrong to defend against them.

The secretary of state took his argument that Armstrong was being derelict in his duty to President Madison, who agreed with him. The President established a new military district. Armstrong was openly hostile to the new unit that was led by William Winder, a successful Maryland lawyer. Armstrong refused to call out his militia to train the men. He also neglected to equip the new unit. President Madison, who was away from the capital, was unaware of Armstrong's obstructionism. When he did learn of it later, he ordered Armstrong to allow the new unit to call on the militia for training—an order that Armstrong ignored. Madison formally reprimanded Armstrong, but before a decision could be made on how to deal with him and his conduct, what the secretary of state had feared all along became a reality.

On August 16, 1814, a flotilla of fifty British ships and a force of nearly five thousand men under the command of General Robert Ross joined up with the raiding squadron of Sir Alexander Cochrane. The unthinkable was happening—the

British were descending on the capital of the United States, and the capital was totally unprepared for the advance.

Reluctantly, Secretary of War Armstrong consented to allow the secretary of state himself to lead a troop of cavalry on a scouting mission. So desperate was the situation that nobody thought it was at all odd that a member of the President's cabinet was personally leading an intelligence mission. But it was too little too late. The defense of the city fell to Winder. By August 25, the British were advancing up the Potomac towards Washington, D.C. Only the fort that guarded the capital, Fort Washington, stood between the British and the city. When a squadron of British began bombarding Fort Washington, an enormous explosion echoed for miles. Most of the residents of the city who heard the explosion assumed that the British had overtaken the fort and destroyed it, but in fact, the fort was destroyed by its own commander without a single defensive shot having been fired at the British.

The residents of the city were evacuated, and a small resistance was mounted. By the time the British raid was over, Washington was in flames. The Capitol Building burned. The White House burned. Nearly every public building burned. Winds picked up shortly after the raid, and fire swept across other parts of the city, burning many private homes. But although the city was raided, the British were not able to occupy it. The secretary of state took over the city's defenses. Most of the defenders were convinced that surrender was the only way to save what was left of the capital. Furious, the secretary of state responded to these calls for capitulation by saying that if "any deputation moved towards the enemy it would be repelled by the bayonet." The British were held back by the secretary of state's last-minute defense and were unable to advance beyond Alexandria. Secretary of War Armstrong resigned and never held public office again. The secretary of state assumed a second cabinet appointment as secretary of war after Armstrong left.

★ GREAT AMERICAN FREEMASONS ★

The secretary of state who defended Washington, preventing both its occupation by enemy forces and its surrender to that enemy, and who possibly prevented the United States from once again being under the thumb of the British crown was James Monroe. Later, he would become the fifth President of the United States.

James Monroe was born in Westmoreland County, Virginia, on April 28, 1758, the son of Spence Monroe and Elizabeth Monroe. Westmoreland County, one of the oldest settled areas of Virginia, was the birthplace of two other Presidents—George Washington and James Madison. Monroe, as a boy, was allowed great freedom. He enjoyed riding and hunting. His father was a modest planter, and young Monroe developed an interest in agricultural matters. Years later, Monroe was happiest when engaged in the day to day management of his estates—much like his friend, Thomas Jefferson.

Monroe entered the College of William and Mary in July, 1774. But in the spring of 1776, he became caught up in the patriotic fervor of the Revolution and enlisted in the Third Virginia Regiment. As a lieutenant, Monroe saw action in the battle of New York. In the famous painting of George Washington crossing the Delaware, it is Monroe standing behind Washington in the longboat, holding the American flag. Monroe distinguished himself in service at Trenton, where he was seriously wounded. He was also present during the winter at Valley Forge and participated in the Battle of Monmouth.

In 1780, Monroe returned to Virginia to study law under Thomas Jefferson, who became a lifelong friend and a major influence on him intellectually and politically. Monroe was elected to the Virginia House of Delegates in 1782. His abilities and total dedication to public service won him a seat in the Confederation Congress in 1783. The Congress was meeting in Annapolis, Maryland, at that time, having fled Philadelphia because of threats from unpaid troops who had mutinied. Monroe served in the Confederation Congress until 1786.

★ THE ERA OF GOOD FEELINGS ★

While in Congress, Monroe advocated a stronger government. At that time, there were two factions in Congress: the Nationalists, who wanted to expand and strengthen the central government, and the group that opposed them, generally referred to as the anti-Nationalists. Monroe's early opinions about a government with expanded authority, however, seemed to change when, as a member of the Virginia ratifying convention, he joined Patrick Henry and George Mason in opposing the ratification of the United States Constitution, primarily because of the excessive power it granted the Senate. He would later remark, "The best form of government is that which is most likely to prevent the greatest sum of evil."

In 1789, Monroe settled in Albemarle County to be close to Jefferson. Monroe had married Elizabeth Kortright of New York. She was regarded as one of the most beautiful women of the day but reserved and somewhat cold in her manner. They had two daughters, Eliza and Maria Hester. Their only son, James Spence, died in infancy.

Monroe was elected to the United States Senate in 1790. There he joined James Madison in combating Alexander Hamilton's domestic measures which emphasized centralization of powers in the federal government. Monroe, once again showing that his politics had changed, was opposed to centralized power. He, along with Jefferson and Madison, organized the Republican Party.

In 1794, Monroe was named minister to France by President Washington. There was concern that America's relationship with France was beginning to deteriorate because of Washington's seemingly pro-British stance. Because Monroe saw his task as the preservation of Franco-American diplomatic relations with France in the face of Washington's pro-British stance, he acted more as a Republican Party spokesman than as the representative of his government. Dissatisfied with Monroe's performance, Washington recalled him from France in 1797. Monroe, upset at being recalled, defended himself by publishing a harsh attack on Washington's foreign policy.

After the debacle in France, Monroe returned to Virginia and served as governor of Virginia from 1799 to 1802. His superb political savvy and administrative ability won him praise for his decisive action in suppressing a slave uprising in 1800.

President Jefferson called on Monroe in 1803. Jefferson wanted him to go to France to negotiate the purchase of a port on the French-owned lower Mississippi River. During the negotiations, much to Monroe's surprise, Napoleon presented Monroe with the choice of buying either all of Louisiana or none of it. Monroe quickly agreed to purchase all of the Louisiana territory, and Jefferson, in spite of his doubts about the constitutionality of such an expansive territorial acquisition, quickly approved it before Napoleon had a chance to change his mind. The Louisiana Purchase was an enormous success and a vital link in the Western expansion of the United States. The Purchase and the attention it received established Monroe securely as a national figure, whose elevation to the Presidency was only a matter of time.

Monroe held a number of positions in the following years. From 1803 to 1807, Monroe served as minister to Britain. In 1808, he ran against James Madison for President. Monroe and Madison got into a debate over a treaty with Britain that would relax some of Britain's commercial restrictions. Monroe ran against Madison more as a form of protest than as a serious run for the Presidency. Monroe received little support, and Madison was elected.

Monroe served in the Virginia assembly in 1810 and 1811. Then President Madison, apparently not holding a grudge against Monroe for their previous disagreement over the treaty with Britain, appointed him secretary of state. The appointment ended the long debate with Madison.

In 1814, Secretary of State Monroe would become the secretary of war as well after the raid on the capital city by the British. Monroe's dual service in Madison's cabinet made him an obvious choice for President in 1816. The Democratic-Republican congressional caucus chose him as the party's

★ THE ERA OF GOOD FEELINGS ★

candidate. Monroe easily defeated the Federalist candidate, New York Senator Rufus King, by 183 to 34 in the Electoral College to become the nation's fifth President. The Federalist Party had been so badly damaged by its opposition to the War of 1812 that the election of 1816 was the last time it was able to run a candidate.

James Monroe came into the White House amidst reconstruction following the British burning of the city in August, 1814. The new President adopted a reconciliatory policy toward the Federalist critics of the war. He ushered in an era of partisan cooperation that led to the passage of many important policies that helped America establish a national identity in its early years. Monroe's Presidency was referred to as "The Era of Good Feelings." The American government had been plagued almost from the beginning by partisan politics, internal divisions, and external threats. Monroe was determined to change that. Instead of focusing on where the parties disagreed, he sought to find broad national goals that were generally agreeable even across the party lines. He hoped that focusing on the areas where government could agree would help bridge the animosities that had existed since the beginning.

By far, Monroe's greatest achievements as President lay in foreign affairs. Supported by Secretary of State John Quincy Adams, Monroe gave American policy a distinctly national orientation, but he had to do so very carefully because of the wide divisions between the parties in office. Monroe wanted to press Spain to cede Florida and to redefine the boundaries of Louisiana. His chance came when General Andrew Jackson invaded Florida in 1818 in pursuit of hostile Indians. Seizing the posts of St. Marks and Pensacola, Jackson took control of Florida. Many considered Jackson's acts as violations of congressional war powers, but it was exactly what Monroe had wanted. It was no longer an issue of acquiring the territory. They already had it because Jackson had felt it necessary to take it during his pursuit of hostile Indians. All Monroe had to do was figure out how to keep it, and Jackson had given him the political room to work that out.

In his cabinet, Adams, an expansionist, urged Monroe to completely and publicly vindicate Jackson while Crawford and Calhoun demanded that Jackson be reprimanded for exceeding his instructions. Monroe took the middle ground. The posts Jackson took at St. Marks and Pensacola were restored to Spain, but Monroe's administration would accept Jackson's explanation that his actions had been justified by the course of events in Florida at the time. The incident, however, led Spain to finally cede Florida to America and, to America's great advantage, allowed the government to redefine the boundary of the Louisiana Purchase in the Adams-Onís Treaty in 1819 to include the entire territory of Florida.

The Missouri Compromise was another of Monroe's successes. Although the compromise allowed Missouri to enter the Union as a slave state, the success was that the wording in the compromise allowed the government to control and to restrict the institution of slavery in the new Louisiana territories, including any states that might be formed in that territory later on. The Missouri Compromise offered a solution to a question that had been a Constitutional argument for many years: Could the government regulate slavery? It was, in essence, America's first anti-slavery legislation.

In 1823, Monroe made one of the most important speeches in American history to date. It would later be called the Monroe Doctrine. Since the discovery of the New World, European powers were constantly seizing lands for colonization. This colonization was putting the security of the United States at risk as Europeans expanded these territories and encroached on the areas held by the United States. Monroe decided to put a stop to it, and he did it in one speech. The Monroe Doctrine made three very important points. First, Monroe declared that the entire Western hemisphere including Southern, Central, and North America was closed to further colonization from European countries. The second point was a

★ THE ERA OF GOOD FEELINGS ★

reaffirmation of one of the points George Washington had stated in his famous Farewell Address—that the United States of America would become involved in foreign conflicts only if its own rights were disturbed. Finally, Monroe stated that any attempts made by European nations to colonize in the Western hemisphere would be seen as a threat to the national security of the United States. But the Monroe Doctrine was not laying claim over the entire Western hemisphere in the name of the United States. It only stated that the countries in the Western hemisphere had as much right to rule over themselves as the United States did, without fear of being invaded and colonized by European governments, and the United States would back up their rights to freedom with military action if necessary.

During his long career in public service, Monroe accomplished many important goals in creating the national identity of the United States. He demonstrated how a government with two parties with opposing views about government and its role could still come together and agree on issues important to all Americans, regardless of party politics. He helped to redefine the borders of the United States and to put the world on notice that the entire Western hemisphere was off limits to foreign interference. He also took the first tentative steps towards expanding the basic human rights of all Americans, including those trapped in the institution of slavery.

Monroe died from heart failure and tuberculosis on July 4, 1831, fifty-five years to the day after the Declaration of Independence was signed. He was the third former President to die on that important national holiday. Thomas Jefferson and John Adams had died on exactly the same day five years earlier—July 4, 1826.

Monroe was originally buried in New York at the Gouverneur family vault in the New York City Marble Cemetery. In 1858, his remains were moved to the President's Circle at Hollywood Cemetery in Richmond, Virginia.

★ GREAT AMERICAN FREEMASONS ★

Brother James Monroe was initiated November 9, 1775, in St. John's Regimental Lodge, a military lodge attached to the Continental Army. After the Revolutionary War, Brother Monroe became a member of Williamsburg Lodge No. 6 in Williamsburg, Virginia.

SEVEN

Old Hickory

"Any man worth his salt will stick up for what he believes right, but it takes a slightly better man to acknowledge instantly and without reservation that he is in error."

Dickinson was known as an expert shot with a pistol, but the man he quarreled with had a reputation too. His foe was a seemingly fearless, hard man with a bad temperament, especially harsh and unyielding when insulted. After Dickinson publicly called his foe a coward and a worthless scoundrel, he ignored several opportunities to retract the statement. His foe had no intention of letting the remarks go unchallenged. The quarrel between the two men resulted in a challenge—a duel.

The site of the duel was a full day's ride from Nashville. As Dickinson stopped with his party for rest and food at local inns, he demonstrated his remarkable skill with a pistol. At one inn, while standing twenty-four feet away, he place four balls from his pistol in an area so small the holes could be covered with a silver dollar. Several times he cut a string with a pistol ball at the same range, saying to the innkeeper that if his foe "comes along this road, show him that!" But his foe was apparently unimpressed.

As the two men later faced each other across the field of honor, his foe stood unflinching—determined to let Dickinson fire first—his thin figure somewhat distorted by his loose coat. When the word was given, Dickinson carefully aimed his pistol and fired. A puff of dust flew from the breast from the foe's coat, but to Dickinson's shock, the man remained standing. "Great God," Dickinson said faltering from the line, "have I missed him?"

As Dickinson began to move, Overton, the foe's second, said with his hand on his pistol, "Back to the MARK, sir!" The duel was not over until the other man fired. If Dickinson had tried to leave the field, Overton would have had every right, according to the rules of honor, to shoot him himself.

Dickinson stood, shaken, with his eyes averted, still reeling from the idea that he had somehow missed his mark. He waited as his foe took deliberate aim and pulled the trigger. The gun neither snapped nor fired. Realizing the pistol was on half-cock, the foe pulled the hammer all the way back and aimed again, his blue-grey eyes sighting down the pistol barrel at Dickinson. He fired. Dickinson's face paled. He reeled backwards as his friends rushed to him, catching him before he fell. The shot had found its mark—Dickinson was mortally wounded.

As Dickinson lay dying, his foe walked from the field with Overton on one side and a surgeon who had accompanied the party on the other. Noticing that one of the foe's shoes was full of blood, the surgeon asked if he had been hit. The foe replied, "Oh! I believe he has pinked me a little. Let's look at it. But say nothing about it." He wanted no one to know that Dickinson's ball had not missed, nor did he wish for Dickinson himself to have the satisfaction of knowing, as his life ebbed away, that he had actually hit him.

Dickinson's ball had struck him right where Dickinson believed the heart was, but the thinness of his foe's body and the looseness of his coat had deceived him. Later, it was found that the ball had broken a couple of ribs and painfully raked the breastbone. It was an ugly wound, but it was far from fatal. Even though he survived the injury, it healed badly, causing him pain and complications for many years to come.

But that day the man had hidden his pain well from Dickinson and his party, walking from the field seemingly uninjured. Dickinson had made a serious error in judgment in quarrelling with this battle hardened legend—a man so tough he was called "Old Hickory." The man that fired the shot that ended Dickinson's life was none other than General Andrew Jackson.

Many years later, Jackson faced danger again as he had done so often during his life. It was after a solemn occasion in 1835—the memorial service for a statesman at the United States Capitol. As Andrew Jackson, the seventh President of the United States, left the memorial service and walked out into the Capitol Rotunda, the unthinkable happened. A man quietly approached him from the throng of spectators that had gathered to catch a glimpse of him. When less than ten feet away, the man pulled out a pistol and fired into Jackson's chest. The shot exploded then echoed through the Rotunda, freezing everyone in place, including Jackson. Before anyone could react, the man pulled out a second pistol and fired it, creating the same resounding thunder as before.

The people inside, as well as those gathered outside, were convinced the President had been shot. Jackson believed the same thing until he realized he did not feel any pain. Charging forward, he assaulted the shooter with his cane. This action by Jackson broke the paralysis of the crowd. As his aides pulled Jackson back to protect him, others, including Davy Crockett who had accompanied Jackson out of the service, apprehended the shooter.

During his life, Jackson had been no stranger to gunfire. It was hardly the first time a gun had been leveled at him in anger; in fact, it was said that he had been in so many duels that he "rattled like a bag full of marbles." But, of course, it had been many years since the Hero of New Orleans had last looked down the barrel of a gun. That day in 1835, as a man of sixty-eight, Jackson had not reacted as quickly as he might have in his youth.

The would-be assassin was Richard Lawrence, an out-of-work house painter with a serious mental illness. His motive for assassinating Jackson was his psychotic belief that Jackson had prevented him from becoming the King of England. Lawrence spent the rest of his life in an asylum.

When the police examined the pistols used in the attack, they discovered that both priming caps had gone off, but they had failed to ignite the powder. The explosive sounds that convinced witnesses that Jackson had been shot had been only the sounds of the caps going off. Upon closer inspection, it was discovered that both pistols seemed to have been loaded correctly. When recapped and tested by police later, both pistols fired flawlessly. As news of this got out, many believed the President had been very lucky, but even more believed that Divine Intervention had stepped in to save him. To this day, there is a statue of Andrew Jackson in the Capitol Rotunda where the attack took place.

By the time Jackson ran for the Presidency in 1824, he was already a very famous man. He had started his military career as a courier in the Revolutionary War. Andrew and his brother Robert were captured by the British and held as prisoners of war. Both contracted smallpox in prison. Andrew recovered, but Robert died just days after his mother had arranged for their release. Andrew blamed the British for the loss of his brother. That event festered into a great hatred of the British.

The Battle of New Orleans was Jackson's first entry onto the world stage. Using bales of cotton for protection against the British attack, his militia fought off ten thousand British regulars with a militia of only four thousand men and sixteen cannons. The British suffered two thousand casualties to

Jackson's seventy-one. The battle was a total American victory. It was the last time the British would attempt to encroach on American soil.

Later, in the First Seminole War, Jackson was ordered to end the uprising of Seminole and Creek Indians in Georgia and, at the same time, to prevent Spanish-held Florida from being used as a safe haven for escaped slaves. Jackson determined the best way to do that was to take the entire territory of Florida from the Spanish for the United States, which is exactly what he did. He ran the Indians out of Georgia and the Spanish out of Florida in short order, which was what President James Monroe had wanted without saying it. As a shrewd politician, Monroe had been vague enough in his orders to Jackson to give himself deniability later on. When Jackson delivered Florida to the United States, he was praised as a man of action, full of bravado and confidence, but by the time he ran for President, the very qualities that had made him so admired were the very things his critics claimed made him unsuitable. He was seen in Washington, D.C., as an uncultured but effective tool of war but hardly one of the genteel aristocrats of the political spectrum.

He was nominated by the Tennessee legislature in 1822. He was the first man to run for President of the United States from the West. As a man who had grown up in the wilderness, who had made his own way in the world, and who had met those challenges with such resounding success, he was beloved and revered by the common masses. But amongst the elitist in Washington, D. C., he was thought to be a brash, unintelligent, and uncivilized man, totally unfit for the highest office in government. Even Thomas Jefferson was reputed to have told Daniel Webster that Jackson was a dangerous man and unsuitable for the Presidency. But Jackson was determined to win—to win government back for the people and to make government truly representative of the people.

Jackson ran against three other candidates in 1824: Henry Clay, who was Speaker of the House of Representatives at the time, William Crawford, and John Quincy Adams. Andrew Jackson received the largest share of the popular vote and the most electoral votes as well, but with four candidates, no candidate had the majority, so it was up to the House of Representatives to decide the election. Jackson had ninety-nine electoral votes, John Quincy Adams eighty-four, Crawford forty-one and Clay thirty-seven. Clay's votes, however, were not considered because he was Speaker of the House. Since most of Clay's backers considered Jackson their second choice for President, the general consensus was that Clay's votes would go to Jackson and that he would win the Presidency. However, in what was later dubbed a "corrupt bargain," Clay gave his votes to John Quincy Adam—an act which surprised many. Very shortly after John Quincy Adams was announced the winner of the election, he made Henry Clay the Secretary of State. It was pretty obvious even to the elitists in government that Adams and Clay had made a deal.

Jackson was outwardly calm. He even attended a reception for the President-elect given by President Monroe. Adams wrote in his diary, "It was crowded to overflowing. General Jackson was there, and we shook hands. He was altogether placid and courteous."

But Jackson was livid. He was convinced, as were his many supporters, that Henry Clay had traded his votes for the Secretary of State position. Jackson later said, "The Judas of the West has closed the contract and will receive the thirty pieces of silver. His end will be the same." Jackson supporters claimed they had been robbed. The *Nashville Gazette* declared Jackson a candidate for President in 1828 without even consulting him, but Jackson was more than willing to make another run for the Presidency. It was the beginning of one of the longest and ugliest campaigns in the history of American politics—even by today's standards.

For the next four years, shots were exchanged between Andrew Jackson and John Quincy Adams in the press. Jackson accused Adams of being a dishonest and corrupt politician—a perfect example of what was wrong with government. Adams accused Jackson of being a murderer and a dangerous militant, as well as immoral in his personal life. One of the ugliest accusations made during the campaign was about the marital status of Jackson's wife, Rachel, early in their courtship. The Adam's camp claimed she was not divorced from her first husband when her relationship began with Jackson. Of all the accusations back and forth, this one seemed to upset Jackson more than any other—perhaps because it was true. It took a very serious toll on his wife, Rachel, as well.

Jackson won a sweeping victory in the second election. Rachel died less than two months before he took office. Because Adams' supporters had made the crude and insidious suggestion about her in the papers, Jackson blamed Adams for Rachel's death. He never forgave him.

Jackson was the first "man of the people" to win the office. He had his share of resounding successes as President and his share of failures. He strongly supported the elimination of the "spoils system." He believed that limiting the number of terms a politician could serve in office would reduce corruption and the trading of favors amongst politicians—favors like the one he believed Clay had traded with Adams in the 1824 election.

Jackson also sought to destroy the United States Bank. He was critical of it for a number of reasons. He didn't trust the bank. He believed it was wrong for a single institution to have control over the majority of the nation's financial strength. He believed the main objective of the United States Bank was to make the rich even richer. He believed that by having the entire nation's security under the control of one entity left the nation open to the possibility of foreign control should that bank change hands in the future. He believed the bank held too much sway and influence over Senate members. Finally, he believed the United States Banks favored Northern industrial states over Southern and Western states. Jackson favored giving control of the nation's financial security to a host of state and local banks. In 1832, Jackson successfully destroyed the United States Bank by blocking the renewal of its charter. While Jackson's plan succeeded in the short term, it did lead to a major depression in 1834. He was censured by Congress for defunding the bank, but that was later expunged from the record by the "Jacksonians" when they won control of the Senate. In the long run, Jackson proved correct.

During the Presidential race in 1828, Jackson's detractors had called him a "jackass." While such a term might have been taken as an insult by politicians of that day, Jackson saw it as a compliment. He liked the term, and used it. Later, the jackass became the symbol of the Democratic Party that he founded.

Though much can be said about Jackson, both against him and in his favor, he was a remarkable symbol to a young nation. Jackson was the first common man to pull himself up by his bootstraps to become President. He demonstrated to the nation that America was the land of opportunity and that government belonged to the American people. From his humble birth in South Carolina (or North Carolina, as both claim him), he was the last President to have been a participant in the Revolutionary War and the only President to have been a prisoner of war. He was a general and commander of American forces at the Battle of New Orleans, a lawyer, a judge on Tennessee's Supreme Court, the military governor of Florida, the first congressman from Tennessee, and, later, the first "frontier" President. Jackson's portrait has appeared not only on the modern twenty-dollar bill, also on the five, ten, fifty, and the ten thousand dollar bills in the past. His portrait was on the Confederate one thousand dollar bill, a fact that would have been very much to his disliking as he was a firm and uncompromising Unionist.

Brother Andrew Jackson was raised in Harmony Lodge #1 in Nashville, Tennessee. He was also an Honorary Member of Federal Lodge #1 of the Free & Accepted Masons in Washington, D.C., and of Jackson Lodge #1 Free & Accepted Masons, which was named in his honor, in Tallahassee, Florida (which belonged to Spain before he "liberated" it). He also served as Grand Master of Masons in the State of Tennessee in 1822-1823.

EIGHT

The First Modern President

*"Our differences are politics.
Our agreements are principles."*

The nineteen-year-old quartermaster sergeant had already been warned by two officers that the field he intended to cross was impassable, but he had a mission to complete. It was his job to see that his units were fed and had other provisions. When several units had been cut off after crossing Antietam Creek during the Battle of Antietam, he rounded up several stragglers from the fighting. They prepared hot food and coffee for the trapped men. The only way to get the provisions to the men was by crossing an open field controlled by Confederate fire. The sergeant loaded the wagons, asked for a volunteer to accompany him, and, despite the officers' warnings, took off hell bent for leather towards the other side, as the countryside shook from the incoming artillery fire. Despite the back of the wagon being taken off by a small cannonball, they made it to the other side. His commander, Colonel Rutherford B. Hayes (later President of the United States), recommended him for a lieutenancy. The army wanted to award the

★ THE FIRST MODERN PRESIDENT ★

young sergeant the Congressional Medal of Honor for his valor, but he refused the honor.

The young man went on to serve a distinguished career in the military during the Civil War, but he declined a peacetime lieutenancy in the army when the war ended. Instead, he opted to finish the education he had just begun when the war broke out. He mustered out of the army in September of 1865 as a captain and brevet major. He went on to be a congressman, a governor, and finally, the President of the United States. After being elected President, he was asked "How shall I address you?" by a fellow veteran of the Civil War. "Call me Major," he replied. "I earned that. I am not so sure of the rest."

This man was the twenty-fifth President of the United States—William McKinley.

McKinley's political career began when he was elected as a Republican to the United States House of Representatives with the assistance of his former commander in the army, Rutherford B. Hayes. He served first between 1877 and 1882, and again between 1883 and May 27, 1884. He lost his seat to Jonathan H. Wallace when the results of the 1883 election were successfully contested. Undeterred, McKinley ran for the House of Representatives again and won, serving from 1885 to 1891. He served as chairman of the Committee on Ways and Means between 1889 and 1891. He authored the McKinley Tariff, which raised rates to the highest in history. It was a very unpopular, widely criticized bill, which led to the Democratic landslide victory of 1890. McKinley narrowly lost his seat by a margin of only three hundred votes. He returned to Ohio, where he was elected to two terms as governor of Ohio.

McKinley's great strength was in his character. He was honest to a fault. He believed in doing the right thing. He was seen as an amiable, intelligent, and deliberate man of impeccable character. In all of his years in the military and in public office, he was never mired by any kind of a scandal, which at that time of political treachery, deceit, and outright fraud was a remarkable accomplishment.

A good example of his character was his conduct at two Republican National Conventions. By the time he ran for President in 1896, he had been involved in Republican National Conventions since 1880. Twice he had nearly been nominated as the Republican candidate for President. The first time his name was suggested for candidacy was in 1888 when a delegate from Connecticut threw McKinley's name out to the cheers of many of the other delegates. McKinley stood, a representative from Ohio, and said he had been instructed by his state, without one dissenting voice, to cast his vote for John Sherman; therefore, he could not allow himself to be a candidate. Speaking to the convention delegates, he said, "I cannot with honorable fidelity to John Sherman, who has trusted me in his cause and with his confidence; I cannot consistently with my own views of my personal integrity consent, or seem to consent, to permit my name to be used as a candidate before the convention."

Four years later, in 1892, he was the chairman of the convention. During the first ballot, the leader of the Ohio delegation announced their full vote for McKinley. The convention erupted in activity as other states consulted with their delegates and one leader after another changed their vote to McKinley. But McKinley, an Ohio delegate himself, knew Ohio could not have a "full vote" because he knew his vote had been for Harrison. McKinley challenged the vote; the leader argued that McKinley was not a member of the delegation at the present time—his alternate had voted for him. "I am a delegate from that State," McKinley shouted over the roar of the crowd, "and I demand that my vote be counted."

When the vote was polled, it was discovered that one of the votes was for Harrison—it was McKinley's vote. McKinley moved to have the nomination made unanimous, which cinched the nomination for Harrison. Declining the nomination again was another example of McKinley's unwavering principles and honesty; it most assuredly paved the way for his nomination four years later.

McKinley's nomination and eventual election in 1896 was a major breakthrough for the Republican party. McKinley's campaign was the first modern one. His manager, Mark Hanna, raised 3.5 million dollars, and using new marketing and advertising techniques, his staff got their message out to the people in a variety of media newly available at the time. Theodore Roosevelt commented that the 1896 campaign sold McKinley like soap. The image the campaign advertised, however, was not an image the campaign created. McKinley was a well known, powerful, and extremely popular candidate. He secured his party's nomination on the first ballot as New York's choice for President, not by playing politics with the well established Eastern political machine but by defeating it with overwhelming popular support. McKinley had earned his reputation by through his own consistent actions, his loyalty to those he served, and his unwavering commitment to his own principles and ideals. His supporters knew it, his party knew it, and even his detractors and political adversaries knew it. He easily won the election of 1896.

It was the first time since Abraham Lincoln's day that the Republican Party was able to solidify its majority; as a result, it dominated American politics for a generation. Much of this confidence and success was undoubtedly due to McKinley's image—the people put tremendous faith in him. They knew that McKinley, without question, would always do what he believed was right and honorable.

President McKinley's America was a nation on the verge of change. It was beginning to see a period of prosperity and recognition as a world power. Many have argued that both of these developments were because of McKinley and the confidence everyone seemed to share in the new McKinley administration. The political agitation and suspense between parties ended for a time; as a result, business, agriculture, and individuals all enjoyed a period of growth and prosperity.

In addition, technology was beginning to change the world. McKinley was the first President to use the telephone extensively. During the Spanish American War, he was the first President to manage a war from a White House war room. He had instant contact to the front lines both by telephone and telegraph. He also kept the American people well informed about what his administration was doing, further cementing the trust the nation already had in him. He turned the White House into a news center, releasing printed news summaries to the press on a regular basis.

He was the first President who travelled extensively—putting himself out there for the American people to see, to hear, and to talk with one on one. He was the first President to visit California, for example. He also had plans to travel abroad. Since America was becoming a world power, McKinley felt it was time to secure a place on the world stage by visiting other nations.

Shortly after his second term began, President McKinley visited the Pan-American Exposition in Buffalo, New York, on September 5, 1901. The Pan-American Exposition was filled with displays of America's pre-Industrial Revolution technological advancements. These expositions were popular all over the world. Paris had held an exposition the year before in 1900 where the American pavilion had been a major draw. Americans seemed to be leading the pack in technological advancements. The modern marvels on display at these scientific expositions stunned the world.

McKinley, as a modernist, wanted to visit the exposition, not only to enjoy seeing the wonders on display himself but also to talk to the American people about the future. This kind of exposition was obviously the best place to do that. On the first day, McKinley made a speech in which he seemed to question his own past views of supporting tariffs in this new modern technological society. He was beginning to see that American's exclusivity was changing. He said, "We must not repose in fancied security that we can forever sell everything and buy little or nothing. The Period of exclusiveness is past."

McKinley, the modern President, saw the world was on the verge of change, and America had to change with it. In that same speech, he encouraged the growth of the Merchant Marine and supported the building of an Isthmian canal. His words were received with tremendous support, but fate would see his vision of the future carried out by the hands of others.

The following afternoon, McKinley was standing on the steps of the Temple of Music, shaking hands with the public. One of the men standing in line to meet the President, Leon Frank Czolgosz, had intentions other than just shaking hands with McKinley. When Czolgosz got to McKinley, he used the pistol he had concealed in his right hand with a handkerchief to shoot McKinley twice at close range.

The first bullet, which did little damage, was easily removed. The second bullet passed through McKinley's stomach and kidney and lodged in the muscles in his back. Fearing that nineteenth century surgery might do more harm than good, doctors decided to leave the bullet where it was. Oddly enough, one display at the exposition was of the newly invented X-ray machine, which could have easily located the second bullet, but the side effects of X-rays were unknown so it was not used. Another ironic note is that the exposition was lit by thousands of light bulbs, but there was no lighting in the exposition's emergency hospital. Medical personnel were unable to use candle light because ether, a highly flammable substance, was being used to keep McKinley unconscious. Instead, instrument pans were used to reflect light from a window while McKinley's wounds were being treated.

After a week, McKinley seemed to be recuperating. Doctors thought he would make a full recovery. But McKinley took a sudden turn for the worse and went into shock. He died on September 14, 1901, eight days after he was shot, from gangrene which surrounded his wounds. He was buried in Canton, Ohio.

While modern technology could not save McKinley's life, it did play a role in that of Leon Frank Czolgosz, who was found guilty of assassinating McKinley. Czolgosz was introduced to a brand new modern marvel himself—Sparky. He was electrocuted in the chair, instead of being hanged at the gallows.

William McKinley is often overlooked as a major American President. There are two reasons for this. McKinley was a manager more than he was a politician. He most often kept his own counsel, which made him difficult to know—he listened much more than he spoke. McKinley was also a very careful, deliberate policy maker. As a result of the time and care he took in making major decisions, he sometimes appeared to others as indecisive. Because of his somewhat stiff, circumspect personality, he was later viewed as more of a product of the past—a Victorian era President. His administration, for many years, has been seen as somewhat lackluster and unremarkable, and he has been, at best, considered a mediocre President.

Perhaps this image of McKinley is because he was assassinated, and his full vision was never carried out in his lifetime. Another reason McKinley is so often overlooked for his accomplishments is that he was, and still is, overshadowed by his larger-than-life successor and second term vice president, Theodore Roosevelt. Many of McKinley's plans were carried out, but they were carried out by his energetic and extroverted successor, who, more often than not, is remembered for accomplishing so many of the things that McKinley began.

McKinley's popularity was unrivaled; in fact, he was so popular early in his second term in 1901 that he felt it necessary to squash rumors that he would run for a third term. McKinley helped usher the United States into an era of prosperity and patriotism. He also helped the nation take its first tentative steps towards being a recognized world power. He renewed, through his own impeccable character and example, the nation's belief in its government officials and restored its faith in the political system. And he accomplished all of these things in just over one Presidential term. Few other Presidents

★ THE FIRST MODERN PRESIDENT ★

in history have accomplished so much in so short time. McKinley should rightly be recognized as one of America's Presidential greats. McKinley's views, policies, and attitudes helped to bring America into the modern age; in fact, history in recent years has begun to view McKinley much differently as, if not as a great President, certainly as a near-great one.

Brother William McKinley is sometimes said to have become a Master Mason in Hiram Lodge No. 10 in Winchester, West Virginia, in 1865. Later research however, seems to indicate he actually received his degrees at Hiram Lodge No. 21 in Winchester, Virginia. McKinley was also affiliated with Canton Lodge No. 60 in Canton, Ohio, and was later a charter member of Eagle Lodge No. 43. He received the Capitulary degrees in Canton in 1883 and was made a Knight Templar in 1884.

NINE

The Rough Rider

"Speak softly and carry a big stick."

A dark cloud of grief had descended suddenly and unexpectedly on the nation. The same nation had just recently celebrated the end of a long and bloody war, but with a single gun shot, the victory celebration had ended in a horrible national tragedy. On June 25, 1865, a six-year-old boy watched silently from the second floor of his grandfather's house in New York as 75,000 people marched by in procession behind a funeral cart drawn by sixteen horses. Through the glass panels on the cart, the boy saw the coffin that carried the remains of Abraham Lincoln. It was a moment that would leave a lasting impression on him.

The boy was pale and sickly, and suffered frequent asthma attacks. Often, he had to sleep sitting up because of the difficulty he had breathing. His mother and father were both very concerned about the young boy's future. His father frequently took him on carriage rides around the streets of New York, and the family often went on outdoor trips to help force air into his lungs. The boy was also treated with black coffee and nicotine from a cigar, which were common treatments at the time. However, nothing worked for very long.

What the boy lacked in health, he made up for in intelligence. He was fascinated with nature. Even before he could read, he would ask his mother and sister to read to him from Dr. David Livingstone's *Missionary Travels and Researches in Southern Africa*. Beginning with the skull of a seal that was given to him, he began collecting and preserving specimens of every animal he could find. He would record detailed notes about his specimens in his notebooks. Much to his mother's displeasure, many of these specimens wound up stored in her icebox.

But his health continued to be a major concern. By the time he was twelve, his asthma showed no signs of improvement. Despite a long trip to Europe and daily twenty-mile walks with his father, he was often unable to blow out a candle.

Afraid for him, his father finally took him aside and said, "You have the mind but not the body, and without the help of the body, the mind cannot go as far as it should. You must make your body. It is hard drudgery to make one's body but I know you will do it."

The young boy looked up to his father, smiled enthusiastically, and replied "I'll make my body."

And he did, with unrestrained enthusiasm. Almost immediately, he began strength training at a local gym. Later, he would have his own gym at home. His health improved dramatically. Within a year, he was well enough to go on a camping trip with his family. He had a great time canoeing the river, climbing mountains, and sleeping outside on the ground—activities he would have been incapable of only a few months earlier. Around this time, he went an entire month without a single asthma attack. He continued to work out with weights, swing on bars, and use a punching bag. His energy increased and his health improved until he became a model of healthy youthful exuberance.

At the same time, his interest in nature expanded to include hunting and taxidermy. In the beginning, he was not a very good shot with a rifle and managed to hit very little. Later, it was discovered that he was extremely nearsighted. Once he was fitted with eyeglasses, his aim became markedly better—and the size of his specimen collection began to increase. The thick round glasses and the seemingly inexhaustible supply of energy would later become his trademark. One can almost see this man charging up San Juan Hill in Cuba at the head of his volunteer regiment of Rough Riders during the Spanish-American War—he was Theodore "Teddy" Roosevelt, the twenty-sixth President of the United States.

Theodore Roosevelt, Jr. was born on October 27, 1858, into a wealthy family, the second of four children of Thee and Mittie Roosevelt. He was nicknamed Teddy by his family. Three years after his birth, the nation was plunged into the Civil War. Theodore's father was a Unionist who supported the policies of Abraham Lincoln. His mother, originally from Savannah, Georgia, quietly supported the Confederacy. Thee wanted to join the Union army, but afraid that joining would cause a riff with his wife, he hired a soldier to fight in his place, as many men of wealth and privilege did in those days, and spent the war years helping to get financial aid to the families of Union soldiers. As a result of his efforts during the war, Thee became close friends with Abraham and Mary Todd Lincoln.

Once Theodore Roosevelt, Jr. overcame his health problems, he was off and running. Often compared to a steam locomotive or a tornado, he became a man of tremendous energy and enthusiasm with a wide variety of interests and an insatiable appetite for success.

While at Harvard University, Roosevelt was active in many clubs, such as rowing and boxing. He was the editor of a student magazine and a member of both the Alpha Delta Phi and Delta Kappa Epsilon fraternities. He graduated Phi Beta Kappa and *magna cum laude* from Harvard in 1880.

He married Alice Hathaway Lee, on October 27, 1880. He was advised by a doctor after a physical that due to a serious heart condition, he should find a desk job and avoid strenuous exercise—advice he completely ignored. He entered Columbia Law School, but when an opportunity to run for New York assemblyman came up in 1881, he dropped out to pursue a new goal of entering public life. He won a seat in the assembly and served until 1884. Four days after the birth of his daughter, also named Alice, his wife Alice passed away. Roosevelt was deeply affected by her death. Overcome with grief, he refused to speak her name again, even omitting her name from his autobiography. Though he would later remarry and have more children, his daughter Alice would never be called Alice. Instead, she was always called Sister by her half-brothers and sisters.

Shortly after his first wife's death, Roosevelt left the New York Assembly, put his daughter into the long-term care of his sister, Bamie, and sought a simpler life in the Badlands of the Dakota Territory. Roosevelt built a ranch he named Elk Horn, where he lived as a rancher, hunter, and deputy sheriff. He learned to ride, rope, and hunt. Once as a deputy sheriff, Roosevelt tracked down three outlaws who had stolen his river boat. After capturing them, he decided that instead of hanging them, he would take them back to Dickson for trial. After sending his foreman back up the river with the boat, Roosevelt set out with the three outlaws over land. Reading first Tolstoy and then a dimestore western one of the outlaws was carrying, he guarded them for forty straight hours without sleep as they traveled to Dickson.

After a bad winter wiped out his cattle herd and his investments in 1886, he returned to Sagamore Hill, a home he had bought in 1885 in Oyster Bay, New York. This would remain his home for the rest of his life. In 1886, he married his childhood sweetheart, Edith Kermit Carow, with whom he would have five more children.

By the time Theodore Roosevelt became President at age forty-two, he already had an impressive resume. He had become a published writer at age eighteen, a husband at twenty-two, a New York State assemblyman at twenty-three, a father and a widower at twenty-five, a rancher at twenty-six, a New York mayoral candidate at twenty-seven, a husband again at twenty-eight, a Commissioner of the United States at thirty, a police commissioner at thirty-six, an assistant secretary of the Navy at thirty-eight, a colonel of the U.S. Volunteer Cavalry regiment the Rough Riders at thirty-nine, and upon his return from Cuba, the governor of New York in 1898 still only thirty-nine years old. But Roosevelt had his eye on the Presidency even then. With his tremendous popularity as a war hero, the way to the White House seemed clear.

Roosevelt supported fellow Republican William McKinley's campaign for a second term as President in 1900, touring the Midwest in 1899 as if he were a candidate for President himself. One political cartoon at the time depicted Roosevelt as a tornado racing across the prairie, blowing away the Democratic candidate, William Jennings Bryan. Roosevelt had quietly begun working on his own plans for running for President in 1904. But even though he was a very popular war hero, he knew America's attention span was short. He wondered if he would have that same popularity in another five years.

Henry Cabot Lodge was the first to suggest to Roosevelt that he run as McKinley's vice president. Roosevelt was adamantly against that idea because he felt he could do more as the governor of New York than as vice president of the United States. He said, "I would simply be a presiding officer, and that I should find a bore." Roosevelt even went to Washington, D.C., to tell McKinley he did not want the job. To Roosevelt's embarrassment, he discovered that McKinley was not even considering him since McKinley thought Roosevelt was too brash and too unpredictable to be a running mate. However, the Republican National Convention, which felt differently, nominated Roosevelt as McKinley's running mate in 1900. McKinley and Roosevelt won by the largest vote margin at that point in history. But Roosevelt would not remain vice president for very long.

On September 6, 1901, President William McKinley was shot and mortally wounded in Buffalo, New York, after visiting the Pan American Exposition. When he died on September 14, 1901, Theodore Roosevelt became the fourth vice president to become the President after the death of a President—the third within the previous forty years with the assassinations of Lincoln, Garfield, and then McKinley.

Not everyone was happy. Republican boss, Mark Hanna, was one of Roosevelt's most vocal detractors. He had been against Roosevelt's nomination as vice president to begin with. While riding on McKinley's funeral train, he said, "I told William McKinley it was a mistake to nominate that wild man . . . Now look, that damned cowboy is President of the United States."

Six months after being sworn in as vice president, Theodore Roosevelt became President of the United States. He was an energetic and popular President. In 1904, he was elected to a second term. As President, Roosevelt fought for the regulation of industry which included the Hepburn Act of 1906 that granted the Interstate Commerce Commission (ICC) the power to set maximum railroad rates. Roosevelt also pushed Congress to pass the Pure Food and Drug Act and the Meat Inspection Act, both in 1906. These laws required the labeling of food and drugs, the inspection of livestock facilities, and the establishment and enforcement of sanitation requirements at meat packing plants.

But Roosevelt's most famous foreign policy initiative was the construction of the Panama Canal, which would shorten the length of the ocean voyage between New York City and San Francisco by eight thousand miles. The canal took ten years to build at the cost of over two hundred workers' lives due to yellow fever and malaria.

Roosevelt's love of nature and the outdoors led him to perhaps one of his greatest legacies. In 1905, he urged Congress to create the United States Forest Service to manage government forest lands. As President, he set aside more acres for national parks and nature preserves than those set aside by all of his predecessors combined. By the end of his second term, Roosevelt had created 42 million acres of national forests, 53 million acres of national wildlife refuges, and 18 million acres surrounding areas of special interest including the Grand Canyon. In 1907, with Congress growing impatient with Roosevelt's "land grabs," Roosevelt managed to add another 16 million acres of new national forests to his total. Roosevelt believed in the more efficient use of natural resources by lumber companies and mining concerns. He encouraged more and better usage, less waste, and a long-term plan for conservation. Even during his Presidency, Roosevelt promoted his views of conservation in essays he wrote for *Outdoor Life* magazine.

Roosevelt remained active in politics after he left office in 1909, but by 1918, his health was beginning to fail. Even as he was considering another run for President in 1920, he was having trouble with his balance, had lost the hearing in one ear, and was blind in one eye. He was in and out of the hospital suffering from complications from injuries he had sustained on a tour of South America a few years earlier. He was finally confined to a wheelchair. He died on January 6, 1919, at the age of sixty. His last words to the public were read at a benefit he had planned to attend at the Hippodrome in New York: "I cannot be with you; and so all I can do is wish you Godspeed."

He was laid to rest in a small cemetery overlooking Oyster Bay. Vice President Marshall said in his eulogy, "Death had to take him sleeping, for if Roosevelt had been awake, there would have been a fight."

Brother Theodore Roosevelt was made a Mason on April 24, 1901, at Matinecock Lodge No. 806, Oyster Bay, New York. In 1902, Brother Roosevelt said of Freemasonry, "One of the things that attracted me so greatly to Masonry . . . was that it really did live up to what we, as a government, are pledged to—of treating each man on his merits as a Man."

TEN

The New Dealer

*"I ask you to judge me by the
enemies I have made."*

Despite his seeming boundless energy and his robust appearance, he had health problems as a youth. He was constantly bombarded with illnesses that often put him into bed for long periods of time. As an adult, his health problems continued in a long chain of illnesses starting with a bout of bad sinus problems. The following year, he was bedridden for weeks with typhoid fever. His wife, who was nursing him back to health, also came down with it. He was hospitalized with a severe throat infection a few years after that. A year later, he returned from a trip to the European theater with double pneumonia. He was so weak by the time his ship sailed into port that he had to be taken by ambulance from the ship to his mother's home, where four navy men carried him inside. Even before he had fully recovered from the pneumonia, he caught a strain of virulent influenza that was sweeping both America and Europe.

When the first great polio outbreak occurred in 1916, he feared for his five children. Polio was primarily a children's disease. He was so concerned his brood would be afflicted that he kept them away from the city. The first outbreak had claimed as many as 2,448 children in New York alone. Eventually, he sent his children from Maine to be isolated at the family estate outside New York. The Navy vessel which transported them sailed with strict instructions not to touch land, especially anywhere near New York, for fear of infection.

In 1921, while vacationing at Campobello Island, New Brunswick, the man contracted an illness after a day of jogging, sailing, and swimming in the cold water of the Bay of Fundy. He awoke the following day partially paralyzed. A doctor who was vacationing in the area was called. The first diagnosis was a blot clot, which the doctor felt would clear up on its own. But a second doctor was called. His diagnosis was much more serious: poliomyelitis—polio.

For nearly thirty-six months, the man struggled to recover from the initial illness, but he never again walked unaided. As surprising as it may seem, very few people knew he was seriously debilitated. In fact, he was able to convince many people that he was actually getting better. Successfully hiding leg paralysis would be a challenge for about any person, but most especially for one in a very public, high-profile job. But this man—the man who helped to found the *March of Dimes*—did hide it well. He was also, incidentally, the thirty-second President of the United States and the only President elected to more than two terms in office. He was Franklin Delano Roosevelt.

Roosevelt was born on January 30, 1882, in Hyde Park, New York, to James Roosevelt and Sara Ann Delano Roosevelt. Both of his parents were from wealthy old New York families. His paternal grandmother was a first cousin to Elizabeth Monroe, wife of the fifth President of the United States, James Monroe. His mother's family lineage could be traced all the way back to the *Mayflower* passengers. Franklin was their only child.

Roosevelt attended Groton School, which was an Episcopal school in Massachusetts. He later completed his undergraduate studies at Harvard, where he was a member of Alpha Delta Phi fraternity. While he was at Harvard, his fifth cousin, Theodore, became President of the United States. During a White House reception, Franklin met his future wife, Theodore's niece, Anna Eleanor Roosevelt. They married two years later in 1905 and had six children between 1906 and 1916. Roosevelt entered Columbia Law School in 1905, but he never finished a degree. In 1907, he passed the New York State Bar exam and took a job with a prestigious Wall Street firm, Carter, Ledyard & Milburn.

In 1910, Roosevelt ran for the New York State Senate, representing the district around his Hyde Park home in Duchess County, New York. The seat had not been filled by a Democrat since 1884. The Roosevelt name, along with all the wealth and influence associated with it, carried him by a landslide victory to the state capital of Albany, New York. He resigned from the New York State Senate in 1913 when he was appointed Assistant Secretary of the Navy by Woodrow Wilson.

Roosevelt showed great skill and administrative talent in the job, negotiating with Congressional leaders to get budget items approved to expand the Navy and to found the United States Navy Reserve. He became an enthusiastic advocate of using and developing the submarine to combat the World War I German submarine wolf packs that were having such a devastating effect on shipping in the Atlantic. He also supported a plan to lay a barricade of mines in the North Sea between Norway and Scotland. It was while touring American naval facilities in Britain and France in 1918 that he met Winston Churchill, a fellow Freemason, for the first time. When World War I ended in 1918, Roosevelt was charged with demobilization of the Navy although he opposed the plan to completely dismantle the Navy.

In 1920, Roosevelt resigned from his job as Assistant Secretary of the Navy when he was chosen by the 1920 Democratic Convention to run as the vice president on a ticket with James M. Cox of Ohio. When the Cox-Roosevelt ticket was badly defeated by Warren Harding, Roosevelt returned home to Hyde Park and a legal practice, but few doubted that he would eventually run for public office again.

It was at this point in his life, in 1921, that Roosevelt contracted the paralytic illness diagnosed at the time as polio. Studies since have indicated that Roosevelt's illness was more likely Guillain-Barre syndrome and not poliomyelitis. During the three years when he struggled to recover from the disease, Roosevelt was fitted with iron braces on his hips and legs. He worked tirelessly to teach himself to walk short distances by swiveling his hips while balancing on a cane. He felt it was absolutely essential to hide the seriousness of his condition if he were to ever successfully run for public office again. In public, he usually appeared standing, with the support of an aide or one of his sons. He used a wheelchair in private, but he was careful not to be seen in the wheelchair in public. There are very few photographs of him in his wheelchair.

But while Roosevelt may have hidden his condition, he truly believed it was possible to recuperate. Refusing to accept the condition as permanent, he tried a wide range of therapies, including hydrotherapy. In 1926, he bought a dilapidated resort in Warm Springs, Georgia, where he established a hydrotherapy center that treated polio patients. The center still operates as the Roosevelt Warm Springs Institute for Rehabilitation.

After the long and painful three-year recovery time, Roosevelt made his first public appearance at the 1924 Democratic National Convention in New York. He gave a famous speech, referred to by historians as "the happy warrior" speech, to nominate Alfred E. Smith. By 1928, Roosevelt had recovered enough to resume his political career. He ran for governor of New York in 1928, an election he narrowly won.

In 1929, while Roosevelt was governor of New York, the stock market crashed, and the Great Depression began. Roosevelt established a number of new social programs to aid in the poor economic climate, and he assembled a team of crack advisors—advisors he would take with him four years later to the White House. They would become known as Roosevelt's Brain Trust. By the time the 1932 Democratic National Convention was underway, Roosevelt was an obvious candidate along with Al Smith, whom he had supported in 1928. Roosevelt, however, had established a very powerful coalition with Irish leader Joseph Kennedy, newspaper magnate William Randolph Hearst, and California leader William G. McAdoo. When the Texas leader, John Nance Garner, threw his support to Roosevelt, the nomination was cinched. Garner was nominated as the vice presidential candidate.

Roosevelt, running for President in the poverty-stricken shadow of the Great Depression, made a pledge to the American people: "I pledge you, I pledge myself, to a new deal for the American people." Roosevelt's New Deal resonated with the American people, especially those most impacted by the economic blight—the poor, organized labor unions, ethnic minorities, urbanites, and Southern whites. Roosevelt mobilized these New Dealers into a coalition that remained a political force until the early 1960s. Promising, among other things, a reduction in public expenditures and the elimination of redundant and unnecessary bureaucracy in government, Roosevelt drew strong support. He solidified his lead with the promise of repealing prohibition, which he noted would bring in increased tax revenue. With the "wet vote" secure, Roosevelt won 57 percent of the vote and carried all but six states in the election.

Roosevelt's first term as President was a flurry of activity aimed at getting the nation's economy going again. In his first one hundred days, he focused on immediate relief for the people hardest hit, sending to Congress a number of bills that passed easily. Much of the problem with the economic recovery was due to the fact that the American people had lost confidence in the banks. People were neither investing nor spending. In a famous speech on the subject, Roosevelt said, "The only thing we have to fear is fear itself." Roosevelt's optimism and confidence in the nation's recovery did much to reassure the nation.

Much of Roosevelt's time during his first two terms as President was dedicated to economic recovery. Many of the programs Roosevelt and his Brain Trust came up with were aimed at providing jobs, stabilizing depleted markets, and helping the people hardest hit. One of Roosevelt's favorite agencies was the Civilian Conservation Corps (CCC), which hired a quarter million unemployed to work on public projects. In addition, Congress gave the Federal Trade Commission broad powers to provide mortgage relief to millions of farmers and homeowners at risk of losing their homes and property to foreclosure. To further help farmers, the Agricultural Adjustment Administration tried to increase the low prices of farm commodities by paying subsidies to take land out of production and to reduce the size of livestock herds. Some of Roosevelt's programs worked better than others, but slowly the economy began to turn around.

One of Roosevelt's most popular campaign promises was that he would push to repeal prohibition—a promise he intended to keep. In 1933, he issued an Executive Order redefining the standard for alcohol, making 3.2 percent alcohol legal for purchase and consumption. Hard liquor was another subject altogether. There was still staunch opposition against legalizing it. However, once Roosevelt legalized 3.2 percent alcohol, cracks began to form in the foundation of the arguments to maintain the prohibition on hard liquor, much of that in the form of popular public opinion. Later in 1933, the Twenty-first Amendment repealed what was left of prohibition.

The Anheuser-Busch Company of St. Louis, which had survived prohibition by manufacturing everything from bottled soda to ice cream, decided to show Roosevelt its appreciation.

It must have been quite a spectacle, even in Washington, D.C., when the famous red Budweiser beer wagon, pulled by a team of Clydesdale horses, turned onto Pennsylvania Avenue and made its way towards the White House to present President Roosevelt with the first case of beer produced by the company since prohibition had begun. As a popular song used in Roosevelt's first election campaign stated, "Happy days are here again!"

It had been an unwritten rule, ever since George Washington had declined a third term as President, that two terms were the limit for a President. When both Ulysses S. Grant and Theodore Roosevelt had attempted to run for a third nonconsecutive term, each received harsh criticism. Roosevelt wanted a third term. He quietly undercut prominent Democrats who were seeking the nomination while saying publicly he would not run again unless drafted. He encouraged the delegates at the 1940 Democratic National Convention in Chicago to vote for whomever they wanted. Then, during the convention, the delegates were stunned when a voice over the loud speaker shouted, "We want Roosevelt . . . The world wants Roosevelt!" The auditorium erupted in enthusiastic cheers, and his nomination was cinched, 946 to 147. He won a third term and then four years later, an unprecedented fourth term.

While Roosevelt's first two terms were dominated with economic issues, his third term was dominated by war. By 1940, the German blitzkrieg was sweeping across Europe. American public opinion was isolationist. Americans saw the war as a European problem, which Europeans should fight. Roosevelt, however, was determined to help Churchill defend Britain. At one point, Roosevelt openly violate the 1935 Neutrality Act, which banned the shipment of arms from the United States, by giving Britain fifty American destroyers in exchange for the right to build bases in the British Caribbean islands. By 1941, Germany had invaded Russia, and America was taking a more active role to support the Allies, secretly helping to ferry troops and to provide supply and repair assis-

★ THE NEW DEALER ★

tance at American naval bases. Roosevelt had committed to helping the Allies with a policy of "all aid short of war." But that would soon change.

The sudden, unexpected attack on Pearl Harbor stunned America. The words of Roosevelt's speech are immortal: "Yesterday, December seventh, 1941, a date which will live in infamy, the United States of America was suddenly and deliberately attacked by naval and air forces of the Empire of Japan." A sleeping giant had been awakened—America was at war.

There was no question in Roosevelt's mind that the Japanese would be dealt with, and furious fighting in the Pacific began almost immediately. However, the focus of America's first involvement in World War II was to defeat the greater menace—Adolph Hitler. The Big Three leaders—Roosevelt, Churchill, and Stalin—put differences aside and worked together against a common enemy. Their cooperation in organizing the war effort into a united front had already begun to chip away at the Third Reich's hold over Europe. Even before the Americans landed on D-Day, Adolph Hitler had taken notice that his enemies—so close to crushing defeat only a couple years earlier—were beginning to fight back in earnest with coordinated attacks, by cutting off oil supplies, and with the Allied invasion of French Morocco and Algeria. After D-Day, Hitler's fate was sealed. But Roosevelt would not live to see the end of World War II.

Shortly after being elected to a fourth term as President, Roosevelt's health began to deteriorate significantly. Many were shocked to see how thin and frail he looked. He was so weakened that when he addressed Congress for the last time, he did so seated. However, even though his health was poor, he was obviously still very much in command until the end of his life. Franklin Delano Roosevelt died suddenly on April 12, 1945, at his resort in Warm Springs, Georgia—just months before D-Day, the surrender of Germany, the atomic bombing of Hiroshima and Nagasaki, and finally the surrender of Japan.

Roosevelt's importance and popularity as an American President has not faded over time. He is still considered one of the top five Presidents of all time, rivaled only by Washington, Jefferson, Lincoln, and Kennedy. For twelve years, his leadership and determination brought America through the Great Depression and through one of the most horrific wars in world history. Those challenges made the nation economically stronger and restored the people's belief in America.

Brother Franklin Delano Roosevelt became a Master Mason in Holland Lodge No. 8 in New York, New York, in 1911. He became a member of the Scottish Rite Albany Consistory in 1929 and joined the Shrine in 1930.

ELEVEN

Where the Buck Stops

"My choice early in life was either to be a piano-player in a whorehouse or a politician. And to tell the truth, there's hardly any difference."

His vision had been bad ever since he was a child. When he was eight years old, his mother had taken him to be fitted with spectacles, which was a rarity in the 1890s. The doctor somewhat over emphasized to his mother the dangers involved with breaking the glasses. As a result, the young man was prevented from taking part in many of the rambunctious, rough-and-tumble games enjoyed by other boys his age. He spent his youth learning to play the piano and reading history—pursuits he came to love greatly.

The boy also dreamed of applying to West Point Academy and becoming an officer, but he knew his vision was bad—20/50 in his right eye and 20/400 in his left without glasses. That was far too bad for the young man to get into the military as an enlisted man, let alone ever to become an officer, so he did perhaps the most dishonest thing he would ever do in his lifetime. In order to pass the eye exam for the Missouri National Guard, he memorized the eye chart. It worked. He was accepted into the Guard in 1905. This young man—Harry S. Truman—would go on to become the thirty-third President of the United States.

Harry S. Truman was born on May 8, 1884, in Lamar, Missouri, to John and Martha Truman. His parents gave him the middle name "S" after both his paternal grandfather Anderson Shipp Truman, and his maternal grandfather, Solomon Young. Although using a letter for a name was not an uncommon practice, his middle name often caused confusion. Truman sometimes joked that since S was his middle name and not an initial, it should not have a period. However, Truman himself used a period when he signed his name. To this day, his name in print can be found written both ways. Soon after Harry's birth came a brother, John Vivian, and a sister, Mary Jane.

Harry's father, John, was a farmer and livestock dealer. John was known as a man quick with his words and handy with his fists when crossed. Once he was called as a witness in a law suit. During questioning by an over zealous attorney, John became angry that the attorney as much as called him a liar. John jumped out of the witness chair and chased the attorney out of the courthouse.

Harry's mother was a self-admitted "un-reconstructed Rebel." She had a general distrust of Yankees. Her family farm had been robbed by Northern soldiers during the Civil War—an act she never forgot nor forgave. She was a very intelligent woman with a great fondness for reading as well as being a very talented musician. She was the one who encouraged young Harry in both of those pursuits. He became a voracious reader and took piano lessons twice a week until he was fifteen, getting up at 5:00 each morning to practice.

Truman's education began when he was six. His family had moved to Independence, Missouri, so that he could attend the Presbyterian Church Sunday School. He did not attend a traditional school until he was eight years old. Truman graduated from Independence High School in 1901. After graduation, he took a job with the Santa Fe Railroad as a timekeeper, then worked a variety of clerical jobs until 1906 when he returned to the family farm near Grandview, Missouri.

Truman worked on the farm until 1917. Later, he frequently spoke nostalgically about the years he spent toiling on the farm. His formative years of physically demanding work on the farm and for the railroad gave him a real appreciation for the working classes. It was also during these years that he met Bess Wallace. He even proposed marriage to her in 1911—an offer she declined.

Truman had served in the Missouri National Guard from 1905 – 1911. At the onset of World War in 1917, he rejoined the Guard. Much to his delight, he was chosen to be an officer and later a battery commander in an artillery regiment in France. When the Germans attacked his battery in the Vosges Mountains, the men in the battery started to run away from the fight. Truman got their attention by letting loose with a string of obscenities he later said he learned while working on the Santa Fe Railroad. The men, shocked by the outburst from this usually quiet, reserved officer, resumed their positions—not a single man in the battery was lost.

The events of World War I greatly transformed Truman and brought to light his great leadership skills. His war record would make his later political career possible.

After World War I ended, Truman returned to Missouri as a captain. Truman once said, "In my Sunday School class there was a beautiful little girl with golden curls. I was smitten at once and still am." Back home, he found the girl with the golden curls and proposed to her a second time. Bess Wallace accepted the second proposal, and they married on June 28, 1919. They had one daughter, Margaret, in 1924.

Truman did not go to college until the early 1920s when he studied for two years towards a law degree at Kansas City Law School. He did not complete the degree. He worked as a judge in Jackson County, Missouri, and as Missouri's director for the re-employment program, which was part of the Civil Works Administration.

Then in 1934, Truman was elected as a Democratic senator from Missouri. He owed a lot of his early success to Tom Pendergast, who led a very influential political machine—a machine that was about to be exposed as corrupt. When the Pendergast machine crumbled about the time Truman assumed his Senate seat, Truman found himself under the Pendergast cloud. He was called the "senator from Pendergast," but Truman was never charged with any wrong doing. While embarrassed by the fiasco, he did not try to distance himself from the scandal by renouncing Pendergast.

Six years later, Truman's re-election hopes were bleak. The Pendergast cloud still surrounded him, and two Democrats, Lloyd Stark and Maurice Milligan, challenged his seat, using the Pendergast connection to try to oust him. Their attempt failed—they only split the "anti-Pendergast" vote between them, giving Truman just enough votes to win re-election. It was both a personal triumph and a vindication for Truman since at the time of the election, Pendergast was in prison for tax evasion.

One of Truman's most celebrated accomplishments as a senator from Missouri was when his preparedness committee, known as the Truman Committee, began to look into the wastes in military spending. Since this investigation was taking place during World War II, President Franklin D. Roosevelt had originally feared the investigation would hurt the war effort. Secretary of War Robert Patterson was not pleased about the investigation either and tried to derail the committee. Patterson wrote to the President, saying it was "in the public interest" to suspend the committee. But Truman was not about to allow his investigation to be suspended because he believed it was in the best interest of the nation. Truman wrote to the President himself, ensuring him that his committee was completely behind the President's administration and had no intention of making the military look bad. Roosevelt allowed the investigation to continue. Truman's no-nonsense approach to spending is believed to have saved more than 11 billion dollars.

Truman's ability to work on the bipartisan committee, to pose difficult questions to powerful people, and to be fair-minded earned him a great deal of public acclaim—he became a political celebrity. His reputation as being tough but even-handed led to his nickname, "Give 'em Hell Harry." Truman once said, "I never gave anybody hell! I just told the truth and they thought it was hell."

It was undoubtedly his achievements on the Truman Committee that drew the Democratic Party's attention to him as a possible vice-presidential candidate for Franklin D. Roosevelt's fourth term re-election campaign. Roosevelt had agreed to replace his current vice president, Henry Wallace, because he was seen as too liberal by the party. A deal was brokered with Truman, a deal that would later be dubbed the "Second Missouri Compromise." In 1944, the Roosevelt-Truman ticket easily won the election.

Truman was sworn in on January 20, 1945. To the surprise of many and the utter shock of others, a few days after he was sworn in as vice president, Truman re-established his connection with his disgraced patron and friend, Tom Pendergast, by attending his funeral. He was the only elected official there. When asked about his decision to go, Truman said simply, "He was always my friend and I have always been his."

Truman was to serve only eighty-two days as vice president. During that time, he had few conversations with Roosevelt. He was left completely in the dark about the war, world affairs, and domestic politics. In addition, there was one very big secret—a very large bombshell—he knew nothing about either, a secret that would play a central role in his political future. The bombshell Truman knew nothing about was literally that—a bombshell. America was about to test the world's first atomic bomb as part of the top secret Manhattan Project.

On April 12, 1945, President Franklin D. Roosevelt died suddenly at his resort in Warm Springs, Georgia. When Truman was urgently summoned by the White House, he assumed he was going for a briefing with the President. Instead, he was informed by First Lady Eleanor Roosevelt that the President was dead. When Truman asked if there was anything he could do for her, she responded, "Is there anything we can do for you? For you are the one in trouble now."

Truman was sworn in the following day. He said to the press corps, "Boys, if you ever pray, pray for me now. I don't know if you fellas ever had a load of hay fall on you, but when they told me what happened yesterday, I felt like the moon, the stars, and all the planets had fallen on me."

Shortly after Truman assumed the Presidency, Germany surrendered to the allies. Truman was briefed on the existence of the Manhattan Project. Three months after he took office, the first successful atomic test called the Trinity test took place in the desert near Alamogordo, New Mexico. The atomic bomb was a reality. With Germany no longer a threat, the Allies were anxious to end the war. Truman approved the use of atomic weapons against the Japanese in order to force their surrender and to quickly bring about the end of World War II. Truman once said, "Carry the battle to them. Don't let them bring it to you. Put them on the defensive and don't ever apologize for anything." Harry S. Truman never did apologize for his decision to use the atomic bomb.

Although today the decision to drop the atomic bombs on Japan is considered by many to have been morally wrong, it was not a controversial decision at the time. Neither the United States nor any of the Allied countries had any qualms about using any weapon available to end the war. World War II had cost the Allies billions of dollars, had wiped out entire cities, and had destroyed families, cultures, and economies. Even after Adolph Hitler committed suicide and Germany surrendered, it would take decades before Europe recovered from the war. The destruction on the Pacific side of the war was also great. World War II had caused destruction and death on the largest scale the world had ever seen with more than 53 million lives, both military and civilian, lost.

The Allies were anxious to see the end of the war at any cost. A mainland assault of Japan, like the one launched against Germany on D-Day, would have driven the casualty numbers even higher and dragged the war on for possibly years longer. According to Truman, the decision to use the atomic bomb was not a difficult decision; it was a necessary evil to end the war. The technology had been made available, and even though it was known to be a terrible weapon of mass destruction, Truman and the Allied nations saw it as "merely another powerful weapon in the arsenal of righteousness."

The two bombs were dropped on Hiroshima and Nagasaki in August, 1945, resulting in the deaths of more than 110,000 people. Japan surrendered. For a short time, the first time in a long time, there was peace on Earth. The weapons of war were silent, and while mankind might never completely recover from the carnage of World War II, the rebuilding began.

Truman would go on to serve another term as President. His second election against Thomas Dewey was so close many national newspapers announced erroneously the following morning that Truman had lost the election. There is a famous photo of Truman, grinning broadly while holding up a copy of the *Chicago Daily Tribune* with the headline DEWEY WINS.

Truman's administration would see, amongst other things, the end of World War II, the beginning of the Cold War, and a police action in Korea that would not be known until years later as the Korean War. There were countless issues at home to deal with as well, including the beginnings of the civil rights movement, the "communist witch-hunts" of McCarthyism, and charges of corruption in his administration that, in one scandal alone, led to the resignation of 166 of his appointees. He accepted both the credit for the good things he was able to do and the blame for the bad things that happened during his administration. As he was so fond of saying, "The buck stops here."

After his Presidency ended, Truman remained active in politics from the comfort of the Truman Library in Independence, Missouri. There, Harry and Bess Truman received such famous guests as John F. Kennedy (for whom Truman campaigned during the 1960 Presidential election), Dwight Eisenhower, Lyndon B. Johnson, and Chief Justice Earl Warren. Harry S. Truman died at the age of eighty-eight on December 26, 1972.

Brother Harry S. Truman was initiated on February 9, 1909, at Belton Lodge No. 450, Belton, Missouri. In 1911, several members of the Belton Lodge separated to establish the Grandview Lodge No. 618, Grandview, Missouri. Brother Truman served as its first master. At the Annual Session of the Grand Lodge of Missouri in September, 1940, Brother Truman was elected by a landslide to be the ninety-seventh Grand Master of Masons of Missouri. He served until October 1, 1941.

While President, Truman was made a Sovereign Grand Inspector General, 33°, and an Honorary Member of the Supreme Council in 1945 at the Supreme Council of the Ancient and Accepted Scottish Rite Masons Southern Jurisdiction Headquarters in Washington, D.C. He was also elected an Honorary Grand Master of the International Supreme Council, Order of DeMolay. On May 18, 1959, the Illustrious Brother Truman was presented with the fifty-year award—the only U.S. President to reach that golden anniversary in Freemasonry.

While President of the United States, Brother Truman once said, "The greatest honor that has ever come to me, and that can ever come to me in my life, is to be the Grand Master of Masons in Missouri.

TWELVE

The Healer

"Government big enough to give you everything you want is a government big enough to take from you everything you have."

The young man excelled at football. He played center on offense and linebacker on defense for his South High School team. During his senior year in 1930, his team won the state championship. After high school, his athletic ability opened college doors for him—Harvard, Northwestern, and Michigan State among them. Ultimately, he decided to attend the University of Michigan where he again played center and linebacker. There he earned the distinction of tackling a future Heisman Trophy winner, running back Jay Berwanger, who won the first trophy in 1935. While still in college at Michigan, he was offered coaching jobs with both the Detroit Lions and the Green Bay Packers. At $200 per game, coaching was a lucrative job for that time—especially attractive since he had been doing dishes at his Delta Kappa Epsilon fraternity house to earn money for school. Even so, he decided a formal education was more important than a career as a coach and stayed in school.

★ GREAT AMERICAN FREEMASONS ★

The young man was a second stringer on the University of Michigan team and did not get a lot of time on the field. In both 1932 and 1933, the team was undefeated in the Big Ten and won the conference championships while he watched from the bench. The young man finally made first string his senior year and was voted Most Valuable Player for 1934. Unfortunately, that year the team lost seven of eight games. But the one game they won was a victory in more ways than one.

Michigan was to play Georgia Tech; however, the Georgia Tech players refused to take the field because Michigan's star receiver, Willis F. Ward, was African-American. When Michigan administrators caved in to Georgia Tech's demands and took Willis F. Ward out of the game, the young man was outraged. He nearly refused to play in the game. But then he realized that taking himself out of the game would only hurt the team, so he played despite his anger about the situation. During the game, one of the Georgia Tech linemen taunted the University of Michigan players over its missing "nigger," and things got ugly. The young man and his teammates blocked the Georgia Tech lineman so savagely that, within a few plays, he had to be carried from the field on a stretcher. It was the only game of the season Michigan won—a 9 to 2 victory.

That young man went on to become the fortieth President of the United States of America—Gerald R. Ford.

Gerald R. Ford was born Leslie Lynch King, Jr. on July 14, 1913, to Leslie Lynch King, Sr. and Dorothy Ayer Gardner King. The couple would separate sixteen days after Leslie Jr. was born. Leslie Sr. was an abusive man who hit his wife at the least provocation. When he flew into a violent rage a few days after Leslie Jr. was born, brandished a knife, and threatened to kill both the new mother and her son, Dorothy moved back to her parents' home in Grand Rapids, Michigan. Later, she would meet and marry Gerald Rudolf Ford, a paint salesman. Young Leslie Lynch King, Jr. was renamed Gerald Rudolf Ford (although he would later change the spelling of his middle name to Rudolph to give it a less Germanic cast). Ford did not realize until he was twelve or thirteen that Gerald R. Ford, Sr. was not his biological father. The revelation made little impact on him because he realized his real father was actually the kind, patient paint salesman who had raised him.

After graduating from the University of Michigan in 1934, Ford hoped to attend Yale Law School starting in 1935, while coaching boxing and being assistant varsity football coach there. Yale Law School, however, rejected him because they felt his full time coaching responsibilities at the school would interfere with his law studies. He attended the University of Michigan Law School in 1937 and was eventually admitted to Yale in the spring of 1938. After Ford graduated from Yale in 1941, he was admitted to the Michigan bar. Ford and friend Philip Buchen opened a law practice in Grand Rapids, but Japan's attack on Pearl Harbor changed Ford's plans to practice law.

While attending Yale Law School, Ford had signed a petition supporting U.S. neutrality in World War II. He strongly believed America had no business in the war. But after the unprovoked bombing of Pearl Harbor, Ford left his law practice to enlist in the Navy. During his service, he earned a number of medals, including the Asiatic-Pacific Campaign Medal with nine engagement stars, the Philippine Liberation Medal with two bronze stars for Leyte and Mindoro, the American Campaign medal, and the World War II Victory medal.

In 1948, Ford married Elizabeth Bloomer Warren. At the time of their engagement, Ford was campaigning for the first of thirteen terms he would serve in the U.S. House of Representatives. Betty Ford later remarked, "Jerry was running for Congress and wasn't sure how voters might feel about his marrying a divorced ex-dancer." Betty was divorced from William G. Warren. She had worked as a fashion model and as a dancer in a troupe of the Martha Graham Dance Company. The voters apparently accepted Ford's marriage. Gerald and Betty Ford had four children, three boys and a girl, between 1950 and 1957.

In 1965, when Ford was House minority leader, he was appointed by President Lyndon B. Johnson to a special task force to investigate the assassination of John F. Kennedy. The Warren Report continues to be a hotly debated document, but Gerald R. Ford never wavered in standing behind its findings.

When Spiro Agnew resigned as Richard Nixon's vice president, party leaders were asked to nominate a replacement. During his eight years as House minority leader, Ford was known as a fair and honest man. Because Ford was admired and respected by members of both parties, he was nominated by his party members under the vice-presidential vacancy provision of the Twenty-fifth Amendment. It was the first time in American history a vice president had been replaced during a term by that Constitutional provision. The confirmation of his nomination for vice president easily passed the United States Senate with a 92-3 vote. Later it was confirmed by the House of Representatives 387-35.

Ford's role as vice president was hardly noted because of the tremendous amount of media coverage of the Watergate scandal. That changed when "smoking gun" evidence implicated Richard Nixon in the scandal. It was becoming very clear that the end of Nixon's Presidency was near. Ford was briefed by Alexander Haig that a videotape would be released on the news. Most assuredly, either Richard Nixon would be impeached or he would resign. Ford could become President. At that time, Ford was preparing to move into the vice-presidential residence in Washington, D.C., but after meeting with Haig, he said to his wife, "Betty, I don't think we're ever going to live in the vice president's house."

When Richard Nixon resigned from office on August 9, 1974, Gerald R. Ford was sworn in as President of the United States. He is the only man in American history to have been both vice president and President without having been elected. Addressing Americans on national television from the East Room of the White House immediately following the swearing in, Ford said, "I am acutely aware that you have not elected me as your President by the ballots, and so I ask you to confirm me as your President with your prayers."

Ford nominated Nelson Rockefeller for the office of vice president, and he was confirmed by both the House and Senate. Ford felt the nation needed to heal from the Nixon scandal in order to get back to the real business important to America.

But within the first few weeks of his Presidency, Ford realized that the national problems were taking a backseat to the Watergate scandal. Huge amounts of his time were spent managing the mess he had inherited. Within his first two weeks in office, Ford began to consider putting the whole matter behind him in order to move forward with more important issues. The nation Ford inherited was on the brink of financial disaster. Rising inflation was pushing the country towards recession. Foreign policy problems loomed on the horizon. Each hour he spent mopping up the Watergate mess frustrated him greatly, but there was no end in sight. There was talk of indictments and a Nixon trial. Ford felt it was up to him to make a decision in the best interest of the nation.

On September 8, 1974, on national television, Ford granted Nixon a full and unconditional pardon, perhaps the most controversial decision ever made by a President. Many Americans were outraged by the unpopular decision. They believed it was part of a dirty deal between Nixon and Ford: Nixon would resign and be pardoned by Ford, who had been elevated to the office of President. This opinion was fueled by the fact Nixon's chief of staff, Alexander Haig, had actually offered the deal. In Haig's opinion, there were only three choices for how Nixon could exit. Nixon could pardon himself and then resign. Nixon could pardon the aides involved in the Watergate scandal and resign. Nixon could resign with a deal in place with his successor that he would be pardoned after he left office. Haig very strongly felt the last option was the best; however, Ford had refused the offer. Later, when Ford saw how much time and energy the scandal was wasting, he independently decided to pardon Nixon so the nation could move on. Many in the nation did not believe that.

In 1976, Ford reluctantly agreed to run for President. The major obstacle in receiving the party's nomination was former California governor Ronald Reagan. Reagan and his right wing conservatives criticized Ford for failing to do more in South Vietnam. They criticized his negotiating to cede the Panama Canal to Panama and the signing of the Helsinki Accords. Reagan won several early primaries, but he withdrew at the Republican Convention in Kansas City, Missouri. The insurgence of Republican conservatives convinced Ford to drop the more liberal Rockefeller and to choose a more conservative running mate, Bob Dole.

That change, however, did not help. Jimmy Carter won the 1976 election by a very narrow margin; in fact, if only 25,000 votes had been shifted in Ohio and Wisconsin, Ford would have won the electoral vote. Carter won the electoral vote 297-240, but he won only 50.1 percent of the popular vote.

Ford attributes the Democratic win, amongst other things, to his decision to pardon Richard Nixon, to bad timing of indications of a national economic recovery, and possibly to his decision to drop Rockefeller as a running mate, which may have made a difference in a couple of key states.

The decision to pardon Nixon, which haunted Ford, very likely cut his political career short, but he never questioned that it was the right decision to make. The fact of the matter is that even if Ford had won the 1976 election, he could have served only one term as President, since he had served more than half of Nixon's second term. In 2001, the John F. Kennedy Library Foundation awarded Ford the John F. Kennedy Profile in Courage Award for his pardon of Richard M. Nixon.

Gerald R. Ford is remembered as the man who helped America heal after the devastating national crisis and who helped put a dark chapter in American history behind them. He was a plain-speaking, unassuming man with a warm, quiet

★ THE HEALER ★

sense of humor, yet he was a brilliant negotiator and communicator. Many have called him the right man at the right time. The American people trusted him, and, regardless of party politics, they liked him. He never shied away from a difficult question poised to him, including personal matters, such as his wife Betty's drinking problems. He never seemed to take himself too seriously, and he could poke fun at himself. For example, in his autobiography, he was able to laugh about his reputation for being a little clumsy. He included a photo of himself falling down the steps of Air Force One.

He lived longer than any United States President, living forty-five days longer than Ronald Reagan. He died at age ninety-three on December 26, 2006, of heart failure. He was the eleventh President to lie in state. His state funeral and memorial services were televised to a large national audience. More than four hundred Eagle Scouts were invited to participate in his funeral. They served as ushers and formed an honor guard as the casket passed by outside the Ford Presidential Museum. In an odd twist of fate, Ford's successor as President, Jimmy Carter, gave the eulogy at the service at Grace Episcopal Church in Grand Rapids, Michigan. According to Carter, the two men had made an agreement decades earlier. Ford had asked Carter if, as his successor, he would consider speaking at his funeral and jokingly offered to do the same for him if Carter went first (the inference in the remark being that Gerald Ford hoped Jimmy Carter would go first for beating him in the election).

The Illustrious Brother Gerald R. Ford became a Master Mason at Malta Lodge No. 465 in Grand Rapids, Michigan, in 1949. His three brothers, Thomas Gardner Ford, Richard Addison Ford, and James Francis Ford, became Masons at the same time. In 1959, he became a Shriner in the Saladin Shrine Temple in Grand Rapids. He later joined the Ancient and Accepted Scottish Rite of Freemasonry, Northern Jurisdiction, and received the honorary title of Sovereign Grand Inspector General, 33rd Degree. The Illustrious Brother Gerald R. Ford, 33rd Degree, was present at the unveiling ceremony of the George Washington Masonic National Memorial in Alexandria, Virginia, in 1975. In a speech he gave at the occasion, he said of Freemasonry, "When I took my obligation as a Master Mason—incidentally, with my three younger brothers—I recalled the value my own father attached to that order. But I had no idea that I would ever be added to the company of the Father of our Country and 12 other members of the order who also served as Presidents of the United States."

Ford, a Navy veteran of World War II, was also a member of several other civic organizations, including the American Legion, Veterans of Foreign Wars, and AMVETS.

AMERICA'S SOLDIERS

"Leadership is intangible, and therefore no weapon
ever designed can replace it."

—*General Omar N. Bradley*
West Point Lodge No. 877

THIRTEEN

The Stand

"We will rather die in these ditches than give them up."

—Jim Bowie (February 2, 1836)

According to the legend, the commander of the fort drew a line in the sand with the end of his sword—the decision was either death later or almost certain death fighting then. The defenders had already survived nearly two weeks of constant bombardment from enemy mortars. They were exhausted and demoralized, with no chance of victory, since they were greatly outnumbered by at least twenty to one. They had held out every hope that reinforcements would come to the rescue, but it was now clear that nobody would be coming to save them. It had been made perfectly clear that no prisoners would be taken—it was either die fighting or surrender and die at the hands of the enemy.

Every defender of the mission, with the exception of one, stepped across the line in the sand. One man, deathly ill with pneumonia and confined to bed, requested he be carried over the line on his cot. That man was legendary fighter and pioneer

Jim Bowie, and the site of the battle, the San Antonio de Valero Mission, has come to be known as the Alamo.

The story of the Alamo is part of the larger story of Texas independence from Mexico. It is a commonly held myth that the Battle of the Alamo was a fight between the Texians (what Texans were called then) and Mexicans. In truth, most of the Alamo's defenders were Mexican citizens. In the early 1800s, Texas was a part of Mexico. In order to attract settlers to the area, a provision of the 1824 Mexican constitution offered settlers of the Texas territory 4,428 acres of free land and exemption from taxes for a decade. Thousands flocked to Texas from Mexico, the United States, and nearly every nation in Europe. It was a promised land with fertile soil, plentiful game, and natural resources.

But by the 1830s, there were no more free land grants. Mexico's president, Antonio Lopez de Santa Anna, began to ignore the 1824 constitutional precedents and started to rule the territory as a dictator. For example, Santa Anna, who disapproved of slavery, outlawed it in 1830, outraging settlers from the Southern states who relied on slave labor to run their farms. Santa Anna also took away the exemption from taxes on imported goods. As Santa Anna began to institute new rules and take away the freedoms promised in the 1824 constitution, many of the settlers—nearly 75 percent of whom were from the United States of America—began to talk about Texas becoming an independent republic. Still others talked about an outright revolution.

Stephen Austin, a leading colonist of Texas, had been responsible for attracting many settlers to Texas. Afraid his fellow Texians would be too quick to mount a rebellion against Mexico, Austin went to Mexico City in 1833 to present Santa Anna with a petition which demanded that Santa Anna restore the rights provided to the Texians under the 1824 constitution. Austin was promptly arrested and thrown into prison for nearly two years. When he was finally released in 1835, he returned to Texas. His attitude toward Mexico and Santa Anna, in particular, was very different. He urged Texians to prepare for war against the dictator.

In October of 1835, a contingent of about one hundred Mexican soldiers was sent to the settlement of Gonzalez to retrieve a cannon Mexico had given to the settlers years earlier. When the soldiers arrived, the cannon was missing. What they found instead was a group of armed Texians who called out that if the Mexican soldiers wanted their cannon, they could "Come and take it!" The standoff lasted for two days. At dawn on the third day, a shot rang out, resulting in an exchange of gunfire. The Mexican soldiers broke and ran. No one was killed and no one was apparently wounded, but the consequences of the rebellion rang all the way to Santa Anna in Mexico City.

Santa Anna had already sent General Cos with his army to occupy San Antonio de Béxar, the territory's largest town and most strategic point. When news arrived that a revolution had started in Gonzales, General Cos moved his nearly one thousand men into the Alamo and began to fortify it.

About three hundred Texians laid siege on Béxar and the Alamo for nearly a month. Texian general Edward Burleson, however, could not bring himself to order an attack. On December 4, a fighter in Burleson's command, Ben Milam, decided it was time to take action. He called out, "Boys, who will come with old Ben Milam into San Antonio?"

The men were ready for a fight. For four days, the battle raged, house to house. Sadly, Ben Milam was killed by a sniper, one of the few Texians killed. Once the town of San Antonio was taken, the men turned to the Alamo. Recognizing defeat, General Cos surrendered.

Furious, Santa Anna decided to return to the Alamo to take the fort and to stomp out the rebellion personally. With a force of several thousand men, Santa Anna began marching towards San Antonio—and the Alamo.

The Texians resumed fortifying the old mission under the direction of Green B. Jameson, who was confident that the Alamo could withstand an assault and that his small force of defenders could "whip 10 to 1 with artillery" from the fortified positions. General Sam Houston was not nearly as confident. His reasoning was that if General Cos had not been able to hold the Alamo with one thousand men against a paltry force of three hundred Texians less than a month earlier, the same paltry force of three hundred would not stand much of a chance against a large force of thousands. In truth, there were far less than three hundred men defending the Alamo. Most of the men had left the fortifications at the Alamo, believing the fight should be waged further south in Matamoros. When they left, they took most of the provisions and ammunition. That left Commander J. C. Neill with about a hundred men—nearly starving, dressed in rags, and without the provisions necessary to mount a defense against Santa Anna.

General Sam Houston had sent Jim Bowie, a famous fighter and adventurer, to the Alamo with orders to blow it up. It was better to destroy it than to leave it for Santa Anna to retake. However, when Jim Bowie arrived, he agreed with Jameson that the Alamo was a perfect place to mount a defense of Texas against Mexico.

Commander Neill was forced to leave the Alamo due to a family emergency. In his place, Governor Smith ordered Lieutenant William Barret Travis to go to the Alamo with reinforcements of about thirty men to take command. Several days later, David "Davy" Crockett arrived at the Alamo from Tennessee with his twelve-man "Tennessee Mounted Volunteers." Crockett was a legendary hunter, fighter, and politician, who had just a month earlier left politics in Washington, D.C., and headed to Texas. Because of his reputation and fame, Crockett's presence boosted the moral of the men defending the Alamo, perhaps fortifying their resolve to defend it against Santa Anna.

By the time Santa Anna arrived in San Antonio on February 24, 1836, there were approximately 250 defenders of the Alamo, from twenty-eight different countries and states. It has never been completely understood what motivated Travis, Bo-

★ THE STAND ★

wie, and Crockett, and all the others to defend the Alamo against such overwhelming odds. Perhaps it was the belief that it was a defensible position, or perhaps it was the American ideal of independence and liberty over tyranny. Santa Anna's revocation of the rights under the 1824 constitution had enraged Texians, perhaps to the point where they were not going to budge any further. One fact is certain—the only thing that stood between Santa Anna and Texas was the Alamo. If the Alamo fell, General Sam Houston did not yet have a force capable of winning against such a large army. All hopes of an independent republic of Texas rested on the Alamo.

When Santa Anna arrived in San Antonio, he ran a red flag up the tower of the San Fernando Cathedral a mile away. The message was crystal clear. If the Texians at the Alamo decided to fight, no prisoners would be taken—they would all die. However, if the Texians surrendered, they would do so on Santa Anna's terms, and the defenders of the Alamo knew that too meant death.

The Alamo defenders delivered to Santa Anna an equally crystal-clear reply. Travis answered Santa Anna's demand for surrender by firing an eighteen-pound cannonball from one of the Alamo's cannons at the Mexican army, which responded at once, beginning a bombardment of the Alamo that would last nearly two weeks. As the bombardment continued day after day, Santa Anna's ranks continued to swell to over five thousand soldiers in San Antonio.

Travis and the defenders of the Alamo held out hope during the bombardment that reinforcements would come. When James Butler Bonham returned to the Alamo with news that no reinforcements were coming, this is when, according to legend, Travis drew his line in the sand and requested volunteers to stay to defend the Alamo.

On the evening on March 5, 1836, the cannons suddenly stopped firing. Exhausted, many of the men in the Alamo instantly fell asleep. They woke the following morning to bugle calls and the sound of thousands of voices yelling, "Viva Santa Anna!" The Mexican assault of the Alamo had begun.

It is believed that fifteen hundred Mexican soldiers besieged the Alamo. Travis was one of the first casualties—shot in the head with a single musket ball. Bowie, who had been gravely ill with pneumonia for days, defended himself from his cot with pistols and his famous knife. Crockett and his men defended the palisades that connected the church to the compound's gate.

While the first few waves of attackers were successfully fought off, very soon, because of the sheer numbers of attackers, the Mexican soldiers were streaming over the walls of the Alamo. The Alamo's biggest gun, the eighteen-pounder that had been used to so clearly answer Santa Anna's demand for surrender, was turned around by the Texians and used to fire at the swarms of Mexican soldiers inside the mission. After those manning the cannon were killed, the Mexican soldiers took charge of it. With devastating effect, the Mexican soldiers used it to blast away doors and defenses and to kill and maim the defenders.

Davy Crockett, his ammunition exhausted, used his rifle "Old Betsy" as a club and continued to fight until he was finally overpowered and killed. Legend has it that there were more than twenty dead Mexican soldiers found near Crockett's body. Even in his weakened condition, Bowie defended himself from his cot to the bloody end. He was found, also surrounded by dead Mexican soldiers—his pistols empty and his knife bloody.

It was over very quickly but at a high price for Santa Anna, who had lost some six hundred soldiers in the assault on the Alamo. He ordered the captured defenders, who were wounded or exhausted, to be summarily executed. All the bodies of the defenders, except one, were unceremoniously burned in funeral pyres. The one defender allowed a proper burial was Gregorio Esparza, whose widow had plead with Santa Anna that her husband be taken from the fort and given a decent burial. Esparaza's brother, Fernando, had served as an *activo* in the Mexican army during the Texian Siege of Béxar. It is likely that this was the only reason Santa Anna permitted the widow to take her husband from the Alamo.

Santa Anna considered the siege a small though costly affair. But the two weeks Santa Anna spent laying siege to the small force of brave defenders at the Alamo gave General Sam Houston time to raise a real army. Six weeks later, Houston's army, enraged and infuriated by the events at the Alamo, attacked Santa Anna's army at San Jacinto. As they prepared for the attack, Houston shouted to his men, "Remember the Alamo!" As the Texian army swarmed down the sloping hillsides, nearly every man was shouting the new battle cry, "Remember the Alamo!" They threw themselves at Santa Anna's massive force, defeating his army in under fifteen minutes.

The following day, the Texians rounded up a group of stragglers from the battle. They heard some of the Mexican soldiers addressing one of the prisoners who was dressed in a regular army jacket as "El Presidente." The Texians immediately took the prisoner to General Houston, who discovered that he was none other than President Antonio Lopez de Santa Anna. He had tried to escape, but his horse had gotten stuck in a bayou, and his attempt to disguise his identity had failed because of his men's reverence for him. Santa Anna surrendered his remaining forces to Houston.

Texas was an independent republic for nine years until being admitted into the United States of America as the twenty-eighth state on December 28, 1845.

The Alamo is great American legend with many different versions of what actually happened on that Sunday morning in 1836. Why the defenders of the Alamo were so willing to sacrifice themselves to such an overwhelming force is open to conjecture—nobody really knows for certain. What is certain is that the Battle of the Alamo forever changed the history of Texas and the United States of America. It has captured the imagination of Americans for generations. It has been written about in everything from novels to comic books, memorialized in movie adaptations and television programs, and celebrated in songs, poems, and art. Thousands from every state and every nation still flock to the mission in San Antonio to view—in hushed silence with hats in hand—the sites where the defenders of the Alamo gave their lives for Texas independence.

Brother David "Davy" Crockett was made a Mason in Weakley County, Tennessee. The lodge was burned during the Civil War, so the only real evidence he was a Mason was a Masonic apron given to him when he was serving in Congress.

Brother James "Jim" Bowie was made a Mason in Humble Cottage Lodge No. 19 in Louisiana. The records for that lodge were also destroyed by fire in 1850.

Brother William Barret Travis was made a Mason in Alabama Lodge No. 3.

Brother Samuel Houston was made a Mason in Holland Lodge No. 36 of Louisiana that later became Holland Lodge No. 1 of Texas. In 1837, he presided over a meeting that established the Grand Lodge of Texas. He later became a member of Forest Lodge No. 19 in Huntsville, Texas. He was knighted in Commandery No. 1, Washington, D.C., on February 23, 1853.

Brother Antonio Lopez de Santa Anna, as cited in *10,000 Famous Freemasons* by William R. Denslow, was also a Mason. According to some sources, that may have been the reason he was spared by Samuel Houston when captured; however, most historians believe he was spared because Sam Houston and the other leaders in Texas did not wish to make him a martyr. It is commonly held that his acts of brutality against humanity placed him well outside the tenets of Freemasonry and any protection from the Masonic obligations of Freemasonry.

FOURTEEN

The Charger

"Up men to your posts! Don't forget today that you are from old Virginia."

When the young cadet graduated from West Point, he had outdone all his classmates and had earned the most impressive resume in West Point history—a resume of misconduct, that is. At the time of his graduation, he had earned 195 demerits—just short of the 200 in a single year which would have led to his expulsion. The list of demerits from just his last year filled four legal-sized sheets with two columns per page.

The young man's misconduct covered a range of indiscretions from using tobacco to sneaking out at night to visit Benny Havens' Tavern. He also seemed to be perpetually late for just about everything—roll call, drill, chapel, meals, and reveille. Besides the drinking and the smoking and his difficulty with being on time, he was also a clown. He often swung his arms comically while marching in drill, flaunting authority and racking up demerits in large numbers. Many of the demerits were also for being out of uniform and for the length of his hair. The cadet uniform at the time was extremely uncomfortable with stiff collars and woolen scarf-like stocks. He could not stand them. From the beginning of his West Point career, he wore the soft collars he preferred and often a cravat—earning black marks in record numbers.

As a youth, he had a genuine distaste for authority. One possible explanation for his behavior might be his belief that the rigid standards robbed cadets of their individuality, initiative, and self-expression, which he thought were important characteristics for leaders of men. He knew the rules; he did not try to change them, and he accepted the penalties for breaking them. Whether his conduct was a form of protest or the result of youthful exuberance, history may never know.

The young man, however, knew the limits—two hundred demerits and a cadet was out. He never passed that number. Instead, as he approached it, he would suddenly curb his bad behavior and snap into line until the end of the year. Then, when the new year would begin with his slate clean, he would begin racking up a whole new list of demerits.

Normally, such a dubious record would condemn a cadet to a lackluster career in a relatively unimportant assignment, but fortunately for the young man, war had broken out during his last year at the academy. He was given an opportunity to prove himself as an officer in battle. His irreverence for authority dissipated immediately. There is nothing in his service record that indicates he was ever insubordinate or failed to carry out an order. Though he had been a rebellious youth, he was a very subordinate officer, never questioning the assignments or missions he was given. He undertook each challenge with enthusiasm and without question.

Though his behavior changed, his manner of dress did not. His appearance was always described as flamboyant. He wore a small blue cap and buffed gloves over the sleeves of his immaculately tailored uniform, which had a double row of gold buttons on the coat. He wore shiny gold spurs on his highly polished boots. He held an elegant riding crop. His mustache,

★ THE CHARGER ★

which was meticulously trimmed, turned upward at the ends. His hair was the talk of the Army. A newspaper reporter once described it as, "Long ringlets flowed loosely over his shoulders, trimmed and highly perfumed, his beard likewise was curling and giving up the scent of Araby."

One can only imagine what he must have looked like, sitting atop his sleek black charger named Old Black during the final battle at Gettysburg, where he had planned the assault on the Union lines. Never had the strength of the Confederate Army been greater and their chances for real victory closer to realization than at Gettysburg, and never was the risk of Union defeat so great. But victory for the Confederacy slipped away in one fateful decision. Neither the Confederate Army nor the young man ever recovered from it.

The famous last assault at Gettysburg bears the young man's name, and the tragedy of that fatal attempt to break the Union line is legendary. The young cadet who caused so much grief to his instructors at West Point was George E. Pickett, and the assault on the Union center was later known as Pickett's Charge.

George Edward Pickett was born on January 25, 1825, in Richmond, Virginia, to Robert and Mary Pickett, the first of eight children. He was born into a prominent family of Old Virginia. His family, however, was deeply hurt by the financial panic in 1837 and thus was unable to send him to the Richmond Academy as planned. He was sent to Springfield, Illinois, instead to study law under his uncle's tutelage. Pickett was not very fond of the idea of becoming a lawyer. At the age of seventeen, he received an appointment to the United States Military Academy. Legend has it that Pickett's West Point appointment was secured for him by Abraham Lincoln; however, Lincoln, as an Illinois state legislator at the time, could not nominate candidates. It is known that Lincoln gave the young man advice after he was accepted, but Pickett was actually appointed by Illinois Congressman John T. Stuart, a friend of Pickett's uncle and the law partner of Abraham Lincoln.

Upon graduation from West Point, Pickett was commissioned a brevet second lieutenant in the U.S. 8th Infantry Regiment. He served in the Mexican-American War. He first gained national attention when he climbed a parapet during the Battle of Chapultepec, retrieved the American flag from his wounded colleague—future Confederate general James Longstreet—and raised it over the fortress while under enemy fire. For that effort, he received a brevet promotion to captain. After the war, he was promoted to first lieutenant while serving on the Texas frontier and finally to captain in the 9th U.S. Infantry.

In January, 1851, Pickett married Sally Harrison Steward Minge, the daughter of Dr. John Minge of Virginia and the great-great-grandniece of President William Henry Harrison. Her great-great-grandfather was Benjamin Harrison, one of the signers of the Declaration of Independence. She died during childbirth in November, 1851.

Captain Pickett next served in the Washington Territory. In 1856, he was stationed in what became Bellingham, Washington. The house he built there still stands, the oldest house in Bellingham. While on a survey mission along the Canadian border, he met a Native American woman from the Haida tribe of "Russian America"—a territory later known as Alaska. They were later married, and she gave birth to a son, James Tilton Pickett. She also died from complications from childbirth. Having lost two wives in six years, Pickett was overcome by oppressive loneliness and abandonment. He seemed to deal with this depression by throwing himself into his duty in the army.

In 1859, Pickett once again became the focus of national attention. Pickett, who was in command of Fort Bellingham, occupied San Juan Island. Occupation of the island led to a territorial dispute with Great Britain, which has been nicknamed the Pig War because an American farmer killed a pig that had gotten loose and rooted up his vegetable garden. As it turned out, the pig belonged to the British-owned Hudson Bay

★ THE CHARGER ★

Company. The British wanted the man to stand trial, but the Americans resisted their efforts to arrest him. The confrontation escalated. While commanding a garrison of only sixty-eight men, Pickett stood up to a British force of three warships and a thousand men who threatened to land and occupy the island. Pickett's stubborn presence and his unwillingness to turn the man over to their custody—along with British orders that called for no confrontations—prevented the British from landing on the island. Once again in the national limelight, Pickett stated defiantly, "We'll make a Bunker Hill of it." President James Buchanan dispatched Lieutenant General Winfield Scott to negotiate a final settlement of the dispute.

After the Confederates fired on Fort Sumter in 1861, Virginia seceded from the Union. Pickett left Washington State to begin a journey home to Virginia. Despite Pickett's personal distaste for the institution of slavery, he was a Virginian. He felt his loyalties, therefore, were with the Confederacy. Arriving after the First Battle of Bull Run, he resigned his commission in the United States Army on June 25, 1861. Within a month, he was appointed colonel in the Confederate Army in command of the Rappahannock Line. He was under the command of Major General Theophilus H. Holmes, whose influence obtained Pickett a commission as a brigadier general on January 14, 1862.

Pickett's first combat command during the Civil War was during the Peninsula Campaign, leading a brigade that was nicknamed the Gamecocks. This is the same brigade that would eventually be led by Richard B. Garnett during Pickett's Charge at Gettysburg. The Gamecocks performed well in several engagements including Williamsburg, Seven Pines, and Gaines' Mill. Pickett was wounded at Gaines' Mill when he was knocked off his horse by a bullet in the shoulder. Pickett, who believed he had been mortally wounded, made a tremendous fuss about it, but a staff officer examined the wound and rode away, stating that he was "perfectly able to take care of himself." However, Pickett was out of action for three months, and his arm would remain stiff for about a year.

When Pickett returned to service in September, 1862, he was given command of a two-brigade division in the corps under the command by his old friend from the Mexican-American War, Major General James Longstreet. Pickett was promoted to major general. At the Battle of Fredericksburg, the men were engaged in a skirmish with no fatalities. They would not see much serious combat until the Gettysburg campaign the following summer. Longstreet's corps was detached on the Suffolk campaign during the Battle of Chancellorsville in May, 1863.

It was during the Suffolk Campaign that Pickett fell in love with a Virginia teenager, LaSalle "Sallie" Corbell. After meeting her, he commuted back and forth from his duties in Suffolk to spend time with her. Pickett was thirty-eight years old and twice widowed when he married Sallie on November 13, 1863.

Earlier that year on July 2, 1863, Pickett's division arrived at the Battle of Gettysburg on the evening of the second day of fighting. Pickett had been delayed, guarding the Confederate lines of communication through Chambersburg, Pennsylvania. After two days of heavy fighting, General Robert E. Lee's Army of Northern Virginia had driven the Union Army to the high ground south of Gettysburg. Lee's efforts to dislodge them from their positions had failed. General Lee's plan for July 3, 1863, called for a massive assault on the center of the Union lines on Cemetery Ridge. He directed General Longstreet to assemble a force of three divisions for the attack. Lee called on Pickett to lead the charge.

Following a two-hour artillery barrage that was meant to soften up the Union defenses, the three divisions stepped off across open fields almost a mile from Cemetery Ridge. Pickett inspired his men by shouting, "Up, Men, and to your posts! Don't forget today that you are from Old Virginia."

★ THE CHARGER ★

Pickett's Charge was a bloodbath. While the Union lost about 1,500 killed and wounded, the Confederate casualty rate was astronomical. All three of Pickett's brigade commanders and all thirteen of his regimental commanders were casualties. Of his three brigade commanders, Kemper was wounded and Garnett and Armistead were killed in combat. Pickett himself has received some unfair criticism for surviving the battle, because he held a position well to the rear of his troops. At that time, however such a position was command doctrine for division commanders.

The crushing defeat had a profound impact on the Confederate forces and on the morale of its officers. They never recovered from the failure of Pickett's Charge. As soldiers straggled back to the Confederate lines along Cemetery Ridge, General Lee feared a Union counteroffensive and tried to rally his center, telling returning soldiers that the failure was "all my fault." Pickett was emotionally devastated by the loss of his forces, and he blamed himself in part for the failure, but he never forgave Lee for ordering the charge.

When Lee told Pickett to rally his division for the expected counterattack, Pickett allegedly replied, "General Lee, I have no division now." Pickett's official report for the battle has never been found. It is believed that General Lee rejected Pickett's original report for its negativity towards Lee's decision to mount the charge. Either Pickett never wrote or Lee never filed an updated version.

To his dying day, Pickett mourned the tremendous loss of his men at Gettysburg. Legend claims that when Pickett and Lee met again, the meeting was "icy." John Singleton Mosby seems to have been the only witness to support this claim of coldness between Lee and Pickett; other witnesses discounted this version. Mosby related that after the meeting, Pickett said bitterly, "That man destroyed my division." Most historians, however, find this encounter unlikely. When asked why Pickett's Charge failed, Pickett is on record as saying, "I've always thought the Yankees had something to do with it."

After Gettysburg, Pickett received no commendation from either Lee or Longstreet, and his career went into decline. He served as a division commander in the defense of Richmond. On April 1, 1865, Pickett's division was defeated at the Battle of Five Forks when Union forces attacked. Pickett was miles away at the time enjoying a shad bake with some other officers. By the time he returned to the battlefield, it was too late. The battle was lost. The defeat led to the unraveling of the Confederate line. It forced Lee to order the evacuation of Richmond, Virginia, and to retreat toward Appomattox Court House. After the Battle of Sayler's Creek, Pickett was relieved of command.

Pickett was paroled at Appomattox Court House on April 9, 1865. Despite his parole, Pickett fled to Canada. He did not return to Virginia until 1866 where he worked as an insurance agent. Pickett had difficulty seeking amnesty after the Civil War. This was a common problem for Confederate officers who had been West Point graduates and who had resigned their commissions at the start of the war. However, former Union officers, including Ulysses S. Grant, supported pardoning Pickett, but he did not receive amnesty until the year prior to his death when it was finally granted by an Act of Congress on June 23, 1874.

Pickett died in Norfolk on July 30, 1875. He is buried in Richmond's Hollywood Cemetery. Pickett's grave is marked by an elaborate memorial commissioned in 1875 by the Pickett Division Association, a group of surviving veterans from his division. It was originally intended to be placed at Gettysburg National Military Park at the "High Water Mark" of Pickett's Charge, but the U.S. War Department refused permission for it to be placed on the battlefield.

There are few events in American history as important as Pickett's Charge. It is difficult to imagine what America would be like today had Pickett succeeded in breaking the Union line in that decisive battle. Pickett's failure at Gettysburg is at the crux of America's continuation and success as a nation.

It was the turning point in the war. The Confederacy never recovered, and neither did Pickett. But regardless of his failures at Gettysburg and later, Pickett was a hero of the Civil War. He was an officer of the highest caliber—even Ulysses S. Grant thought enough of him after the war to work for his amnesty. Pickett earned his position in history through his accomplishments, his great enthusiasm, and his willingness to take on any difficult challenge given to him—often against tremendous odds. He fought for what he believed in. Although his personal ideology was sometimes at odds with the ideology of his Confederate cohorts on the topic of slavery, he sided with his fellow Virginians and vigorously defended his home at any cost.

Brother George E. Pickett belonged to Dove Lodge No. 51 in Virginia.

FIFTEEN

Friendship and War

"If the Confederacy falls, there should be written on its tombstone: Died of a Theory."
—Jefferson Davis

It began with the firing of a single cannon—the signal to begin the assault. It was on the third day of the Battle of Gettysburg, July 3, 1863. Confederate General Robert E. Lee was convinced that the Union line was weak at its center with most of Union General Meade's forces occupied with defending Cemetery Hill on one end and Little Round Top on the other. Lee's plan was an all-out assault on the center of the line after an intense Confederate bombardment by artillery, striking a point on the Union line referred to as "the angle." Once the Confederate soldiers breached the Union defenses at the angle, they would scatter Meade's forces by flanking their defensive positions on the higher ground.

Confederate General Longstreet disagreed with Lee's plan, which he thought was potentially disastrous. Longstreet believed that even if the Confederate assault could break through the Union lines at the angle, with thirty thousand Union soldiers fighting on higher ground on either side, the

Confederate forces could be easily flanked, surrounded on three sides, and then slaughtered. Basically, Longstreet believed the Union line would swing around like a fence gate and crush them as they breached the line. However, Lee was undeterred in his plan—buoyed by the determination and confidence in the plan from the general he had selected to lead the charge, General George Pickett.

Pickett's charge would consist of three brigades led by generals Garnett, Kemper, and Armistead. At least one of the generals leading Pickett's charge was going up against not an enemy but a friend. Brigadier General Lewis A. Armistead knew through his inquiries that the man commanding the center of the Union line was Major General Winfield Scott Hancock. The two generals, although now on opposing sides at Gettysburg, had been close friends since 1844 when they had served together as officers in the Union Army in California. Win Hancock and his wife, Mira, who had opened their home to Armistead, a widower, had enjoyed many dinners and evenings with him. Their close friendship was based in part on the fact that they were both soldiers and Freemasons, Armistead belonging to Washington Lodge No. 22 in Alexandria, Virginia and Hancock to Charity Lodge No. 190 in Norristown, Pennsylvania.

With the secession of the Southern States from the Union, Armistead, a Virginian, decided to join the Confederate Army, while Hancock, a Pennsylvanian, remained loyal to the Union. Armistead was troubled by the fact they would be serving different causes, but he had vowed to Hancock, before they parted ways in California in 1861, that he would never raise a hand against his friend—asking God to strike him dead if he ever caused his friend harm.

It is surprising to some that Lewis Armistead decided to join the Confederacy. His uncle was American patriot Major George Armistead, the commander of Fort McHenry, who so vigorously defended the original Stars and Stripes when the British attacked the fort during the War of 1812. That famous battle witnessed by Sir Francis Scott Key had inspired the poem "The Star Spangled Banner" which would later become the words for our national anthem.

Being on opposing sides at Gettysburg—two years after having last seen Hancock and having made his solemn vow—was hardly the reunion for which Armistead had hoped. Possibly sensing that Longstreet was correct and that, in all likelihood, the assault would fail, Armistead asked Longstreet to ensure the delivery of a package to Mira Hancock, the wife of his old friend, should he not live through the day. The package contained his Bible.

Shortly after one o'clock in the afternoon of July 3, 1863, the sound of the signal cannon echoed through the countryside. It marked the beginning of one of the bloodiest days in American history and the beginning of the end for the Confederate States of America.

Seconds after the cannon signal, the center of the Union line at the angle seemed to explode. The countryside shook as the largest and longest cannonade in the war unleashed a bombardment of shot and shell onto the Union positions.

Moments before the bombardment began, Major General Winfield Scott Hancock had been enjoying a lunch with Commander of the Army, Major General George Meade, several other generals, and members of their staff. Seated behind Union lines on blankets, they were eating off an improvised table made from a cracker box. As they finished the meal, they discussed where the Confederate Army might focus their next attack. Meade was certain the Confederates would renew their attack from the day before while Hancock was certain they would attack the center of the line. Lighting cigars as they departed from the picnic area, the generals heard the signal cannon. Suddenly, the air was filled with shells, one of which struck near them, destroying the table where they had all been sitting just moments before. General Pleasonton, one of the members of the meeting, looked back when the shell hit, later describing what he saw flying through the air as "an indiscriminate mass of sandwiches, cheese, crackers and stragglers all mixed up together."

The Confederate cannonade bombarded Union lines for an hour and forty-five minutes. General Hancock said, "It was the most terrific cannonade I ever witnessed, and the most prolonged."

As the shells exploded all around the Union positions, there was nothing more for the men to do than to seek cover and wait for the shelling to stop. General Hancock started to ride along the lines of defense. A regimental band began to play "The Star Spangled Banner." Although it was not the national anthem at the time, the swelling of the music over the exploding shells caused Hancock to pause and remove his hat in reverence. As he worked his way up and down the Union defenses, he smiled and waved his hat at the men huddled around him, seemingly unconcerned with the falling shells. The men were steadied by the sight of the man they had begun calling "Hancock the Superb." Then, after what must have seemed to be an eternity, the cannon fire ended, and Pickett's charge began.

During the fighting, Hancock was badly wounded when a bullet struck the pommel of his saddle, driving a nail, bits of wood, and the bullet deeply into his leg. Hancock would survive the wound and the war. He would go on to run for President in the 1880 election against James A. Garfield, but he would not witness the end of the fighting at the Battle of Gettysburg nor would he have the opportunity to reunite with his old friend Lewis Armistead.

The cannonade Lee had ordered to soften up the Union lines had not had the effect Lee had been counting on. As nearly twelve thousand Confederate soldiers streamed across the field toward their objective—the angle—they were bombarded with an inferno of shot and shell from the Union positions on the higher ground. The smoke was so thick it was difficult to navigate through it to their objective.

General Armistead's was the only brigade that had not fallen apart as the men crossed the fields. As the other two brigades began to scatter under intense fire, he saw the nerve of his own men beginning to falter. Armistead removed his hat, stuck it on the end of his sword, and, waving it in the air, shouted, "Behind me Virginians!" He charged forward towards the angle. His ranks, greatly thinned by the intense fighting, followed him, screaming a blood-curdling Rebel yell as they closed the distance across the field to the stone wall that protected the Union position.

When they reached the stone wall, Armistead jumped onto it. Still waving his hat on the end of his sword, he turned to cheer on his men "Give them the cold steel, boys!" he yelled. Of nearly twelve thousand men in Pickett's charge, only Armistead, with less than two hundred men behind him, reached the objective of the stone wall at the angle. As he placed his hands on one of the Union guns, he was struck by Union fire. As he fell, he made a gesture—the meaning of which was unknown to many of the witnesses but not to those who were Freemasons. Armistead crumbled to the ground, mortally wounded. The Rebel victory lasted only minutes as Union forces fired into the small group of men from three sides—just as General Longstreet had predicted. The position was quickly retaken by the Union Army.

Union Captain Henry A. Bingham, a Mason himself and General Hancock's aide, was at the angle during the battle. Seeing that Armistead was an officer and a Mason, Bingham rushed to his aid. When Bingham introduced himself as General Hancock's aide, Armistead asked Bingham to "tell General Hancock that General Armistead sends his compliments." When Bingham told Armistead that Hancock had been wounded and taken from the battlefield, Armistead became greatly distressed. Realizing he had broken his oath and had possibly caused the death of his good friend, he said, "Tell General Hancock for me that I have done him and done you all an injury which I shall regret the longest day I live."

At Armistead's request, Bingham collected several items from Armistead, including Armistead's watch, spurs, and pocketbook. Then Bingham ordered that Armistead be taken to a nearby hospital where he later died. Bingham rode to find Hancock and to deliver Armistead's possessions. When Bingham found Hancock, lying wounded in a field hospital, he gave his report to Hancock. Hancock's reaction to the report is unknown, but it can be assumed he felt great sorrow at the loss of his old friend and fellow Mason. As a soldier, Hancock must have been impressed that of the three excellent generals leading the assault of more than twelve thousand men against the Union lines, only his friend, Lewis Armistead, with less than two hundred men left, had managed to breach the Union defenses at the angle.

The following day, Independence Day, the Confederate forces withdrew. The Union Army did no pursuit them—perhaps the greatest mistake made in the war. The fighting would continue for nearly two more years, and many more were to die on both sides before it ended at Appomattox Courthouse in April, 1865.

Much has been said and written about this incident at the angle on the last day of the battle at Gettysburg, and many variations of the story exist. One thing that cannot be called into question is the incredible horror of war, most especially the Civil War that turned brother against brother. It is fortunate, in fact miraculous, that America as a nation was able to reconcile in the wake of such a horrible tragedy when so many on both sides were lost in the struggle. There were many great men wasted, split by ideology. Perhaps Sam Watkins of the 1st Tennessee put it best when he said, "America has no north, no south, no east, no west. The sun rises over the hills and sets over the mountains, the compass just points up and down, and we can laugh now at the absurd notion of there being a north and a south. We are one and undivided."

Four months after the Battle of Gettysburg, President Abraham Lincoln delivered one of the most famous speeches in

American history. It was written in Lincoln's own hand on the train during his journey to Gettysburg for the dedication of the Soldier's National Cemetery in Gettysburg. No story of the American Civil War can be complete without Lincoln's touching words. It was the tragic loss of Lincoln's own life by an assassin's bullet—the last fatality of the Civil War—that may have ensured that "a government of the people, by the people, for the people, shall not perish from the earth."

THE GETTYSBURG ADDRESS
November 19, 1863

Four score and seven years ago our fathers brought forth on the continent, a new nation conceived in Liberty, and dedicated to the proposition that all men are created equal.

Now we are engaged in a great civil war, testing whether that nation, or any nation so conceived and so dedicated, can long endure. We are met on a great battlefield of that war. We have come to dedicate a portion of that field as a final resting place for those who here gave their lives that the nation might live. It is altogether fitting and proper, that we should do this.

But, in a larger sense, we cannot dedicate—we cannot consecrate—we cannot hallow—this ground. The brave men, living and dead, who struggled here, have consecrated it, far above our poor power to add or detract. The world will little note, nor long remember what we say here, but it can never forget what they did here. It is for us the living, rather, to be dedicated here to the unfinished work which they who fought here have thus far so nobly advanced. It is rather for us to be here dedicated to the great task remaining before us—that from the honored dead we take

★ FRIENDSHIP AND WAR ★

increased devotion to that cause for which they gave the last full measure of devotion—that we here highly resolve that these dead shall not have died in vain—that this nation, under God, shall have a new birth of freedom—and that government of the people, by the people, for the people, shall not perish from the earth.

Brigadier General Lewis Addison Armistead belonged to Washington Lodge No. 22 in Alexandria, Virginia. Major General Winfield Scott Hancock was a member of Charity Lodge No. 190 in Norristown, Pennsylvania. Captain Henry H. Bingham was a member of Chartiers Lodge No. 297, in Canonsburg, Pennsylvania.

The following is a list of officers in the Battle of Gettysburg, both Union and Confederate, known to be Freemasons:

Brigadier General William Barksdale, Columbus Lodge No. 5, Columbus, Mississippi.
Major General David B. Birney, Franklin Lodge No. 134, Pennsylvania.
Major General Daniel Butterfield, Metropolitan Lodge, No. 273, New York.
Colonel Joshua Lawrence Chamberlain, United Lodge No. 8, Brunswick, Maine.
Brigadier General John W. Geary, Philanthropy Lodge No. 255, Pennsylvania.
Brigadier General John B. Gordon, Gate City Lodge No. 2, Atlanta, Georgia (unconfirmed).
Brigadier General Harry T. Hays, Louisiana Lodge No. 102, Louisiana.
Major General Henry Heath, Rocky Mountain Lodge No. 205, Utah Territory.
Brigadier General John D. Imboden, Stuanton Lodge No. 13, Virginia.

★ GREAT AMERICAN FREEMASONS ★

Brigadier General Rufus Ingalls, Williamette Lodge No. 2, Oregon.

Brigadier General Alfred Iverson, Columbian Lodge No. 108, Columbus, Georgia.

Brigadier General James L. Kemper, Linn Banks Lodge No. 126, Virginia.

Brigadier General Joseph B. Kershaw, Kershaw Lodge No 29, South Carolina.

Brigadier General Solomon Meredith, Cambridge Lodge No. 105, Indianapolis, Indiana.

Major General George E. Pickett, Dove Lodge No. 51, Virginia.

Major General Alfred Pleasonton, Franklin Lodge No. 134, Pennsylvania.

Major General Carl Schurz, Herman Lodge No. 125, Philadelphia, Pennsylvania.

Brigadier General George J. Stannard, Franklin Lodge No. 4, Vermont.

Brigadier General George T. "Tige" Anderson, Lodge affiliation is unknown.

Brigadier General Alfred T. A. Torbert, Temple Chapter No. 2, Delaware.

Brigadier General John H. H. Ward, Metropolitan Lodge No. 273, New York, New York.

SIXTEEN

The Raider

"The first lesson is that you can't lose a war if you have command of the air, and you can't win a war if you haven't."

At seven a.m. on Sunday morning, December 7, 1941, the sun rose on the Hawaiian Islands—a paradise of tremendous beauty and tranquility. Most of the Pacific fleet lay at anchor. The enemy was believed to be thousands of miles away and no threat to the American base. No one could imagine, as the sun rose to begin what promised to be another perfect day that within two hours, the date and the harbor would be linked to events that would change American history forever.

At 7:55 on that quiet morning, the sound of planes could be heard over Pearl Harbor. As the men of the United States Navy looked overhead, they saw the inconceivable—waves of Japanese planes. The first wave was focused on Hickam Field in order to keep the Army Air Corps from getting off the ground. The attack was well planned. The planes at Hickam had no opportunity to scramble as the Japanese decimated them on the ground. The scene was utter chaos. American forces tried to deal with the attack on the airfield, but things were about to get much worse.

Five minutes into the attack, a desperate message that would shock the world was sent to Washington, D.C., from the U.S. Navy's Pacific fleet headquarters: "AIR RAID. PEARL HARBOR. THIS IS NO DRILL." Within ten minutes of the attack on the airfield, Japanese torpedo bombers began their run across Pearl Harbor with the helpless, anchored ships of the Pacific Fleet in their sights.

One hour and forty-five minutes later, Pearl Harbor lay in smoking ruins. Eighteen American ships were sunk or badly damaged, the majority of the American planes had been destroyed on the ground, and more than 2,400 men had been killed. During only the last half hour of the attack had the American forces mounted any kind of defense. About thirty American fighter planes were able to get airborne, and eleven Japanese fighters were shot down. But it was too little, too late. The damage had already been done. The empire of Japan, in one surprise attack, became the dominant power in the Pacific.

By 9:30 a.m., Air Force patrol planes were in the skies, looking for the Japanese. But the search proved fruitless. After fifty sorties, the search was abandoned. The American forces had been not only surprised but also mystified as to where the attack had come from. The Japanese fleet escaped undetected to the north and returned home to a heroes' welcome.

America was stunned. The answer to the attack was a declaration of war on Japan. America, the sleeping giant, had been roused from its isolationist views of World War II. Americans finally understood that either they were going to have to take the fight to the enemy or they were going to have to fight that same enemy on American soil. America decided to take the fight to the enemy.

On April 18, 1942, less than four months after the attack on Pearl Harbor, the Japanese in Tokyo, Kobe, Osaka, and Nagoya experienced the same confusion and surprise the Americans had experienced at Pearl Harbor. At noon, the Japanese looked up to see the inconceivable—American B-25 bombers passing overhead as 500-pound bombs rained down on their cities. The questions of how the Americans had gotten there and where they had come from were as big a mystery for the Japanese as they had been for the Americans facing the attack at Pearl Harbor. Later, when reporters asked the President from where the bomber attack had been launched, President Roosevelt boasted that the flight had taken off from Shangri-La—the mythical place featured in James Hilton's novel *Lost Horizon*.

Roosevelt's cryptic answer confounded the Japanese, who began wondering if the Americans had a secret base in China or elsewhere. The Japanese never considered that the attack could have been launched from aircraft carriers, since they accepted the conventional wisdom of the day that bombers were too large and too heavy to be launched from carriers.

The raid on Japan was America's reply to Pearl Harbor. It told the Japanese, in no uncertain terms, that America was in the war to win. The daring attack on the Japanese cities was called Doolittle's Raid. The leader of this daring raid was Lieutenant Colonel James H. Doolittle.

James H. Doolittle was born in Alameda, California, on December 14, 1896. He spent a good part of his youth in Nome, Alaska, where he earned a reputation as a boxer. After graduating from Manual Arts High School in Los Angeles, he attended Los Angeles City College. Later, he won admission to the University of California at Berkley where he studied in the School of Mines. At the beginning of World War I, he took a leave of absence from college to join the United States Signal Corps Reserve, where he enlisted as a flying cadet. Commissioned as a second lieutenant, he trained at the University of California School of Military Aeronautics at Rockwell Field.

During World War I, Doolittle stayed in the United States as a flight instructor. At the end of the war, he qualified for retention and received a regular army commission of first lieutenant. Doolittle became a very famous pilot after World

War I. In 1922, he made the first of many pioneering flights in a DeHavilland DH-4. For example, he made the first cross-country flight from Pablo Beach, Florida, to San Diego, California, in twenty-one hours and nineteen minutes with only one refueling stop. The army awarded him a Distinguished Flying Cross.

Doolittle was awarded a Bachelor of Arts degree by the University of California even though he had never finished his studies there. In July, 1923, after he had served as a test pilot and aeronautical engineer at McCook Field, the army gave Doolittle two years to complete his master's degree. Doolittle entered the Massachusetts Institute of Technology. In March, 1924, he conducted aircraft acceleration tests at McCook Field, which became the basis of his master's thesis and led to his second Distinguished Flying Cross. He received his master's degree in aeronautics in June, 1924. Since the Army had given him two years to get his degree and he had finished it in only one, he immediately started working on his doctoral degree in aeronautics, which he received in June, 1925.

Doolittle's contributions to aviation were numerous. He worked as a test pilot, broke speed records, and helped design and build military air fields. He was also instrumental in convincing Shell Oil to develop high octane aviation fuels, which would become vital to the high performance engines being developed by the end of the 1930s.

But by far, Doolittle's most important contribution to early aviation was the development of instrument flying. He was involved in the invention of the artificial horizon and the directional gyroscope. These instruments made it possible to operate an airplane with limited or no visibility. In 1929, he became the first pilot to fly with no outside view from the cockpit. He took off, flew, and landed the airplane depending solely on the instruments. His "blind flying" received wide newspaper attention, and he received the Harmon Trophy for his experiments. The ability to fly in all conditions made all-weather airline operations practical.

★ THE RAIDER ★

After the bombing of Pearl Harbor and America's entry into the war, Doolittle planned the raid on Japan, but his plan hinged on an idea first conceived by Navy Captain Francis Low, who believed that under the right conditions twin-engine bombers could be launched from an aircraft carrier. It was an idea never considered before, but Doolittle also believed the plan could work. When tests were conducted, it was discovered that the B-25, with some modifications, could be successfully launched from the deck of an aircraft carrier. The B-25s had the necessary range of 2,400 miles and could carry a 2,000 pound payload. But there was one problem with the plan—it would be a one-way mission. The planes would fly to Japan and drop their bombs. Then, with what fuel remained, they would fly to Ally airbases in China.

Despite the risks, on April 1, 1942, sixteen modified B-25's were loaded onto the deck of the *USS Hornet* at Alameda, California. Each aircraft carried four specially-constructed 500-pound bombs—three were high-explosives, and one was an incendiary. Each plane had a crew of five men for a total of eighty Doolittle Raiders.

The *USS Hornet* set sail the following day. Several days later, she met up with the *USS Enterprise* and her escort of cruisers and destroyers. The *USS Enterprise* would provide protection during the raid since the *USS Hornet's* fighter planes were stored below deck because of the bombers. The American force proceeded in radio silence to their intended launch point in enemy controlled waters.

On the morning of April 18, the mission was compromised when the ships were sighted by a Japanese patrol boat, which radioed an attack warning. The Japanese picket boat was quickly destroyed by the *USS Nashville*, but Doolittle decided to launch the attack immediately in the event the message from the Japanese boat had been received. The planes left the carrier ten hours early and more than 170 miles further off shore than what had been intended. The extra distance was the major concern. The calculations for the fuel required for the mission were very tight. With the added distance, it was uncertain, in fact doubtful, whether the planes would have enough fuel to deliver the attack and to reach the landing bases in China.

Despite the fact that none of the crews had taken part in the previous tests and none had ever before flown off the deck of an aircraft carrier, all sixteen bombers successfully took off from the *USS Hornet*, flying toward Japan in a single-file line just a few feet above the waves in order to avoid detection.

The planes arrived over Japan around noon, just six hours after they had departed from the carrier. They bombed ten military and industrial targets in Tokyo, two targets in Yokohama, and one target each in Yokosuka, Nagoya, Kobe, and Osaka. There was little resistance other than some light anti-aircraft fire and a few enemy fighters. None of the American bombers were shot down or badly damaged by the Japanese defenses.

After the attack, fifteen of the bombers fled across the East China Sea towards China while one bomber, critically low on fuel, set off towards Russia. By nightfall, the crews heading to China were very low on fuel, and the weather was deteriorating. It was becoming obvious they would not make it to the Chinese bases where they had planned to land. Some of the bombers opted to crash land while other crews parachuted out of the doomed planes over eastern China near the border. Three of the Raiders were killed.

All sixteen B-25s were lost, but most of the crew members made their way back home with the help of the Chinese. Helping the Raiders escape the Japanese came at a high price, however, since it is believed over 250,000 Chinese were killed by the Japanese as they relentlessly pursued Doolittle's men. Eight of the Raiders were captured by the Japanese. Three were executed, and one later died as the result of starvation and mistreatment—the remaining four survived the war.

At first, Doolittle considered the raid to be a miserable failure. It did very little damage to the Japanese, and all the

★ THE RAIDER ★

planes were destroyed along with cost in human lives. Doolittle fully expected to be court-martialed upon returning to the States. Instead, Doolittle's Raid bolstered American morale to such an extent that Doolittle was awarded the Medal of Honor by President Roosevelt. He was also promoted two grades to brigadier general. During the next three years, he went on to command the 12th Air Force in North Africa, the 15th Air Force in the Mediterranean, and the 8th Air Force in England.

In addition to Doolittle being awarded the Medal of Honor, Corporal Dave Thatcher and Lieutenant Thomas White each received the Silver Star for helping several wounded crew members evade Japanese troops in China, and all the remaining Raiders were awarded the Distinguished Flying Cross. Those who were killed, wounded, or injured as a result of the raid also received the Purple Heart. And every Doolittle Raider was honored by a decoration from the Chinese government.

The Doolittle Raid, as Doolittle himself knew, did little damage to the Japanese materially. However, when the news of the raid was released, the United States was swept up in a great patriotic fervor. America mobilized itself for war. Its great manufacturing plants began to create the weapons of war needed to win. After the devastating attack at Pearl Harbor, the success of Doolittle's Raid was the first good news Americans had to celebrate about and is considered the first military victory of World War II.

The raid also had another important strategic impact besides what it had done for American morale. The raid had the opposite effect on the Japanese, who, not understanding how American aircraft could attack from such a distance, assumed that America had developed a new, extremely long-range aircraft or that America possessed secret air bases. Because the Japanese could not determine where the attack had come from, fighter units were recalled to the home islands out of fear of another raid. This pulling back of forces subsequently weakened Japan's air capabilities against the Allies at the Battle of Midway and later during the Pacific Theater campaigns.

Doolittle's Raid, while not as devastating to Japan as Pearl Harbor had been to the United States, still served a vital purposes—it was a message to the Japanese. And it not only convinced Americans but also the Japanese that America could win the war.

The Doolittle Raiders have held an annual reunion almost every year since the late 1940s. At each reunion, there is a solemn, private ceremony in which the surviving Raiders perform a roll call. Then they toast those Raiders who have passed away during the previous year with individual silver goblets—one for each of the eighty Raiders. The goblets of those who have died are turned upside-down in the special case that houses them. When only two Raiders remain alive, they will drink a final toast using the vintage 1896 bottle of Hennessy cognac that is also stored in the case along with the goblets—the 1896 vintage is in commemoration of the year of their leader's birth. Only fourteen Raiders were still alive as of the 65th anniversary reunion held in San Antonio in April, 2007, and only eight were able to attend. The case that houses the bottle of cognac and the goblets is on display at the National Museum of the United States Air Force in Dayton, Ohio.

The *USS Hornet* from which the raid was launched was lost during World War II at the Battle of Santa Cruz Island in October, 1942. In September, 1944, the new aircraft carrier *USS Shangri-La* was launched—an obvious reference to the Doolittle Raid and to the cryptic answer President Roosevelt had given when asked from where the raid on Japan had been launched.

On May 10, 1946, Doolittle reverted to inactive reserve status. He became the vice president of Shell Oil, later serving as director. In 1947, he assisted in forming the United States Air Force Association, and he was the first president. In March, 1951, he was appointed a special assistant to the Air Force chief of staff, serving as a civilian in scientific matters which led to the Air Force ballistic missile and space programs. He retired from Air Force duty on February 28, 1959, but he con-

★ THE RAIDER ★

tinued to serve as chairman of the board of Space Technology Laboratories.

On April 4, 1985, the U.S. Congress promoted Doolittle to full general on the Air Force retired list. In a later ceremony, President Ronald Reagan and Senator Barry Goldwater pinned the four-star insignia on Doolittle.

James H. "Jimmy" Doolittle died in California in 1993. He was buried at Arlington National Cemetery. After the brief graveside service, one of the Doolittle Raiders tried to play "Taps," but he could manage only a few notes. He passed the bugle to Doolittle's great-grandson, who finished "Taps" flawlessly, as the few remaining B-25s in the United States flew overhead in General Doolittle's honor.

Brother James Doolittle became a member of Hollenbeck Lodge No. 319, Los Angeles, California during World War I, but was actually made a Mason at the Lake Charles Lodge No. 16 in Louisiana. Doolittle was stationed in Louisiana in the Air Force prior to being shipped overseas to serve in World War I. By special dispensation by the Grand Lodge of California and the Grand Lodge of Louisiana, Doolittle was permitted to become a California Mason in Louisiana. He was also a 32° Scottish Rite Mason and a Shriner.

SEVENTEEN

The Hero

"Lead from the front."

The boy was small for his age, one of twelve children in a very poor family. His home life was depressing. He grew up in an environment where there was no money and often little food. His family had a reputation for being both poor and dirty. When one of his sisters got a house cleaning job, the woman who hired her often made her take a bath before allowing her to clean the house.

The boy's second grade teacher remembered him as a bright, energetic child, who often stayed after school to help her pound out erasers. The cleanliness of the classroom seemed to appeal to him. Because he often did not have any food for lunch, the teacher many times rushed home after school feeling famished since she had given her lunch to him.

The young boy helped feed the family by hunting. He was a very good shot with a very unlikely weapon—a slingshot. He killed rabbits for his family to eat with the makeshift weapon. One afternoon, a young man from town was home from college when he saw the young boy heading towards the woods with his slingshot. Knowing the family was very poor, the young man asked the boy if he would like to borrow his .22 rifle. The young boy did borrow the rifle along with eight shells. When the boy left the woods later to return the rifle, he had only four rabbits. Before the young man could tease him about his aim, the young boy handed him back four unused shells.

Later, as a young man, he became a deadly shot with both a rifle and a shotgun. It is said he very rarely missed what he aimed at, whether it be a rabbit or a squirrel. Shells were cheap, but because of his family's poverty level, every shot counted. The young man could shoot a darting rabbit with a .22 rifle from the window of a moving car—no small feat.

When he later found himself a soldier in World War II, that deadly accuracy would come in handy. It would save his life and the lives of many others. He would become a hero and the most decorated solider of the World War II—Audie Murphy.

Audie Leon Murphy was born near Kingston, Texas, to Emmett Berry and Josie Bell Murphy. He grew up in extreme poverty near Celeste, Texas. Audie dropped out of school in the eighth grade in order to help support his family. He worked for a dollar a day, performing grueling work for any farmer who would hire him—sometimes plowing and sometimes picking cotton. He became very skilled hunter, providing small game to help feed the family. Audie was the sixth of twelve children, only nine of whom survived to adulthood.

During the 1930s, Audie worked in a combination general store, garage, and filling station in Greenville, Texas. In 1936, his father deserted the family, never to return. When Audie was sixteen, his mother died on May 23, 1941. Because he was unable to care for his younger siblings, he was forced to put the three youngest into an orphanage. But he would not forget about them; he would reclaim them after returning from World War II.

After the Japanese attack on Pearl Harbor on December 7, 1941, Murphy tried to enlist in the military, but he was rejected because he was only seventeen. He waited until his eighteenth birthday. In June, 1942, Murphy tried to join the Marines, but he was rejected again, this time because of his small size. He was only five foot five and weighed only one hundred ten pounds.

But Murphy did not stop trying to enlist. Finally, the United States Army accepted him. He was sent to Camp Wolters, Texas, for basic training. During a training session, he passed out. His company commander was concerned that he was too small to be a combat soldier and tried to have him transferred to a school for cooks and bakers, but Murphy insisted on becoming a combat soldier. When his commander gave him another try, Murphy worked very hard to prove himself, and he succeeded. After graduating from basic training, he was sent to Fort Meade, Maryland, for advanced infantry training.

In early 1943, he was shipped out to Casablanca, Morocco, but Murphy saw no action in Africa. Instead, he participated in extensive training maneuvers along with the rest of the 3rd Division. His combat initiation finally came when he took part in the liberation of Sicily on July 10, 1943. Murphy was promoted to corporal shortly after arriving for having killed two Italian officers who were trying to escape on horseback. Possibly because of his size and his need to prove himself as a solider, Murphy seemed to work overtime to succeed.

After Sicily was secured from the Germans, the 3rd Division invaded the Italian mainland, landing near Salerno in September, 1943. While leading a night patrol, Murphy and his men were ambushed by German soldiers. Able to fight their way out of the ambush, they took cover in a nearby rock quarry. The German command sent a squadron of soldiers to the quarry to wipe them out, but the Germans were stopped by Murphy's patrol. The German squadron came up against intense machine-gun and rifle fire. Three German soldiers were

★ THE HERO ★

killed and several others captured by the patrol. For his actions at Salerno, Murphy was promoted to sergeant.

Murphy distinguished himself several more times in combat while in Italy, fighting at the Volturno River, at the Anzio beachhead, and in the Italian mountains. While in Italy, his skills in combat earned him several promotions and decorations.

After the Italian campaign, the 3rd Division next invaded southern France on August 15, 1944. Murphy's best friend, Lattie Tipton, was killed. Tipton and Murphy were approaching a German machine gun nest when a soldier began waving a white flag. Not trusting the Germans' intent to surrender, Murphy urged Tipton to stay down. But Tipton disagreed. He was starting towards the position when he was shot and killed. In a rage, Murphy charged the machine gun position and single-handedly wiped out the entire German machine gun crew that had just killed his friend. Murphy then turned the German machine gun against several other nearby enemy positions, destroying them as well. For this act, Murphy received the Distinguished Service Cross, an award second only to the Medal of Honor.

Just weeks later, he received two Silver Stars for further actions. He had also been promoted to staff sergeant and held the position of platoon sergeant. Then he was awarded a battlefield commission to second lieutenant, which elevated him to the platoon leader position. Shortly after he was promoted, he was wounded in the hip by a sniper and spent ten weeks recuperating. Within days of returning to his unit, he became the commander of Company B. A few days later, he received minor wounds from a mortar round which killed two other soldiers nearby. The wounds were not serious enough for him to leave the battle.

The following day, January 26, Murphy would take part in the actions that would earn him the Medal of Honor. The citation on the Medal of Honor records the events as follows:

Second Lt. Murphy commanded Company B, which was attacked by six tanks and waves of infantry, 2d Lt. Murphy ordered his men to withdraw to a prepared position in a woods, while he remained forward at his command post and continued to give fire directions to the artillery by telephone. Behind him, to his right, one of our tank destroyers received a direct hit and began to burn. Its crew withdrew to the woods. 2d Lt. Murphy continued to direct artillery fire, which killed large numbers of the advancing enemy infantry. With the enemy tanks abreast of his position, 2d Lt. Murphy climbed on the burning tank destroyer, which was in danger of blowing up at any moment, and employed its .50 caliber machine gun against the enemy. He was alone and exposed to German fire from three sides, but his deadly fire killed dozens of Germans and caused their infantry attack to waver. The enemy tanks, losing infantry support, began to fall back. For an hour the Germans tried every available weapon to eliminate 2d Lt. Murphy, but he continued to hold his position and wiped out a squad that was trying to creep up unnoticed on his right flank. Germans reached as close as 10 yards, only to be mowed down by his fire. He received a leg wound, but ignored it and continued his single-handed fight until his ammunition was exhausted. He then made his way back to his company, refused medical attention, and organized the company in a counterattack, which forced the Germans to withdraw. His directing of artillery fire wiped out many of the enemy; he killed or wounded about 50. 2d Lt. Murphy's indomitable courage and his refusal to give an inch of ground saved his company from possible encir-

★ THE HERO ★

clement and destruction, and enabled it to hold the woods which had been the enemy's objective.

Murphy was credited with destroying six tanks as well as killing over 240 German soldiers and wounding and capturing many others, nearly single-handedly. He received thirty-three United States military medals, plus five medals from France and one from Belgium. It has been said that Murphy received every medal available at the time from the United States military except the Good Conduct Medal, which was ironic because, at the time, the Good Conduct Medal was considered the easiest medal for a combat solider to earn. Murphy became the most highly decorated soldier of World War II.

In early June, 1945, one month after Germany's surrender, Murphy returned from Europe to a hero's welcome in his home state of Texas. He gained nationwide recognition when his picture appeared on the July 16, 1945, cover of *Life* magazine. That picture of the freckled face boy who had won a Medal of Honor made him a national hero. Shortly after he returned, Murphy was discharged from active service with the U.S. Army as a first lieutenant. Later, he was discharged from the military on September 21, 1945.

After seeing the *Life* cover photograph, actor James Cagney invited Murphy to Hollywood in September, 1945. Cagney thought Murphy, with his youthful good looks and his national fame, could be a huge success as an actor. But the next few years in California were difficult for Murphy as he trained to become an actor. Even with Cagney's help, he had difficulty getting parts, and he was financially broke. He was sleeping on the floor of a gymnasium owned by his friend Terry Hunt when he finally received small parts in the 1948 films *Beyond Glory* and *Texas, Brooklyn and Heaven*. In 1949, Murphy starred for the first time in *Bad Boy*, his third movie.

In 1948, with the help of his writer friend "Specs" McClure, Murphy began writing his autobiography. The book was a modest description of his exploits during World War II.

He did not portray himself as a hero, nor did he mention any of the decorations he had received as a result of his actions. Instead, Murphy praised the skills, bravery, and dedication of the other soldiers in his platoon.

Murphy's 1949 autobiography, *To Hell and Back*, became a national bestseller. About the same time that he was both acting and working on his book, Murphy met actress Wanda Hendrix. In 1949, they married. Even though things were beginning to look up for Murphy, not all was well. Murphy was plagued by insomnia, serious bouts of depression, and horrendous nightmares related to his experiences during World War II. He was suffering from what was called "shell shock" or "battle fatigue" in that day. Those conditions are now known as post-traumatic stress disorder (PTSD). His wife often talked about how Murphy struggled with this condition. It was an illness that, at the time, was not talked about; in fact, it was sometimes seen as a sign of weakness. Murphy struggled silently with the symptoms of the disease for years. Wanda claimed that due to his illness, he had once held her at gunpoint. They were divorced in 1951. Later, he would remarry and have two children with former airline stewardess, Pamela Archer.

In 1955, he made his most successful film, playing himself in an adaptation of his best-selling book, *To Hell and Back*. He expressed great discomfort in playing himself. He even suggested that Tony Curtis might be a better actor for the role. However, he finally agreed to play the part. Part of his reluctance may have been related to his illness. It was an emotional ordeal for Murphy to relive the battles and events he took part in during World War II. But *To Hell and Back* grossed almost ten million dollars during its initial theatrical release. It was Universal Studio's biggest hit in its history—surpassed only by *Jaws* more than twenty years later.

In the twenty-five years Murphy spent in Hollywood, he made a total of forty-four feature films—thirty-three of them Westerns. Even though Murphy saw a great deal of success,

★ THE HERO ★

his illness continued to plague him. In the 1960s, Murphy became addicted to the pills he was taking because of his problems sleeping. When Murphy finally realized he was an addict, he knew he had to stop taking the sleeping pills. He took matters into his own hands. Locking himself in a motel room for a week, he suffered terrible withdrawal symptoms from the drug, but he came out free from addiction.

One of Murphy's great legacies was that he finally broke the taboo about publicly discussing war-related mental conditions. In an effort to draw attention to the problems of war veterans returning first from the Korean conflict and later from the Vietnam War, Murphy spoke out candidly about his own problems with post traumatic stress disorder. Murphy called on the United States government to give increased consideration to the emotional impact of combat experience. He urged the government to extend health care benefits to address PTSD and the other mental-health problems of returning war veterans. His fame and his reputation as a solider went a long way in changing the perceptions about PTSD and helped bring about changes in how veterans suffering from the disorder are treated, even to this day.

While Murphy was on a business trip on May 28, 1971, his private plane crashed into Brush Mountain near Catawba, Virginia. The pilot and all five passengers, including Murphy, were killed. A large granite marker now marks the site of the crash. Murphy was forty-six years old.

On June 7, 1971, Audie Murphy was buried with full military honors at Arlington National Cemetery. The official U.S. representative at the ceremony was decorated World War II veteran and future President George Herbert Walker Bush.

The tombstones at Arlington National Cemetery for Medal of Honor recipients are normally decorated in gold leaf. Murphy had specifically requested that his stone remain plain and inconspicuous—the stone of an ordinary soldier. Later, however, a special walkway was constructed at Arlington due to the large number of visitors who came to pay their respects.

Murphy's grave is the second most-visited gravesite at Arlington National Cemetery, second only to that of President John F. Kennedy.

Brother Audie Murphy was a member of North Hollywood Lodge No. 542 in North Hollywood, California. He became a Master Mason on June 27, 1955, and later became a dual member, joining Heritage Lodge No. 764 in North Hollywood, California, in 1956.

Murphy was extremely active in the fraternity, taking part in parades and guest speaking at Masonic events. As he was in the military, he became highly decorated in the fraternity as well. He joined the Scottish Rite in 1957 and received the 32° at the Scottish Rite Temple in Dallas, Texas. He became a Shriner at Hella Temple in Dallas, Texas, in 1957. Murphy was made a "Master of the Royal Secret" in the Valley of Dallas, Orient of Texas, on November 14, 1965. He was also decorated a Knight Commander of the Court of Honor (KCCH) on December 11, 1965.

Shortly after Murphy's death, the Long Beach California Scottish Rite Bodies of the Masonic Order honored Brother Audie Murphy by naming the 111th Scottish Rites Graduating Class the Audie Murphy Memorial Class. One of the highlights for the members of the Audie Murphy Memorial Class was a special showing of the film *To Hell and Back* to give the candidates a much better understanding of the character and background of their most distinguished member.

In 2000, during the November Ladies Night Dinner of the Valley of Long Beach, Audie Murphy was posthumously honored with the 33° cap, the fraternity's top honor, which was presented to his widow, Pamela Murphy.

ENTERTAINERS

"I personally believe that each of us was put here for a purpose—to build not to destroy. If I can make people smile, then I have served my purpose for God."

—*Red Skelton*
Vincennes Lodge No. 1, IN

EIGHTEEN

The Musician

"Composers are the only people who can hear good music above bad sounds."

The man was considered one of the best trapshooters in America. He enjoyed the sport a great deal primarily because he felt that it equalized and leveled all ranks. It was also something he could continue to enjoy as he got older. He won trophies and medals in many of the national competitions in which he competed. It was not unusual for the man to shoot more than 15,000 targets in a single season with an average shooting accuracy at competitions between 75 and 98 percent. In fact, he was such a good shooter that the Ithaca Gun Company named one of its high-end guns after him. He also wrote articles about trapshooting and lent his image and remarks for use in advertisements for products related to the sport.

The man belonged to several trapshooting organizations. In 1916, he was elected president of the American Amateur Trapshooters' Association. In 1917, he became the chairman of the National Association of Shotgun Owners. He was also a member of a group of elite crack shots known as The Indians.

Once, an English minister, having read that the man had shot many thousands of "pigeons," wrote to him, urging him to repent and to stop with his wholesale slaughter of the poor creatures. Amused, the man sent a box of broken clay "pigeons" to the minister with instructions that they should be boiled before being eaten.

As handy as this man was with a gun, it should not be surprising that he was in the military nor that he was rarely seen out of his uniform. What might be surprising is that this man, as a Marine, never carried a gun—he carried a baton. He was the man who wrote much of the patriotic music that has given Americans something to wave their flags to for years. He was none other than John Philip Sousa.

Sousa is still considered one of the most prolific composers in American history and one of the most famous in his lifetime. In total, he wrote 136 marches, 15 operettas, and 70 popular songs, waltzes, humoresques, and incidental music. Sousa once remarked, "I can almost always write music; at any hour of the twenty-four, if I put pencil to paper, music comes." He also wrote more than 130 articles on everything from music to trapshooting.

But Sousa was best known by his nickname, the March King. Many of the patriotic-themed marches are still played by bands today. His music is particularly enjoyed on patriotic holidays, at summer band concerts, and during military ceremonies. Very few high school marching bands in America today do not have at least a couple John Philips Sousa marches in their repertoire—including, most likely, "The High School Cadets."

While best known for his patriotic marches, Sousa dedicated marches to just about any topic that caught his attention. For example, in 1925, to honor his favorite game of baseball, he wrote a march entitled "The National Game." As an extremely active Freemason, he wrote a march in 1923 in their honor entitled "Nobles of the Mystic Shrine." He also wrote a number of marches for state universities, including the University of Illinois, the University of Wisconsin, Kansas State University, and the University of Nebraska, to name a few. In addition, he wrote marches about things like the famous Revolutionary War ship the *USS Constitution*, also called *Old Ironsides*, and places like the New York Hippodrome. He wrote marches for the Boy Scouts of America, the Salvation Army, and even a wedding in 1918. Sousa once said, "Anybody can write music of a sort. But touching the public heart is quite another thing."

John Philip Sousa was born to John Antonio and Maria Elisabeth Trinkhaus Sousa on November 6, 1854, in Washington, D. C. He was the third of ten children. His father played the trombone in the U.S. Marine band. When John Philip started his music training at age six on the violin, he was found to have "perfect pitch." That meant he could hear a note, and without the aid of a pitch pipe or musical instrument, he could immediately identify the pitch. At a very young age, John Philip accompanied his father and the U.S. Marine band to Gettysburg where Abraham Lincoln gave his famous "Gettysburg Address." A few years later, he attempted to run away from home to join a circus band, so his father enlisted him in the Marines as an apprentice. During the seven years he served in the U.S. Marine band, he learned to play all the wind instruments and received scholastic training along with the music training. He also learned advanced music subjects from private teachers and performed in local theater orchestras at night.

In 1875, Sousa left the U.S. Marine band at the age of twenty. He set out to expand his career as a violinist and conductor. He later worked as the director of a company which was performing the extremely popular Gilbert and Sullivan musical *HMS Pinafore*. The musical was so popular new companies were being formed in great numbers. The performance directed by Sousa was one of the most successful and one of very few about which Gilbert and Sullivan commented favorably.

Sousa met his wife-to-be when the production moved to Philadelphia. The daughter of a carpenter, she joined the cast as an understudy. Although she was not a gifted vocalist, Sousa adored her from their first meeting and made sure she stayed on with the cast. Sousa married Jan van Middlesworth Bellis, whom he always called Jennie, on December 30, 1879. She was sixteen (or seventeen) and he was twenty-five.

During the spring of 1880, Sousa was asked to compose music for a variety show *Our Flirtations*. The production was first performed in Philadelphia and later went on tour. While in St. Louis, Sousa learned that he was being considered for the conductor's position for the U.S. Marine Band. Although his father was retired by that time, he had some influence in having his son considered for the post, but he was not totally responsible for securing the position for John Philip. The commandant of the Marine Corps, having seen one of Sousa's performances of *Our Flirtations* in Philadelphia, was impressed with Sousa's abilities as a director. Through a series of telegrams back and forth with his father, Sousa accepted the position by proxy, despite having some difficulty in getting released from his obligations to his theatre company. At the age of twenty-five, John Philip Sousa became the seventeenth leader of the U.S. Marine Band.

When Sousa assumed leadership of the band, it was composed of approximately forty members, mostly older men of German and Italian descent. Sousa made several changes in the band. He updated an antiquated library with some modern compositions. He also began a rigorous rehearsal schedule. In addition, he changed how parts were split. He believed that two instruments playing the same part, which was standard at the time, was a waste. He once remarked, "Two parts for two players seems to me to be correct. But a good deal of talent is lost in doubling men for each part." These changes upset some of the older members. Instead of trying to pacify these musicians, he arranged for their discharge upon their written request. The ranks of the U.S. Marine Band temporarily shrank to around thirty members, but the improvements in the sound were dramatic. Even with fewer members, the band sounded fuller because the doubling up of parts had been eliminated. Sousa filled in the vacancies left by older members by recruiting younger players, including some of his friends from Philadelphia. After only a year, the band performances were notably different from what they had been. Many people took notice of the changes, leading to well-attended performances.

Sousa's conducting style was a performance art in itself. In what seemed to be a music-driven trance, he conducted with energetic motions and gyrations few had seen before. Crowds were mesmerized not only by the music but also by his style. He was usually sweating profusely and exhausted after a performance.

The U.S. Marine Band performed at White House events. In twelve years as the leader of the U.S. Marine Band, Sousa served five Presidents: Hayes, Garfield, Arthur, Cleveland, and Harrison. He maintained close friendships with most of these Presidents. In his autobiography, *Marching Along*, he gave rarely related insights into their characters. By far his closest friendship was with President James Garfield, who was a member of the same Masonic lodge as Sousa. Upon receiving news of Garfield's death, Sousa walked aimlessly around Washington all night. When he returned home, he composed a dirge entitled "In Memoriam," which was played by the U.S. Marine Band during the funeral services.

As the leader of the U.S. Marine Band, Sousa endeared himself to the musicians in the band by keeping their welfare at heart. He pushed to have their salaries increased and allowed them to take other jobs to supplement their poor military salaries. The morale of the band was also greatly increased by the fame of their conductor, who was becoming world renown as the March King, and by the privilege and prestige of premiering many of his original marches, such as "The

Washington Post" and "Semper-Fidelis," which were rapidly becoming famous.

Sousa was also very kind to musicians when an error was made during a performance. He was credited for having an ear that never missed a sour note and a memory that never forgot from performance to performance exactly who in the band had made the error and where in the piece it was made. But during the performance, he would not make any indication that he had even heard the wrong note. However, during the next performance, a few measures before they arrived at the same place where the sour note had been hit in the last performance, he would look directly at the offending musician, then glance towards heaven and make a brief gesture of prayer.

During the last two years Sousa was conductor, the U.S. Marine Band, without Sousa's active participation, made entertainment history by making numerous recordings. The phonograph had been recently invented. Only about a third of the band could fit inside the recording studio. Ten mikes were used to record the band, each making only a single recording, so if three hundred recordings of a song were wanted, the band had to record the same song thirty times. Sousa did not like the tinny recordings because he felt they were a poor representation of the band's actual sound. Sousa was also against the recordings because there was no consideration under copyright laws at that time for the composer's rights for the new recording technology. The only ones to benefit financially from the musical recordings were those selling them. Sousa said, "When they make money out of my pieces, I want a share of it." He later appeared before Congress, and the laws were finally changed to give composers rights to their recorded music. Although Sousa never liked the recordings, they did help him achieve tremendous popularity and fame as well as make many of his marches accessible to those who normally would never have had the opportunity to hear them. Even a poor quality recording of a John Philip Sousa march was still something unique, and enough of the music came through to make the recordings very popular.

Sousa left the U.S. Marine Band in 1892 to form his own band. The U.S. Marine Band had traveled very little, but with his new civilian band, he took his music all over the United States. At first, his decision to leave the U.S. Marine Band was received with public outrage, but eventually, his civilian band achieved tremendous fame and popularity, making Sousa a millionaire. His largest performance was during the Chicago World's Fair where, at an open-air concert, the band entertained a crowd of more than ten thousand with a medley of popular songs. Sousa's band not only toured in the United States but also in 1900, represented the United States at the Paris Exposition and then completed a tour of Europe.

John Philip Sousa died on March 6, 1932, at the Abraham Lincoln Hotel in Reading, Pennsylvania, after conducting a rehearsal of the Ringgold Band he was to guest conduct the next day. The last song he conducted at the rehearsal was "Stars and Stripes Forever." He was laid to rest in the Congressional Cemetery in Washington, D.C. Thousands lined the streets and attended the memorial service. The U.S. Marine Band played, among other pieces, "In Memoriam," the dirge he had composed for his friend, President James Garfield. At the gravesite, Masonic rites were held and a prayer was given. After a navy squad fired a salute and a single bugler played "Taps," America's March King was laid to rest. Along the bottom of his stone, a musical staff was engraved with a fragment of his most famous piece, "Stars and Stripes Forever."

But only the man had died. His music lives on today. It has become the soundtrack of the American experience and tradition—a sound that has never gone out of style. Throughout the world, his music is still played by bands big and small, professional and amateur. It would hardly be the Fourth of July in America without a marching band playing "Stars and Stripes Forever." In 1987, fifty-five years after Sousa's death,

★ GREAT AMERICAN FREEMASONS ★

President Ronald Reagan signed a bill making "Stars and Stripes Forever" the national march.

Brother John Philip Sousa was a very active Freemason. He was raised a Master Mason at Hiram Lodge No. 10, Washington, D. C., on September 16, 1886. He received Capitular Degrees and exalted in Eureka Chapter No. 4 (later Eureka Naval Chapter) on December 3, 1886. He also received the Order of the Red Cross on December 10, 1886. He was knighted in Columbia Commandery No. 2 of the Knights Templar in Washington, D.C., on April 21, 1922. He joined the Shrine, initiated in the Ancient Arabic Order of the Nobles of the Mystic Shrine, Almas Temple, Washington, D. C., and wrote a march entitled "Nobles of the Mystic Shrine" in 1923 in their honor. He was named honorary leader of Almas Temple Band on March 10, 1932.

NINETEEN

The Writer

"I remember when I had just written Innocents Abroad *when I and my partner wanted to start a newspaper syndicate. We needed three dollars and did not know where to get it. While we were in a quandary I espied a valuable dog on the street. I picked up the canine and sold him to a man for three dollars. Afterward the owner of the dog came along and I got three dollars from him for telling where the dog was. So I went back and gave the three dollars to the man whom I sold it to, and lived honestly ever after."*

There is only one man that can be introduced by one of his own stories and whose life story can be told through his own words. William Faulkner called him "the father of American Literature." His satirical humor went on to define the American style of writing, and to this day, his humor and satire captivate his readers. He was not only a commentator on the world in his time but also the first writer to find humor in the truth and to poke fun at us—the American people.

He was Samuel Langhorne Clemens—a.k.a. Mark Twain.

"[Jane Clemens] was very funny at times, but her humor was often entirely unconscious. When she was visiting in Kentucky in her later years she heard two men behind her in the train arguing about Mark Twain's birthplace, one insisting that he had been born in Tennessee, the other that it was Kentucky. Mrs. Clemens said to the man who was traveling with her, 'Tell them he was born in Florida, Missouri.' The man complied but it did not settle the discussion, one of the disputants insisting, 'I'm sure you're mistaken. He was born in Kentucky.' It was too much for Jane Clemens. Without the slightest intention of being humorous she turned around and said, 'I'm his mother. I ought to know. I was there!'"

She was right! Samuel Langhorne Clemens was born in Florida, Missouri, on November 30, 1835, the same year Halley's comet made an appearance into the galaxy. He was born to John Marshall Clemens and Jane Lampton Clemens, the sixth of seven children, only two of whom survived to adulthood. When he was four years old, his family moved to Hannibal, Missouri, which later became the inspiration for the fictional town of St. Petersburg he used as the backdrop for his novels *The Adventures of Tom Sawyer* and *The Adventures of Huckleberry Finn*. It was there that young Samuel Clemens became familiar with the institution of slavery, as Missouri was a slave state at the time, and developed a strong opinion of slavery, which he later explored in his fiction.

> "It is a wise child that knows its own father, and an unusual one that unreservedly approves of him."

In 1847, shortly after his father passed away, Samuel became a printer's assistant. In 1851, he became a typesetter and a contributor of articles and humorous sketches to the *Hannibal Journal*, which his brother Orion owned. At eighteen, Samuel left to ply his trade as a typesetter in New York, Philadelphia, St. Louis, and Cincinnati. But he returned to the Mississippi at the age of twenty-two.

★ THE WRITER ★

Inspired by a river boat pilot, Bixby, Samuel was determined to become a river boat pilot. At the time, being a river boat pilot was the third highest paying job in America with pilots earning 250 dollars per month. Samuel trained to become a pilot and convinced his brother Henry to join him. Because riverboats were made of dry wood and thus were very susceptible to fire, lamps were not permitted at night, which made navigating the river a very precarious occupation. Even so, Samuel urged his brother towards a life on the river. When Henry was killed in a riverboat explosion in 1858, Samuel blamed himself for involving his brother in such a dangerous occupation. Though guilt-ridden, Samuel continued to work on the Mississippi until the Civil War broke out on 1861 and the traffic on the Mississippi dried up.

Missouri did not join the Confederacy, but Clemens and his friends formed a Confederate militia that was later involved in a skirmish that resulted in the death of a man. Clemens decided he was not a soldier. Since he did not want to be responsible for the deaths of others, he deserted.

Joining his brother Orion, he headed west. That trip would later become the inspiration for his book *Roughing It*. Samuel tried his hand at mining in Nevada, but he failed. His writing career began when he started to work for the Virginia City newspaper *The Territorial Enterprise*. In 1863, he wrote an amusing travel piece for the paper, signing it Mark Twain. It was the first time he had used that moniker.

Samuel had used other pen names, like Josh or Thomas Jefferson Snodgrass prior to 1863, but the name Mark Twain, which he would use consistently after 1863, came from his years on the riverboat. Two fathoms, which was considered the safe water depth to operate a riverboat, was measured on a sounding line. When the two fathom mark was reached on the line, the riverboat man would cry "Mark Twain," or more fully "by the mark twain," *twain* being an archaic word for two.

Samuel Clemens traveled on to San Francisco, where he continued as a journalist and began lecturing. He received an assignment in Hawaii, which became the topic for a series of lectures. Later when he was sent to the Mediterranean by a local paper, he sent back humorous travel letters. Doing much the same thing, he continued writing on a tour through Europe and the Middle East. Later those letters were complied in his book *Innocents Abroad.*

On that trip, he met Charles Langdon and saw a picture of his sister Olivia. Clemens claimed to have fallen in love with her at first sight. They met in 1868, were engaged a year later, and married in 1870. After settling in Hartford, Connecticut, they had four children. Their son, Langdon, died in infancy. Samuel and Olivia Clemens were married thirty-four years. Even though Clemens was self-admittedly a happily married man, it didn't stop him from poking fun at the institution of marriage: "It reminds me of the man who was reproached by a friend who said, 'I think it a shame that you have not spoken to your wife for fifteen years. How do you explain it? How do you justify it?' That poor man said, 'I didn't want to interrupt her.'"

Humorists were a dime a dozen in Clemens' time, but he was unique because he continued to be successful while many others faded away. He called *The Autobiography of Mark Twain* a cemetery because he claimed he had known and been friends with seventy-eight humorists. He said that as quickly as they rose they vanished. He attributed his success to being more than just a humorist. Clemens remarked, "Why have they perished? Because they were merely humorists. Humorists of the "mere" sort cannot survive. Humor is only a fragrance, a decoration. Often it is merely an odd trick of speech and of spelling. . ."

Clemens believed the reason he survived was because he broke the old convention that a novel should be a work of art solely and should not be used as a platform to teach or to preach.

> "I have always preached. That is the reason that I have lasted thirty years. If the humor came of its own accord and uninvited I have allowed it a place in my sermon, but I was not writing the sermon for the sake of the humor. I should have written the sermon just the same, whether any humor applied for admission or not."

Clemens is primarily remembered as a humorist, but his work includes commentaries on politics, anti-war pieces, travel letters, and semi-autobiographical tales of his adventures while traveling the world. As he claimed, his serious fiction is interwoven with his preaching on subjects such as slavery, politics, and life in his times. More often than not, humor did apply for admission into his work. It is the humor that his readers enjoy and that continues to give his work the ability to teach and preach as it entertains his readers.

Most surprising is that Clemens wrote more than charming travel commentaries and heartwarming stories about youth along the Mississippi. In Victorian times, another form of fiction was flourishing, but it was not really talked about. Many writers at that time dabbled in writing more lewd and racy works. In Europe, this pornographic fiction was slowly being looked at as something that might be sold to a mass market. Clemens, having grown up on the river did not seem to have any objection to this form of writing, in fact, he once commented, "There are no people who are quite so vulgar as the over refined ones." But it was believed that Clemens' only contribution to this form of writing was a few lewd jokes and poems in his journal at the time.

However, in the 1880s, a small anonymously authored book called *1601: Conversation, as it was by the Social Fireplace, in the Time of the Tudors* was published. It was a hilarious yet pornographic story that included many popular characters, such as Queen Elizabeth, William Shakespeare, Francis Bacon, and Sir Walter Raleigh, to name a few. Almost as soon as it was published, it was rumored that Clemens had penned it. It was not until 1906—more than twenty-five years after it appeared in print—that Clemens finally admitted that he had written the piece. Mostly to entertain himself and his friend and partner Joe Twitchell, Clemens had penned it many years earlier when he was studying archaic English language in preparation for writing *A Connecticut Yankee in King Arthur's Court.* Clemens and Twitchell would read it aloud to each other during walks in the woods and laugh themselves silly. Clemens had never meant for it to be published, but Twitchell thought it was the funniest thing he had ever heard and shared copies with his other friends. From there, it found its way to John Hay, who set it in type and printed it on fine linen. As the years passed, it became an underground cult classic. Apparently, Clemens was capable of much more than just a few lewd jokes and poems.

To this day, Clemens' books are frequently banned from local libraries, primarily because they use the common language of his time and are sometimes considered offensive and racist. His books causing controversy even now would probably have amused Clemens a great deal. He had seen this reaction to his work himself a few times. In 1885, a library in Concord, Massachusetts, banned *Huckleberry Finn.* Clemens was obviously saw the merit and humor of the situation when he wrote to his publisher, "They have expelled Huck from their library as 'trash suitable only for the slums'; that will sell 25,000 copies for us for sure."

Clemens has a unique voice in literature. He viewed the world with a certain childlike innocence and sense of humor that captivated readers then as it does now. He could preach in his fiction or in his lectures about serious issues of the day, but because of his humor and style, he could say what it was he wanted to say without offending those he was saying it to.

It is ironic that his books are most commonly banned because of their racist language and the "slave dialect" he used because slavery was one of the topics he preached against most often. He rarely stated his opinion outright in his fiction but rather relied on the story and his treatment of various characters to let that opinion form in the minds of his readers. In truth, Clemens had a high regard for the slaves he had known in his boyhood, and those memories stayed with him his entire life. When he was a boy, he knew a slave named Uncle Dan, who became "Jim" in *The Adventures of Huckleberry Finn*.

> "He has served me well these many years. I have not seen him for more than half a century, and yet spiritually I have had his welcome company a good part of that time, and have staged him in books under his own name and as "Jim," and carted him all around… It was on the farm that I got my strong liking for his race and my appreciation of certain of its fine qualities."

Clemens' humor continued his entire life and covered almost every topic, including his own death. He looked at death no differently than any other topic he had ever joked about—cigars, marriage, religion, politics. Death was part of life, and humor was his life. In 1909, he joked about his own mortality during a lecture.

> "I came in with Halley's comet in 1835. It is coming again next year, and I expect to go out with it. It will be the greatest disappointment of my life if I don't go out with Halley's comet. The Almighty said, no doubt: 'Now here are these two unaccountable freaks; they came in together, they must go out together.'"

Samuel Clemens died April 21, 1910—the year Halley's comet returned.

Samuel L. Clemens was a member of Polar Star Lodge No. 79 in St. Louis, Missouri. He was raised to the sublime degree of Master Mason on July 10, 1861. During his trip around the world which became the basis of his novel *Innocents Abroad*, he procured a beautiful gavel which he had inscribed as a gift for his blue lodge. Its inscription read: "This Mallet is of Cedar cut in the Forest of Lebanon, whence Solomon obtained the Timbers for the Temple. The handle was cut by Bro. Clemens himself from a cedar planted just outside the walls of Jerusalem by Bro. Godfrey DeBouillon, the first Christian Conqueror of that City, 19th of July, 1099. The gavel in its present form was made at Alexandria, Egypt, by order of Bro. Clemens. From Bro. Sam'l L. Clemens."

TWENTY

The Raconteur

"If I had to live my life over, I'd live over a saloon."

A man named Bill Daily asked the young boy if he would like to accompany him on a trip to the Trenton Fair in New York City. Daily was a "huckster," or a confidence man, and he intended to ply his trade with those attending the fair. He made a living with three half walnut shells and a small piece of dough rolled up in a ball, which he referred to as "the little pea." It was the shell game. Daily, an expert shell manipulator, was known to his friends as the Professor. The boy agreed to go to the fair with him.

In the wee hours of the morning, Daily and the boy made their way to Wayne Junction, a small suburban train stop outside of Philadelphia where trains stopped to pick up the milk which would be delivered to New York City residences later in the morning. While the crew was distracted with loading the cargo, Daily and the boy sneaked onto the train and hid towards the front behind the tinder box.

Everything went well until the train crossed the Delaware near the place where George Washington had crossed the river during the Revolutionary War, except Daily and the boy were going into New York, unlike Washington who was fleeing from the city. Steam engines of that era needed copious amounts of water to generate steam. The trains used a water scoop that could pick up water from a trough along the tracks as the train continued to move. It was a messy procedure called "taking water on the fly," but it was effective since it did not require the train to stop to fill its tanks from overhead water spouts. That morning, when the train dropped the scoop to fill the tanks, the tanks overflowed as they often did, soaking Daily and his young companion to the skin. Years later, the young boy would remember that day as the one when he developed a strong aversion to water.

Wet, cold and miserable, Daily and the boy departed the train just past the station in New York. They ran for a while, hoping their body heat would dry them out, but that did not happen. Since both were hungry, they decided to enjoy some bread, rolls, butter, and milk for breakfast—all nicked surreptitiously from the front porches of houses where the milkmen and the bakers had left them for the residents.

When they finally made it to the fair, full but still wet and miserable, the Professor went about setting up an improvised table made from a few boxes. Then he began barking to the crowd, "It's an old army game. One will get you two, two will get you four, four will get you eight. Find the little pea. It's the old army game. A boy can play as well as a man."

When Daily said, "A boy can play as well as a man," the boy's part in the ploy began. The boy, playing the role of the "shill," had to get the ball rolling by getting the crowd interested in the Professor's game. The boy stepped forward, as if he were just a member of the crowd, and tossed down a dollar. After the Professor scrambled the shells, the boy found the pea on the very first try, walking off proudly with the two dollars he had just won so easily. The game was on, and all the suckers would gather around the table for a go, intently focused on the slight of hand at which the Professor was so skilled. The shill would repeat the ploy whenever the game slowed down.

Suddenly, a local constable descended upon the pair. The constable probably knew the man and the boy were working the crowd together because both were still wet. He booted the young boy in the rear end, causing the boy to later recall that the constable kicked him so hard in his *fundiment* that "he almost raised me over the fence." The constable grabbed the Professor by the collar and took him away as the boy escaped into the brambles. He did not make it back to Philadelphia until late that night.

Later, the boy would claim that if it had not been for the water, he might have decided to make an honest living out of being a shill, or even possibly, to have his own shells and pea business. But this young boy went in a different direction. As a result of his experiences that day, he learned a valuable lesson. He wrote," I took an oath then never to drink water from that day on."

That young boy would go on to become an American icon—one of the most unique and funny comedians of the twentieth century. That boy was W. C. Fields.

W. C. Fields was born William Claude Dukenfield on January 29, 1880, in Darby, Pennsylvania, to James and Kate Dukenfield. Both his mother and father were of English descent. His father came from a noble English-Irish family; he was a descendent of Lord Dukenfield of Cheshire. But Fields' father hardly lived an aristocratic lifestyle. James was identified as a baker on the 1860 U.S. census and as "a huckster" on the 1870 census. Fields once said, "I am an expert of electricity. My father occupied the chair of applied electricity at the state prison."

Fields was well-known for embellishing the stories of his youth, but the truth is that his home seems to have been a relatively normal one and his family life was happy. His parents supported his show business ambitions. When he was eighteen, they saw him off on the train for his first real stage tour on the vaudeville circuit.

Fields married vaudevillian chorus girl Harriet "Hattie" Hughes on April 8, 1900. By the age of twenty-one, he was traveling as a comedy juggling act. He added Hattie to his vaudeville act as a silent assistant. When Fields would drop an item he was juggling, he would stop and point an accusing finger at the silent assistant standing nearby—getting huge laughs. They worked together on vaudeville until the birth of their son on July 28, 1904. Hattie wanted Fields to settle down into a more respectable trade and stop touring, but Fields was unwilling to leave vaudeville. Then in 1906, he made his Broadway debut in the musical comedy *The Ham Tree*.

By 1907, W. C. and Hattie had separated, and their relationship became very tumultuous; even so, Fields sent voluntary child support payments and maintained close contact with Hattie and his son. Fields once said, "A woman drove me to drink and I didn't even have the decency to thank her."

Though known mostly for his comic acting, Fields got his start as a comic juggler—and he was a good one. He was later inducted into the juggling hall of fame. Fields usually appeared in the makeup of a tramp with a scruffy beard and shabby tuxedo. He juggled things like cigar boxes, hats, and a number of other unique objects. Some of his early juggling acts were reproduced in some of his films. His routine became very successful, and he toured with Irwin's Burlesquers and other vaudeville troupes in the United States, Europe, and Australia.

In 1915, he made it to Broadway as part of Florenz Ziegfeld's famous revue. In 1916, he did something he had never done before—he spoke on stage. He was thirty-six years old. Even though he had been working in vaudeville since he was eighteen, he had never spoken a word on stage. But once W. C. Fields spoke, it was impossible to shut him up. To the delight of audiences, he developed his trademark mumbling patter during this time. A typical remark mumbled on stage during his routine would be something along the lines of, "Always carry a flagon of whiskey in case of snakebite and furthermore, always carry a small snake."

During his ten years as part of the Ziegfield Follies, he developed a hilariously successful pool playing skit, which included gags and stunts that involved bizarrely shaped cues and a custom-built table. Along with his mumbled one liners, this famous pool game skit, which was also reproduced in some of his later films, made him even more famous on the silver screen.

Fields had another little-known talent. He was a cartoonist. While traveling on the vaudeville circuit and later with the Ziegfield Follies, he often created his own advertising with caricatures of himself doing his routine. These caricatures show how his act evolved over time. Early advertisements showed him as a bearded, pudgy clown character, juggling balls and cigar boxes—not at all identifiable with the character he later developed. By the turn of the century, Fields' appearance had not changed much, but he included in his advertisements his new silent assistant, his wife, Hattie. By 1912, however, Fields' image had begun to evolve into the easily identifiable personae of W. C. Fields. The beard was gone, but he often drew himself wearing a curled-up mustache. Instead of juggling, he was often shown at the pool table, wearing a top hat and frumpy tuxedo, smoking a cigar as the smoke rings circled his head. There is no question—these later cartoon characters are the W. C. Fields famous on American stage and screen.

Fields starred in a couple of short comedies filmed in New York in 1915, but his stage commitments prevented him from doing more movie work until 1924. Fields often wore a scruffy-looking, clip-on mustache in his silent films, but he discarded it after his first sound feature film, *Her Majesty Love*.

Fields created one of the great American comic personae—a hard-drinking misanthrope who teetered on the edge of buffoonery but never quite fell in. His character was blind to his own failings. He was a charming drunk, a gambler, and a man who hated children, animals, and women—unless, of course, they were the wrong sort of women. He once said, "Marry an outdoors woman. Then if you throw her out into the yard on a cold night, she can still survive." This characterization was so believable that it was identified as Fields himself. He rarely appeared in public "out of character."

In his films, he most often played hucksters, such as carnival barkers, gamblers, confidence men, and cardsharps, distracting his marks with his buffoonery as he mumbled such gems of wisdom as "Horse sense is the thing a horse has which keeps it from betting on people," and "Never give a sucker an even break." It was often hard to know exactly where the persona ended and the real W. C. Fields began.

At times, it seemed that art imitated life. Fields did begin to drink heavily, and his behavior, at times, could be described as anti-social. He once remarked, "I'm free of all prejudices. I hate everyone equally." Both Madge Evans, an actress who appeared in several films during the 1930s, and Groucho Marx told a similar story about Fields. They claimed that Fields so deeply resented intrusions on his privacy by tourists trespassing on his property that he would often hide in the shrubs and shoot at their legs with a BB gun.

By 1936, Fields was in poor health, exacerbated by his heavy drinking. He became very difficult to work with. He often fought with studio producers, directors, and writers over the content of his films. He was determined to make his movies his way, to write his own scripts, and to choose his supporting players. He made one last film for Paramount, *The Big Broadcast of 1938*. Then, because Fields had become so difficult, the offers mostly quit coming. One offer, however, was the title role of the MGM film *The Wizard of Oz* in 1939—Fields was the original choice for the role of the wizard. For reasons that are not known exactly, he declined the role. One rumor was that he believed the role was too small. However, it is more likely that Fields' asking price of $100,000 was too much more than the $75,000 MGM was offering.

While Fields was out of work, he recorded a short speech for a radio broadcast. His familiar snide drawl registered so well with listeners that he quickly became a popular guest on network radio shows. One of his funniest routines had him trading insults with Edgar Bergen's dummy, Charlie McCarthy, on *The Chase and Sanborn Hour*. Fields would insult Charlie about being made of wood, and Charlie would fire back at Fields about his drinking:

Fields: Is it true your father was a gate-leg table?
McCarthy: If it is, *your* father was *under* it!

Fields' new popularity on the radio re-opened the door to Hollywood. He negotiated a contract with Universal Pictures in 1939. His first feature for Universal, *You Can't Cheat an Honest Man*, carried on the Fields-McCarthy rivalry. In 1940, Fields made *My Little Chickadee* with the perfect actress to play the "wrong sort of woman"—an actress that had created her own persona much as Fields had—Mae West. He also made one of his best-known films, *The Bank Dick*. Shemp Howard, one of the original Three Stooges, played the bartender.

Fields to bartender: Was I in here last night, and did I spend a $20 bill?

Bartender: Yeah!

Fields: Oh, is that a load off my mind . . . I thought I'd *lost* it!

Because things had been running so smoothly in their relationship with Fields, Universal Studios finally gave Fields a chance in 1941 to film a movie version of his book *Never Give a Sucker an Even Break*. The film was a masterpiece of absurd humor in which Fields appeared as himself. The film Fields delivered to Universal was so nonsensical that Universal had to re-cut and re-shoot parts of it. After the studio released the film, they also released W. C. Fields from his contract. *Never Give a Sucker an Even Break* turned out to be Fields' last starring role.

Fields' film career slowed down considerably in the 1940s. His illnesses confined him to brief guest-star appearances. His last film appearance was in the musical revue *Sensations,* released in 1945.

Fields spent his final weeks in a hospital, where a friend, stopping by for a visit, caught him reading the Bible. When asked why, Fields replied, "I'm checking for loopholes." In a final irony, W. C. Fields died on Christmas Day, 1946—a holiday he claimed he hated. There have been stories that he wanted his grave marker to read. "I would rather be dead than play Philadelphia." Whatever his wishes might have been, his stone has only his name and the dates of his birth and death.

Brother W. C. Fields was a member of E. Coppee Mitchell Lodge No. 936 in Philadelphia, Pennsylvania.

TWENTY-ONE

The Cowboy Philosopher

"There is nothing as stupid as an educated man if you get him off the thing he was educated in."

Knowing well the reputation of the famous actor he was working with in his new picture, Director Henry King was prepared for the constant state of chaos this man could create. The plot of his new movie, *State Fair*, revolved around a prize-winning hog. At the Iowa State Fair, the production company had bought the grand champion boar to use in the film. The animal was a behemoth with large tusks and a foul disposition. King was worried that his comic actor, when trying to get laughs, would mess around with the animal and be seriously injured.

King warned his actor that the boar, named Blue Boy, was a dangerous animal and urged him to leave the boar alone. Scratching his head, the actor said, "I've always been on friendly terms with hogs. "Me and him'll get along all right."

When it came time to shoot the first scene with Blue Boy, King could not find his actor and began to search for him. To his horror, he found the actor, apparently asleep with his hat pulled down over his eyes, in the pen with Blue Boy—his head resting on the hog's side. King's reaction was exactly what the actor had expected. Once the actor got his laugh, he climbed out of the pen as the cast and crew howled. What this man knew, which King did not know, was that as long as he didn't disturb the hog, he was safe.

When the picture was concluded, the studio asked the actor if he would be interested in buying Blue Boy since there was a lot of meat on an animal that size. The actor declined the offer, saying, "I wouldn't feel right eatin' a fellow actor." What he did do for his *State Fair* co-star and former state champion was find him a permanent home in California's agricultural schools—pretty typical behavior for one of America's most beloved characters, Will Rogers.

"My ancestors didn't come on the *Mayflower* but they met the boat," Rogers once said. He was born on November 4, 1879, in the Indian Territory that would later become the state of Oklahoma. His father, Clement Van Rogers, and mother, Mary America Schrimsher, were both of Cherokee Indian heritage. Growing up on the Dog Iron Ranch, Rogers learned at a young age to love the cowboy ways. He became an expert roper.

In 1902, Rogers decided to leave the ranch to secure a job with the Argentinean gauchos. When that venture was unsuccessful, he sailed to England and then later to South Africa, where he finally found work breaking horses for the British army. He began his show business career there in Texas Jack's Wild West Circus as a trick roper capable of throwing three lassos at one time. He was billed as the Cherokee Kid.

Returning to America, Rogers worked as a Wild West performer in the Wirth Brothers Circus. Eventually, he began to do his rope tricks on the vaudeville circuits. While his act was just doing rope tricks, his humorous remarks and witty comebacks to the audience when he missed a trick got laughs. Although the main focus of his act remained his remarkable roping skill, he began working into his act more jokes. For example, a quip, such as the following, was bound to amuse an

★ THE COWBOY PHILOSOPHER ★

audience: "Be thankful we're not getting all the government we're paying for."

In 1915, Rogers got his big break. He was booked for a one-week engagement with legendary showman Florenz Zicgfeld in his *Midnight Frolic*, a variety show that started at midnight and drew a very influential and faithful clientele. As a result, Rogers could not just repeat the same show every night as he had done in the past. Instead, Rogers, an avid reader of the daily news, worked up a nightly monologue based on the news of the day and famous newsmakers.

"All I know is what I read in the papers," is often misquoted as one of Will Rogers' punch lines. In reality, that was the way he opened his famous show each evening. Standing on stage while twirling a rope, he would say something to the audience like, "Well, what shall I talk about? I ain't got anything funny to say. All I know is what I read in the papers."

Rogers' "one-week" engagement lasted well into 1916 when he was offered a spot in the even more famous Ziegfeld show, *The Ziegfeld Follies*. Ziegfeld saw comedic acts as nothing more than fillers during stage resets and costume changes, but Rogers managed to achieve star status with his roping demonstrations and his humorous monologues about the daily news. Rogers appeared in nearly every performance of the *Follies* between 1916 and 1925.

Between 1925 and 1928, Will Rogers was dubbed "Ambassador at Large of the United States" by the National Press Club of Washington, D.C. He began traveling the length and breadth of the United States, becoming one of the first entertainers to fly coast-to-coast with pilots during the early days of airmail flights. People loved his humor, and some of his more amusing remarks were often quoted in the newspapers. For example, a remark such as the following, was bound to wind up printed in the newspaper following one of his performances: "Instead of giving money to found colleges to promote learning, why don't they pass a constitutional amendment prohibiting anybody from learning anything? If it works as good as the

Prohibition one did, why, in five years we would have the smartest race of people on earth."

Rogers became one of the nation's most important commentators on the daily state of affairs. He was a popular convention speaker and lecturer, often giving benefits after floods, droughts, and earthquakes. After the Great Depression hit, he took his message to radio audiences, giving regular radio talks about the state of unemployment and the economy with ex-President Calvin Coolidge, President of the United States Herbert Hoover, and former Presidential candidate Al Smith. Many people saw Will Rogers as the conscience of the nation. At the same time he tried to educate his audiences, he continued to amuse them with lines such as this: "The man with the best job in the country is the vice-president. All he has to do is get up every morning and say, 'How is the president?'"

Rogers spent most his time in the early 1930s lecturing and speaking on the radio, but he was also dabbling in motion pictures and writing a regular column. However, he seemed to enjoy radio the most. He had a lot of things to say, and he would often ramble on from one topic to another. This became a problem on the radio when he had an allotted amount of time to speak. It was not unusual for him to go over his time and to get cut off in mid-sentence. By 1935, he had finally bought a wind-up alarm clock. When it began ringing on the air, he knew it was time to begin his wrap up. Soon, his radio show was being announced as "Will Rogers and His Famous Alarm Clock."

Rogers had made a number of silent movies between 1918 and 1924. While he enjoyed the experience of making films and wrote many of the title cards for the films he appeared in, speaking was his strongest skill, not acting. He had even tried his hand at making films, but he nearly went bankrupt. He began to feel like he was wasting his time. After making a dozen pictures for up-and-coming director Hal Roach, he left Hollywood in 1924, not returning until the ad-

★ THE COWBOY PHILOSOPHER ★

vent of "talkies" in 1929. Once he quipped about his work in Hollywood: "I'm not a real movie star. I've still got the same wife I started out with twenty-eight years ago."

When Rogers returned to Hollywood in 1929, it was not as an actor in B-movies—he was considered a real commodity. He was already a very famous and well-liked character, and his voice was familiar to audiences from the radio. More often than not, Rogers played a version of himself in movies. He never followed a script, though he might read through it the evening before, just to get the "gist" of it. The following day, with the aid of a script girl reading what he was supposed to say, he would ad lib his own lines. It was often a harrowing experience for other actors working with Rogers because he never said anything the same way twice and he never did a scene the same way twice. In addition, the other actors often had a difficult time catching their cues because they were never quite sure when Rogers was done.

Rogers was a top box office draw. He worked with some of the biggest names in Hollywood, including Myrna Loy, Hattie McDaniel, Ray Milland, Maureen O'Sullivan, Dick Powell, Mickey Rooney, Boris Karloff, and Bill "Bojangles" Robinson. Several of his films were directed by the legendary director John Ford.

The films that Rogers made were squeaky clean. "I just don't want to play in any picture where folks may think they shouldn't have brought their children," he once said. Because of this reputation, families did go to his films together; in fact, it was not unusual for an entire school class to take a field trip to the local theater to see a newly released Will Rogers film. Rogers believed in strong family values and clean living, which he applied to his every day life and to his professional career. He once said, "Live in such a way that you would not be ashamed to sell your parrot to the town gossip."

About the same time he was achieving such success in films, Rogers began writing a popular syndicated column called "Will Rogers Says." The column, which was actually a telegram he would send out daily to his subscribers, usually appeared on the front pages of the subscribing papers.

On the movie set, Rogers lived out of his car. He would often be found sleeping on the side boards or reading the paper in the front seat or typing out his "telegram" on a portable typewriter he kept in the car.

Rogers' column often expressed his disappointment with big government and its failure to serve the American people. His remarks were not always appreciated, and he often irritated the politicians he frequently called by name. "It's easy being a humorist when you've got the whole government working for you," he once said.

In the summer of 1935, Will Rogers decided to undertake a sightseeing tour of Alaska with Wiley Post, a fellow Oklahoman and world-renowned aviator. Post's plane, which was top-heavy, was an experimental hybrid of a Lockheed Explorer with Orion parts. On August 15, 1935, it crashed near Point Barrow, Alaska. Both Will Rogers and Wiley Post were killed.

It is difficult for people today to understand the place that Will Rogers held in 1935. Between his regular weekly column and his "telegrams," Rogers was the most widely read newspaper columnist in the world; his thirty-minute Sunday night radio broadcasts were also the highest rated radio show, and he was a top box office draw in Hollywood, second only to Shirley Temple—all at the time of his death. Rogers was the "conscience of the nation" who talked plain English to the American people through a variety of media forms and about topics that were important at the time. During the difficult years of the Great Depression, he became a friend of the common masses, concerned with the subjects that concerned them. He not only commented on events of the day but also interpreted the news in ways the American people could grasp. Rogers may have started as an entertainer, but to most Americans, he became a great cowboy philosopher and horse-sense

★ THE COWBOY PHILOSOPHER ★

sage, saying once, "Diplomacy is the art of saying 'Nice Doggie' until you can find a rock."

To this day, Will Rogers is keeping a watchful eye on Congress. Each state is allowed two statues in the United States Capitol Building. There is a story that Oklahomans knew long before Will Rogers died that they wanted his statue to be one of their statues on display. When they asked Will Rogers if having his statue there would be all right with him, Rogers said only if the statue was placed facing the House gallery so he could keep an eye on Congress. As a result, his statue is the only one in Statuary Hall that faces the House gallery entrance. It is also said that since the statue of Will Rogers was put into place, every President has rubbed Rogers' feet for good luck before going inside to deliver the State of the Union Address.

Brother Will Rogers became a Master Mason at Claremore Lodge No. 53 in Claremore, Oklahoma, on March 13, 1906. He was also a member of the Scottish Rite and Akdar Shrine Temple in Tulsa, Oklahoma.

TWENTY-TWO

The Singer

"You Ain't Heard Nothin' Yet!"

The moment in the show the audience has been anticipating, the reason most of them bought tickets to begin with, has finally arrived. The curtain closes on the previous act, and a hush falls over the crowded theater. A small man, only five foot seven, steps through the curtain onto the forestage, dressed in a frumpy oversized suit, a red string tie, and white gloves. His face is blackened with make-up. The audience erupts into applause. Once the applause dies down, sometimes after several minutes, the orchestra begins playing the introduction, and the small performer's huge voice rings throughout the theater.

This performer did not sing songs in the traditional way audiences were accustomed to. Generally, a performer would come onto the stage, stand before the audience, and sing. This performer was much different. The songs seemed to erupt from him with such tremendous energy that the audience became completely hypnotized by the performance. His gloved hands

★ THE SINGER ★

clenched, he would belt out George Gershwin's "Swanee," or, dropping to one knee during "My Mammy," he would weep the lines, half singing and half crying: "Mammy, mammy, look at me. Don't you know me? I'm your little baby. . ." His happy songs were performed with such glee and exuberance the audience was caught up with clapping and singing along. His slow songs were performed with such deep feeling and raw power the audience would find themselves in tears. He sang, he told jokes, he whistled, he danced, and as always, he dazzled crowd after crowd, city after city, year after year—for decades.

There is one thing about this performer that has been written over and over again. Anyone who saw him perform got the impression that he was singing directly to, talking to, and joking directly with that audience member alone—as if there was nobody else in the theater expect that one person.

Such was the magic that was the trademark of the legendary performer, Al Jolson.

Al Jolson was born Asa Yoelson in the small Jewish village of Seredzius in the Lithuanian region of Imperial Russia on May 26, 1886 (this is the date according to Al Jolson, but no records exist to verify it, and some believe he could have been born at any time after 1884). His father, Moshe Yoelson, was a cantor, and the Yoelson children—Rose, Etta, Hirsh, and Asa—were raised in a strictly Jewish orthodox household. When Moshe became a rabbi in 1890, he went to America to get out of tsarist Russia. His wife, Naomi, stayed back with the children. When Moshe became the head of a congregation in Washington, D. C., in 1894, he brought his family to America. Moshe had high hopes of having a normal life in America, but those hopes were destroyed when Naomi died in 1895.

Eight-year-old Asa Yoelson, who was in the next room, never fully recovered from his sense of loss. His mother had been the center of his universe, and she had doted on him. Even with his tough exterior and brash, confident appearance, he would remain emotionally a child for the rest of his life with an inflated ego and fear of being left alone. He lived his whole life for the constant attention his mother had given him. He was at times selfish, self-indulgent, and capable of fits of temper. There was little that he would allow to come between him and what he wanted.

Asa and his brother Hirsh embraced American culture, most especially the music. They began to learn the ragtime songs performed on the streets and in the saloons of Washington, D.C. Moshe was not pleased by this. He remarried, hoping to return some stability to the family, but both the brothers had already caught the show business bug. Hirsh changed his name to Harry, and Asa changed his name to Al. They ran away from home several times. Al even spent time at St. Mary's Industrial School for orphaned boys in Baltimore—the same school Babe Ruth attended later.

Harry and Al finally broke into the business, first in a traveling circus and then in vaudeville acts and burlesque shows. Starting after the turn of the century, Al and Harry began getting regular bookings in a crude act of ethnic comedy called "The Hebrew and the Cadet." At this time, they changed their last name to Joelson. Later, they decided to get cards printed, but for the style of cards they liked, their names were too long, so they changed the name again, dropping the "e" to make it shorter for the printer. Their last name became Jolson.

Al Jolson's first performances were not very memorable because they were not very good. Because he was neither confident nor comfortable on stage, his performances were stilted. The brothers did get recruited into a three-man vaudeville comedy act with wheelchair-bound comic Joe Palmer, but Al's self-conscious performances threatened the success of the act.

Then in 1904, supposedly at the suggestion of veteran blackface comedian James Francis Dooley, Al Jolson donned the blackface makeup for the first time. The makeup acted as a mask behind which Jolson could hide, and his performances improved. In a short time, his confidence soared, his energy exploded from behind his mask, and the act got big laughs.

★ THE SINGER ★

Soon, the three men found themselves booked on vaudeville's Orpheum circuit. The act was becoming a huge success.

Harry eventually withdrew from the act to go out on his own, and Joe Palmer retired, mainly because he could see he was holding Al Jolson back. He was right. After Palmer retired, Jolson began his career as a blackface singing comedian, wearing his famous "uniform." In those days, especially in the West, the houses were tough sells. Very often customers would smoke and thumb through their newspapers until something on stage managed to catch their attention. Jolson would belt out songs, stomp his feet, whistle tunes, and dance. He even told risqué jokes—whatever it took to get their attention. Once he had it, he had it, and he refused to let it go.

Jolson finally got noticed by Broadway, where his legend really began. In 1911, he was hired by Lee and J.J. Shubert on Broadway for the premiere of the stage production *La Belle Paree* at the opening of their Winter Garden Theater. The show was so terrible that even Jolson could not keep the audience in their seats. It was badly panned in the papers the following day. It was a bomb, but the show went on again. During that performance, Jolson, for the first time left the script in the middle of the performance, turned to the audience and began to talk about the bad reviews the show had received. He asked if they would rather see the rest of the show or if they would rather just hear him sing. Of course, the audience wanted to hear Jolson sing, so with the assistance of the orchestra, he finished the show with his own personal concert. It was the first flash of that huge ego for which he would later be known. Although his stopping the show was not popular with the rest of the cast, the critics only encouraged his behavior by giving him good reviews. Stopping the show when the audiences became bored and singing instead became a pattern for which he would also become famous.

Jolson became the star of every production he was in, no matter what part he played. He performed in hit after hit. Recognizing a good thing, the Shuberts, year after year, signed him to a contract that not only retained him for their purposes but also allowed him to go out to perform on his own, increasing Jolson's fame as well as their ticket sales. His extremely successful recording career began during this period. There were few performers in that time more famous or more revered than Al Jolson.

In 1927, Jolson was approached with another interesting project. Warner Studios in Hollywood wanted his voice to be featured in the first talking picture, *The Jazz Singer*. The movie was a huge success. Jolson made numerous "talkies" after that, becoming a big star of the silver screen even though many of his films were not particularly well produced. It was a new entertainment medium, and the American audiences were not that particular about the quality. They only insisted that the films be "talkies," and their favorite star of "talkies" in the early years was Al Jolson.

Jolson went on to enjoy Broadway and film successes. Later, he was a very popular radio personality. He has three stars on the Hollywood Walk of Fame, and his "knees" are forever memorialized in concrete at Grauman's Chinese Theatre in Hollywood.

But Jolson was not always loved by those he worked with. He was often difficult, he had an enormous ego, and he was a shameless self-promoter. He drove directors and producers crazy by constantly leaving the script. Stopping shows to sing to the audience often rubbed his fellow actors the wrong way. But because he was a huge star, he was very seldom corrected for his misdeeds. Jolson was something others just had to endure if they wanted to capitalize on his tremendous popularity. Jolson was out to please Jolson, and what pleased Jolson more than anything was audience applause and adulation.

Not all of Jolson's songs were his to begin with. He made a lot of people angry over the years because he would record a song previously recorded by another artist, and, of course, with the Jolson name, his version would usually become more pop-

★ THE SINGER ★

ular. Jolson's signature song "My Mammy" was not even his song originally. It was first introduced to vaudeville audiences by another performer, William Frawley. When Jolson heard the song, he liked it so much he included it in his hit show *Sinbad*. It was an instant sensation. For the rest of his career, it became the most requested of all of his songs—the song for which Jolson is most remembered. William Frawley, on the other hand, remained in obscurity for years until he met up with a wacky red-head named Lucille Ball. American audiences know him best as Fred Mertz, the cheapskate landlord and former vaudeville performer who lived with his wife Ethel next door to the Ricardos on *I Love Lucy*.

Jolson's career wound down towards the middle of the 1930s. He was virtually forgotten. He was still a producer, but he was out of the limelight. Then in 1946, the film *The Jolson Story* was released. It was a huge hit with Larry Parks playing the part of Al Jolson. Because Jolson's original recordings were considered to be in such poor shape by more modern standards, Jolson was brought out of his retirement to re-recorded all the music for the movie. He even performed in one scene that was filmed at a distance so audiences would not realize they were seeing the real Jolson and not Parks playing Jolson. Jolson enjoyed a huge comeback after the film release. Record sales and a percentage of the film and the music rights made him a tidy bundle. A second film was released in 1949: *Jolson Sings Again*. Once again, Jolson returned to the studio to record all the selections for that movie, and once again, the movie added fuel to his comeback.

To demonstrate how far out of the limelight he had been before his comeback, Jolson told one story about going to see the premiere of the first film, *The Al Jolson Story*. Because he was very nervous, he kept leaving his seat to stand in the back of the theater or in the lobby. One time when he was out of his seat, he heard two ladies talking about what a wonderful film it was and how sad it was that Jolson had not lived to see it.

Jolson went on to entertain troops in Korea. When the Defense Department said it had no budget for entertainers, Jolson paid all his own expenses. During seven days in September, 1950, he gave forty-two concerts for the troops despite a bad cold he could not seem to kick. When he returned to California, he admitted to reporters who commented on how tired he looked that the trip had been difficult.

In October, 1950, he was preparing to make another appearance on Bing Crosby's radio show. While playing cards with friends, he complained of indigestion. Two doctors were called. A short time later, he was joking about his condition with the doctors and his friends, but he was not feeling any better. He kept joking though. He told his doctors, "I'm a real important guy. Hell, Truman only had one hour for MacArthur. I got two." A short time later, Jolson suddenly reached for his pulse. He said, "Oh, I'm going," and slumped over. Doctors tried to revive him, but Al Jolson was dead.

Jolson would probably enjoy more fame today if it were not for the "mask" that had made him a star to begin with. Performance in blackface was a style of entertainment popular from the 1830s through the 1920s. There is no indication from Jolson's actions or opinions that he was ever racist. In fact, there is evidence that Jolson saw America as many immigrants did—as a great melting pot where everyone could achieve the American dream. But those blackface performances and pictures of Jolson posed in blackface makeup make most people uncomfortable today, explaining perhaps why he is not as famous as one might expect. Al Jolson was, after all, one of America's greatest performers and stylists, the first entertainer to sell over 3 million records and a man who had only one great love in his life—besides himself that is—performing before an audience.

★ THE SINGER ★

Brother Al Jolson was made a Master Mason at St. Cecile Lodge No. 568 in New York City, New York, on July 13, 1913. He joined with several friends who were well known at the time in the entertainment business—John H. Bunny, Charles Emmet, David Stamper, and Charles J. Dryden.

TWENTY-THREE

The American

"Life is tough, but it's tougher when you're stupid."

At the top of a hill on a tall horse sits an enormous, broad-shouldered, thin-waisted rider wearing a ten-gallon hat, a red bandana, a denim shirt, and a leather vest. The sun setting over the painted desert below him glints off the tin star pinned on his vest. He sits quietly, rolling a cigarette. The man says little, but what he does say is quoted faithfully by legions of his admirers. For example, he once said, "I won't be wronged, I won't be insulted and I won't be laid a hand on. I don't do these things to other people and I require the same from them."

This is the figure of a man everybody in America knows, a legend everyone recognizes, an icon as much a part of Americana as the Fourth of July and apple pie, but this man never actually existed beyond the over 170 films he appeared in during his fifty-year career from 1926 to 1976. Unless you have been living on a deserted island for the last eighty years, you know that man sitting on his horse, watching the sunset—he is John Wayne.

He was born Marion Robert Morrison on May 26, 1907, in Winterset, Iowa, to Clyde and Mary Morrison. His parents had been married only eight months when the strapping thirteen-pound Marion was born, causing a bit of a small town scandal. When his brother Robert was born four years later, Marion's name would be changed to Marion Michael Morrison.

Both his parents were of Scotch-Irish descent. Clyde Morrison was a handsome, charming man of average height. He was very smart, if not just a little irresponsible. Mary Morrison was a strong-willed, hot-tempered woman. Marion remembered his mother as a women's libber and the first woman he had ever seen smoke. She came to dominate her husband as well as her boys. Marion attributed his hot temper to her.

When Marion was a boy, he was picked on by playground bullies. He frequently found himself involved in fights, becoming more often than not the loser in the end. "Defending that first name taught me to fight at an early age," he once remarked.

When his family moved to California in 1911, he earned a nickname. His constant companion was the family Airedale. When passing the local firehouse each day with his dog on his way to school, the local volunteer firemen began calling the dog "Big Duke" and the boy "Little Duke." Everyone in his family, except his mother, began calling him "Duke." One evening, he showed up at the firehouse with a black eye and a split lip. One of the firefighters, an ex-boxer, began teaching Duke to defend himself. The razzing and bullying stopped when Duke learned to hold his own in a fight. "I really looked up to those guys. They were heroes in my book," he remembers. Marion used the name Duke for the rest of his life.

Duke applied at the U.S. Naval Academy, but he was not accepted. Instead, he went to the University of Southern California where he studied pre-law and joined the Sigma Chi fraternity. The six-foot, four-inch Duke also played football for the Trojan Knights under the well-known coach Howard Jones.

While attending the University of Southern California, Duke began working for a local studio. Legendary film star Tom Mix got him a job in the props department. In exchange, Duke got him football tickets. Soon Duke was acting in bit parts. A lifelong friendship with director John Ford began. About that time, Duke was injured while surfing "The Wedge" off Balboa Pier at Newport Beach, ending not only his football career but also his college scholarship. As a result, he began working at the studio full time in the props department and as a bit actor.

In 1930, he got his first starring role in *The Big Trail*, one of the Western genre's first sound epics. Director Raoul Walsh, who is credited for discovering Marion Morrison, dubbed him "John Wayne" after the Revolutionary War general "Mad Anthony" Wayne. Duke finally established his screen credentials and began his long career as a leading man. Although *The Big Trail* was a commercial failure, he continued to make Westerns and serials. He learned to ride horses and picked up other Western skills from the stunt men working at the studios. Wayne became an extremely skilled equestrian and stunt man. Along with famous stuntman Yakima Canutt, he perfected skills and stunt techniques still in use today. Wayne went on to perform in more than 170 films, starring in more than 140 of them.

His longest and most productive relationship was with director John Ford. He appeared in more than twenty of the legendary director's movies, starting in 1928 and continuing for more than thirty-five years. John Ford's *Stagecoach* in 1939 was the film that made John Wayne a star. Wayne went on to make many more movies with John Ford, including *She Wore a Yellow Ribbon* (1949), *The Quiet Man* (1952), *The Searchers* (1956), *The Wings of Eagles* (1957), and *The Man Who Shot Liberty Valance* (1962).

While Wayne had several controversial aspects to his character and to his politics, the one controversy that persisted is the question of why he did not serve in World War II. In truth, due to his age and family status, he was given a family deferment. Wayne made some calls about enlisting, but he did not follow up on them. He also talked to his friend John Ford about enlisting in his unit, but it seemed that Wayne was always in the middle of a film he wanted to finish first. In 1944, Wayne was reclassified as draft eligible, but his studio arranged to have him reclassified as non-eligible because of his work in "national health, safety or interest." Wayne never dodged the draft, but he never worked very hard at enlisting. His studio also intervened several times to block his enlistment, even threatening his contract if he enlisted on his own—most likely a bogus claim since no studio had followed up on that kind of threat in time of war. Remaining on the home front, Wayne spent the war years supporting the war by promoting America in films.

Not serving in World War II was something Wayne felt guilty about for the rest of his life, but it was not something the veterans of that war seemed to hold against him. He was as much their comrade in arms as if he had served along side them. They called their can openers "John Wayne" can openers because they could do anything, and the crackers in their C-Rations were called "John Wayne crackers" presumably because they were so inedible a man had to be as tough and burly as John Wayne to eat them. They also called their toilet paper "John Wayne toilet paper" because it "didn't take shit off anybody." Even if others were not critical of him, Wayne had problems with his lack of service. His third wife Pilar wrote, "He would become a 'superpatriot' for the rest of his life trying to atone for staying home."

John Wayne was without a doubt a flag-waving, right-wing, Republican conservative. His politics frequently were controversial, but Wayne never apologized for his beliefs. He was a staunch anti-Communist believing that Communism was a major threat to the United States. In 1943, he was one of the founders of the Motion Picture Alliance for the Preservation of American Ideals. In 1949, he became the President of that organization. He became a vocal supporter of the House Un-American Activities Committee. He played a role in blacklisting the screenwriter of *High Noon,* Carl Foreman, for the anti-McCarthyist theme of the film. "I'll never regret having helped run Foreman out of the country," he would say later. While Wayne admitted to playing a role in driving Foreman out of the country, he denied there was any "blacklist." In his typical unapologetic style, Wayne later said, "There was no blacklist at that time, as people said. That was a lot of horseshit. . . The only thing our side did that was anywhere near blacklisting was just running a lot of people out of the business."

John Wayne was approached several times about running for public office, but he always declined because he did not believe people would take an actor seriously in public office. That attitude did not stop him from supporting his friend and fellow actor Ronald Reagan in both of his campaigns for governor of California. He also lived long enough to see his old friends Ronnie Reagan and Nancy Davis blazing a trail towards the White House.

When John Wayne was diagnosed with lung cancer in 1964, it was rumored that filming *The Conqueror* in the deserts of Utah where the government had tested nuclear weapons had caused it. Instead, Wayne publicly admitted the cancer was more likely caused by his five-pack-a-day cigarette habit—a habit that he had begun back when the harmful effects of cigarette smoking were still considered to be a controversial issue. After his entire left lung and four ribs were removed, he survived the cancer, but he never fully recovered from the surgery. He did not want the public to see him in a weakened condition. After the surgery, he walked out of the hospital, smiling, signing autographs, and telling the crowd gathered there that he was fine. But when he got into the car, he collapsed and immediately needed oxygen from his mask.

Less than four months later, he was back on the set. When Wayne was filming a particularly difficult stunt scene in *The Sons of Katie Elder* in 1965, a photographer snapped his picture as he took oxygen from a canister between shots. Wayne snatched the camera from the photographer and smashed it to the ground. Wayne did not seem to mind people knowing he had beaten cancer, but he did seem to have a problem with anyone seeing what it had taken out of him. During the shoot, he insisted on doing all his own fighting and riding. He often made a show of tossing a few pills into his mouth and washing them down with Mescal. "I'm the stuff that men are made of!" he'd say. John Wayne was back.

Another controversial political view Wayne later held went along with the anti-Communist feelings he had had since the 1940s. He supported the Vietnam War. He was disappointed by the country's lack of support for the troops and angered at the protestors. As he had done in World War II, John Wayne decided to try to sway the public into seeing the war in Vietnam in a different light. He passed on the film *The Dirty Dozen.* Instead, he made a pro-Vietnam film, *The Green Berets,* which endeavored to show Americans what they were fighting against in Vietnam. Mostly because of John Wayne's name and the fact that Americans still loved a John Wayne war movie, the movie was a commercial success, but it was panned by critics as ridiculously unrealistic. Wayne was too old to play the part of the tough combat leader, a role he might have been more believable in twenty years earlier. The film was preachy with dialog saturated in patriotism—a patriotism that fell on deaf ears in the rebellious world of 1968. John Wayne had made a World War II movie about Vietnam, but times had changed, and Americans did not hear the message.

For the first time, after forty years on the big screen, it seemed as if John Wayne was out of touch, as if his America no longer existed. He was seen as a relic from the previous generation trying to apply those values to a different time. It seemed like John Wayne was working very hard to play a part he was obviously too old to play—he was trying to be something he was not.

But John Wayne seemed to figure that out on his own, and he was a long, long way from being done.

Wayne returned to his forte, the great American Western. Americans soon learned that their screen hero's best work was not behind him. In 1969, he won the Academy Award for his portrayal of the grizzled, whiskey-swilling, rule-bending, one-eyed lawman Rooster Cogburn in *True Grit*. But he did not rest on his laurels. He went on to make some of his best known movies, such as *Chisum, Big Jake, The Cowboys, Rio Lobo,* and *The Train Robbers*. In 1975, he reprised his Academy Award winning character from *True Grit* in *Rooster Cogburn*, starring with another screen legend his own age, actress Katherine Hepburn.

In 1976, John Wayne began filming the movie *The Shootist*. It is a film about an aging gunfighter, J.B. Books, who learns from the local physician, played by Jimmy Stewart, that he is dying of cancer. Instead of wasting away in bed, the dying gunfighter decides he would rather go out fighting, and, in the process, do the public a great service by taking a few of his old enemies and a few local scoundrels along with him. He arranges a shoot-out in a local hotel saloon.

Wayne's health had been failing badly previous to his taking the role, and it became worse during filming. He had been having increasing pains in his stomach and flu-like symptoms. The director was becoming very concerned that Wayne might not be able to finish the film because of his long absences from the set—first for one week and then for two. The director had to shoot around Wayne's lines and to use doubles, fearful that Wayne might not be able to return to filming. But Wayne did return, and the film was finally finished. Although Wayne did not know it at the time, *The Shootist* would be his last film. He had terminal stomach cancer. Later, he acknowledged the irony of the script with his own situation.

As Wayne's condition worsened, Hollywood knew their favorite leading man was about out of time. In 1979, a stream of actors and actresses went to Washington, D.C., to testify before Congress that John Wayne should be honored for his great contributions to America. On May 26, 1979, his seventy-second birthday, he was awarded the Congressional Gold Medal. Wayne's favorite co-star from several films, Maureen O'Hara, first suggested before Congress the words that should be printed on the medal. The United States Mint agreed with her. On one side of the medal was John Wayne on horseback. On the other side was his portrait and the simple words Maureen O'Hara had suggested to Congress: John Wayne, American.

John Wayne died less than a month later on June 11, 1979.

Brother John Wayne was a member of the Glendale DeMolay Chapter during his high school days. Following in his father's footsteps, John Wayne became a Freemason, receiving his Craft degrees in July 1970 in Marion McDaniel Lodge No. 56, Tucson, Arizona. Being a Senior DeMolay, he was also awarded the DeMolay Legion of Honor in 1970. He joined the York Rite Bodies in California and became a Shriner in Al Malaikah Shrine Temple in California.

AMERICAN LEGENDS

"Ideas control the world."

—*James A. Garfield*
Columbus Lodge No. 30, OH

TWENTY-FOUR

The Explorers

"An intelligence officer, with ten or twelve chosen men . . . might explore the whole line, even to the Western Ocean . . ."
—Thomas Jefferson

The dog was a black Newfoundland, weighing somewhere between 110 and 150 pounds. The occasional journal entries about the dog indicate that he sometimes served as a hunter for the expedition. He caught squirrels, geese, and beavers for the men to eat. Once he took down an antelope in a stream, drowned it, and returned it to the men. He repeated that same action when one of the members of the expedition wounded a deer.

But the dog's most valuable role was as a watchdog. On May 29, 1805, the journal entry read:

> "Last night we were all alarmed by a large buffalo bull, which swam over from the opposite shore, and coming alongside of the White Pirogue, climbed over it to land. He then, alarmed, ran up the bank in full speed directly towards the fires, and was within eighteen inches of the heads of

some of the men who lay sleeping before the sentinel could alarm him or make him change his course. Still more alarmed, he now took his direction immediately towards our lodge, passing between four fires and within a few inches of the heads of one range of the men as they yet lay sleeping. When he came near the tent, my dog saved us by causing him to change his course a second time, which he did by turning a little to the right, and was quickly out of sight, leaving us by this time all in an uproar with our guns in our hands, inquiring of each other the cause of the alarm, which after a few moments was explained by the sentinel. We were happy to find no one hurt."

The dog also protected the camp on several occasions by alerting the men to the presence of grizzly bears and the approach of Native America Indians, who had stolen supplies, horses, and canoes several times during the expedition; in fact, one time, the Indians tried to steal the dog.

There are very few mentions of the dog during the winter at Fort Clatsop when the men were suffering from starvation. Perhaps he was lying low since the men in the expedition had been purchasing dogs to eat from local Indian tribes.

The dog's name was Seaman, but it is not the dog that is famous, although he should be since he was the only dog to complete one of the most famous expeditions in American history. You see, Seaman's master was Meriwether Lewis—half of the famous duo of Lewis and Clark, whose Corps of Discovery expedition into the Pacific Northwest trekked nearly eight thousand miles in two years and opened up a whole new territory for Western expansion.

The expedition was an idea first conceived by Thomas Jefferson while he was serving as an ambassador to France from 1785-1789. He had heard rumors of several plans the

★ THE EXPLORERS ★

French had to better explore the Pacific Northwest. In fact, he later learned for certain that King Louis XVI was planning a scientific expedition to that region. Jefferson did not believe that the mission was primarily for scientific discovery, but rather that it was France's intention to gain a foothold in the region. Fortunately for America, France never launched the expedition.

As President, Jefferson was a great supporter of Western expansion, and he had some real concerns about the territories beyond the Mississippi River. The French had a claim on most of the territory from the Mississippi River west to the eastern slopes of the Rocky Mountains and from the Gulf of Mexico north, to the present day United States-Canadian border.

Jefferson's chief concern was the war between France and Britain. The war effort was not going well for Napoleon. Should the British defeat Napoleon, they would have a claim to that same area, and the United States' chance for Western expansion would be blocked.

An American expedition to the "Western Sea" was already being planned when cash-strapped Napoleon agreed to sell the entire region to the United States in 1803. The Louisiana Purchase included more than 800,000 square miles including all or parts of several present-day states: Arkansas, Missouri, Iowa, North Dakota, most of Kansas, Minnesota, and Louisiana west of the Mississippi River, and the parts of Colorado, Wyoming, and Montana east of the Rockies.

After the Louisiana Purchase, Jefferson still wanted an expedition to explore the Pacific Northwest for several reasons. He wanted to see what the French and the English were doing in the region west of the Mississippi since both British and French Canadian hunters and trappers were well established in the area. He also wanted to find a water route to the Western coast for the purpose of expansion and commerce. In addition, Jefferson wanted knowledge about the native tribes in order to establish possible trade relations with them later.

Finally, he wanted to learn about the geology, wildlife, vegetation, and terrain of the region.

But Jefferson's primary goal was to get to the Pacific Northwest first and stake a claim on it before the French, the British, or the Spanish could beat him to it. Jefferson envisioned a nation that stretched from coast to coast, and while the Louisiana Purchase was an unexpected, but gigantic leap in meeting that goal, there was still the area west of the Rockies the United States needed to claim. Almost nothing had been charted about the terrain in that area. Maps at the time showed very little detail about what lay west of the Rockies, it would later be proved that those maps had greatly underestimated the scope of the Rocky Mountains. Having detailed information about the area, including maps charting the chief water routes, was vital in staking a claim, so the scientific expedition, already approved and underway, was under new pressure to succeed.

To lead the Corps of Discovery expedition, Jefferson selected Meriwether Lewis, his private secretary, who was a former member of the Virginia militia and later a captain in the regular army. Lewis had been instrumental in planning the expedition. To lead it, he had prepared himself by going to Philadelphia to study cartography and to learn other skills he would need to document a scientific expedition.

Lewis then selected William Clark to share the command with him. William Clark had enlisted in the Kentucky militia, which had been formed to defend against attacks by Native American Indian tribes in that region. When the federal government became involved, Clark accepted a commission as a lieutenant in the regular army.

While Clark was technically second in command, Lewis kept this a secret, always referring to him as "Captain." In essence, they shared the command. When the Louisiana Purchase took place, Lewis was already on his way to meet Clark. They met at the falls of the Ohio River on August 31, 1803. Lewis set the departure point at the mouth of the Dubois

River, located on the east side of the Mississippi River across from the mouth of the Missouri River—with the Pacific Ocean as the ultimate goal.

As they traveled down the Ohio River toward that point, they picked up supplies and men for the journey, leading this portion of the expedition to be called the "recruitment phase." During this two and a half month period when the group traveled to reach the mouth of the Missouri River and the official start of the expedition, the men formed tight bonds with one another and became dedicated to the mission. That bonding and dedication helped carry them through all the hardships and difficulties ahead of them. The party wintered over at Camp Dubois (near present-day Hartford, Illinois). On May 14, 1804, the expedition consisting of forty-five men departed, beginning their long trip up the Missouri River.

While Seaman, Lewis's Newfoundland, was a lesser known member of the Corps of Discovery, one of the more famous was Sacagawea, who became a member of the expedition when her husband, Toussaint Charbonneau, joined as an interpreter. In 1804, when the group set out for the unknown West, she was a sixteen-year-old mother with a newborn infant son. She helped the party by scavenging for food and by showing the men how to make leather clothing. Sacagawea, originally a member of the Shoshoni tribe, had been captured by the Hidatsa Indians when she was about twelve years old. Over the years, a misconception has arisen about Sacagawea's status in the Hidatsa tribe. In history texts, she is generally regarded to have been a slave. This is inaccurate as there was no place in the Hidatsa culture for slavery. Instead, it was more like adoption—the taking of a child from another tribe when the parents were unable to care for that child.

On December 3, 1805, the expedition reached the Pacific Ocean. After a harsh winter at Fort Clatsop, the group began the journey home. On the return trip, the expedition split into two groups for just over a month so Lewis, along with three other men, could explore the Marias River. During the exploration, the four men encountered some Indians from the Blackfoot tribe. While the cordial meeting seemed to go well, during the night, the Blackfoot tried to steal the men's weapons. In the struggle, two Blackfoot were killed. Fearful of retaliation, the expedition fled, traveling more than a hundred miles down river in a single day before camping again.

Clark did not have much better luck during the group's separation. He had crossed over into territory dominated by the Crow Indians, who were known as horse thieves. During the night, half of their horses were stolen although nobody had heard or seen anything.

The bad luck continued even when the two groups reunited. They were to meet at the fork of the Yellowstone and Missouri Rivers, but one of Clark's hunters, who was blind in one eye and extremely nearsighted in the other, mistook Lewis for an elk and fired upon him, wounding him in the thigh.

But despite long odds and thousands of miles, the expedition finally made it back to St. Louis on September 23, 1806. During the just over two years they had been gone, they lost only one member of their party. Sergeant Charles Floyd had died from acute appendicitis shortly after the expedition had begun. During their numerous encounters with the local Indian tribes, only one became violent, much to the credit of interpreters Sacagawea and her husband, Toussaint Charbonneau. Their newborn son Jean Baptiste Charbonneau also helped to convince the Indians that the Corps of Discovery's intentions were friendly since no war party would include a mother and her baby.

As a result of the Corps of Discovery expedition, Americans not only gained extensive knowledge of the geography and terrain of the American West through Lewis's maps but also learned about 178 plant species and 122 animal species. Lewis and Clark even sent back to Thomas Jefferson a living prairie dog and many other samples they had collected. Because of Lewis and Clark, the United States was able to establish diplomatic relationships with the Indians, improve the Euro-

★ THE EXPLORERS ★

American fur trade in the West, and strengthen the country's claim to the Oregon Territory. But just as important, Lewis and Clark opened the eyes of Americans about the West. Because of the great amount of attention given to the Corps of Discovery in newspapers and the extensive body of information Lewis and Clark had documented, the idea of Western expansion caught on, and Jefferson's dream of a nation that stretched from sea to shining sea eventually became a reality.

Brother Meriwether Lewis became a Freemason in 1797, receiving his degrees from Door to Virtue Lodge No. 44, in Albemarle County, Virginia. In 1808, Brother Lewis and several of his brothers began to discuss the need for a lodge in St. Louis. They drew up an application for dispensation and submitted it to the Grand Lodge of Pennsylvania. Brother Lewis was nominated to be the first Master of the proposed lodge in St. Louis. The Grand Lodge of Pennsylvania granted the request and issued a warrant for the formation of St. Louis Lodge No. 111 on September 16, 1808.

Brother William Clark, probably at the suggestion of Lewis, petitioned St. Louis Lodge No. 111 for membership and was accepted. Clark's involvement in the lodge continued long after Lewis' death; in fact, he allowed Missouri Lodge No. 12 to hold their meetings for several years on the second floor of his house. When he passed away on September 1, 1838, he was buried with full Masonic honors, and a Masonic monument was erected over his grave.

However, after careful examination of Masonic records, it does not appear that Seaman was ever made a Mason—but he was a very good boy.

TWENTY-FIVE

The Equalizer

"We have seen samples of the invention which is certainly exceedingly ingenious and meritorious. Its advantages are great."

—The Baltimore Republic
March 2, 1836

The young man was not a particularly good student. He spent more time in school getting into trouble than he spent on his studies. The trouble more than once involved the discharging of his large caliber horse pistol, which he had found when he was six years old. According to legend, he rebuilt it into a serviceable firearm using cannibalized pistol parts discarded as junk by a local gunsmith.

His strength was a unique natural understanding of mechanics which he may have discovered during the time he spent with the machinery in his father's automated silk factory. Another influence on his understanding of mechanics came from time he spent on a farm in Connecticut, where he was sent by his new step-mother. Among the volumes in the farmer's library was an encyclopedia entitled *Compendium of Knowledge*, which he read instead of doing his homework and Bible studies. He was mesmerized by what he read about how applied practical science had been used to solve so many practical problems. He also learned that many of the scientific discoveries and inventions in existence were deemed impossibilities until they were actually accomplished. That idea fascinated him.

Even considering the trouble the young man had been in, his father never discouraged his enthusiastic study and experimentation on topics from gun powder to nitrous oxide. In July, 1829, the fifteen-year-old boy was passing out handbills, claiming he would "Blow a Raft Sky-High on Ware Pond, July 4, 1829." The town came out to see the spectacle, dressed in their Fourth of July best. As promised, there was a huge explosion, but the raft was by no means blown "sky-high." The explosion completely missed the raft floating in the pond. In fact, the only thing accomplished by the explosion was the creation of a huge geyser that completely covered the assembled crowd with mud and water.

Convinced they had fallen prey to an intentional prank rather than a failed experiment, the crowd threatened the young man with a thrashing. A young mechanic, Elisha Root, rescued him from the beating. After the mud-spattered crowd dispersed, Root examined the young man's experiment, determining that he had detonated the bomb remotely by running an electrical current under the water. Root realized at once the importance of what the young man had done.

This was an invention many at the time were struggling to perfect. For some time, inventors, including Robert Fulton—inventor of the paddle-wheel steamboat, had been working unsuccessfully on an underwater mine to protect harbors. What these great inventors had failed to do—to run an electric current underwater—had just been successfully accomplished by a fifteen-year-old boy. When Root asked the boy how he had solved that problem, the boy replied, "Simple. I wrapped the wire in tarred cloth."

That fifteen-year-old boy would go on to become an important inventor of his time, perfecting one of the most important advances in firearms design in American history. His name was Samuel Colt.

Samuel Colt was born on July 19, 1814, into a very dangerous world. Despite many modern ideas and scientific discoveries, there was one technology that was woefully deficient and badly outdated—the flintlock rifle, a direct descendent of the muskets brought over on the *Mayflower*. The rifle, which had been virtually unchanged for generations, was a single fire, slow-reloading cannon that, while accurate at up to 150 yards, provided little protection against the settlers greatest risk—Indian raids. It was not the accuracy of the rifle that was the chief weakness of the weapon but its slow reloading time. It took an expert marksman twenty seconds to reload. During that time, the rifleman was helpless—an easy target for the enemy. Considering the conditions on a battlefield, it is easy to imagine why rifles were found after the Battle of Gettysburg with their barrels packed with numerous rounds. Green troops, swept up by panic and fear, would forget to fire their rifles before loading them again.

Aware of the weaknesses of the flintlock rifle, the native Indians developed a simple yet effective strategy against it early on. During an Indian raid, the white settlers would wait until the natives were within range, then fire a large volley to take out as many natives as possible, hopeful that the volley would slow their advance. The natives learned, however, that after the initial volley, it would be twenty or thirty seconds before the settlers could fire again. In that amount of time, the natives could cover 150 yards, or roughly the effective range of the rifle. The natives invented strategies to trick the settlers into firing that first large volley. Once it was fired, the natives would initiate a devastating attack before the settlers could reload—an attack the settlers stood little chance of surviving. Even Benjamin Franklin recognized that slow reload speed was a major weakness of the flintlock rifle. He suggested that the military be trained to carry bow and arrows because they were just as accurate at the same distance and could be fired at a more lethal rate of speed.

Prior to blowing up Ware Pond, Samuel Colt sometimes left the farm to run errands in town. There he heard the soldiers tell stories about the early successes of a new double-barreled rifle, but, in their opinion, they needed a repeating rifle capable of more than just a couple shots and with a faster reload speed. Most of them believed that a true repeating rifle was an impossibility. Samuel Colt, inspired by what he had read in the *Compendium of Knowledge* and already knowledgeable about how guns worked, decided to become the inventor who would build that "impossible" gun.

In 1832, a few years after the incident at Ware Pond, Sam's father arranged for him to take a job aboard the sailing ship *Corlo* to learn the seaman's trade. On his voyages aboard *Corlo*, Sam thought a lot about the repeating gun. One day, as he watched the wheel of the ship, the idea of how the repeating gun might work finally came to him. He wrote, "Regardless of which way the wheel was spun, each spoke always came in direct line with a clutch that could be set to hold it . . . the revolver was conceived!"

The rotating chamber was not a new idea. There was already a rifle designed by Elisha H. Collier utilizing that technology. Although Colt later denied having seen Collier's rifle, it is possible that he saw a model of the rotating chambered breech rifle in London or Calcutta. What was new with Colt's design was the use of a pawl and ratchet. The chamber would work much the same way the pawl and ratchet gear on the capstan of a ship worked to prevent the running away of a cable under pressure. The very simple mechanism rotated the cylinder as the hammer was pulled back, lining up a round with the barrel. Thus, depending on how many rounds the cylinder would hold, the rifle could be fired rapidly and repeatedly. During the ocean voyage, Sam Colt, using his jackknife, carved a model of his idea into a discarded chunk of wood. The idea which took form, however, was not a repeating rifle—it was a six-chambered pistol.

When Colt returned from his ocean voyage, his father, who was always a supporter of his son's ideas, financed the building of two prototypes of the pistol, but he hired only cheap mechanics to build them because he questioned the validity of the design. Because of poor workmanship, one pistol exploded on firing, and the other wouldn't fire at all.

Colt was forced to start working in his father's factory again. During this time, he began experimenting with nitrous oxide, now known as laughing gas, after learning about it from a chemist in the factory. Colt went on the road, giving demonstrations of nitrous oxide and its anesthetic qualities. In the process, he raised money to apply for a U.S. patent for his pistol. Later, in 1835, he traveled to England to apply for a patent there also.

Colt formed a corporation of New York and New Jersey capitalists in order to built a plant outside Patterson, New Jersey, called the Patterson Manufacturing Company. By agreement, Colt would receive a commission on the sale of every gun in exchange for his share of the patent rights, but it was stipulated that should the company fail or disband, his patent rights would be restored.

Finally, on February 25, 1836, the United States Patent Office issued Samuel Colt a patent which protected the basic principles of his revolving-breach loading, folding-trigger firearm called the Patterson Pistol. The patent depended on three innovative design features: the rotation of a many-chambered cylinder actuated by the cocking of the hammer, the locking and unlocking of the cylinder by the cocking of the hammer, and the placement of partitions between the nipples to prevent the powder flash out the sides of the cylinder from igniting all the rounds in the cylinders at once.

Samuel Colt had several ideas about factory innovations. Even though some gun parts were being made by machine at that time, he wanted all the parts made by machine so that there would be no man-made, or hand-fitted, parts. Machined parts could be made absolutely identical, with no variations in size or shape, and it would mean that every gun could be made exactly identical. It meant that parts could easily be made to replace parts when they wore out, without the necessity of a gunsmith. It would also open the door to another innovation. Using only machined parts would permit the adaptation of another of Colt's ideas about a new assembly method—the assembly line—which he explained to his father in a letter: "The first workman would receive two or three of the most important parts . . . and would affix these and pass them on to the next who add a part and pass the growing article on to another who would do the same, and so on until the complete arm is put together." This assembly method would allow guns to be mass produced on a scale not previously possible.

But Colt ran into problems with the company's owners. They were reluctant to invest in the machinery necessary to make all the parts interchangeable. It was the beginning of many problems in the early days of the repeating revolver. Colt tried selling the weapon by demonstration. He even visited President Andrew Jackson to demonstrate the pistol. Jackson, who liked the pistol, put a bill through Congress for a demonstration of the pistol to the military, but no money for purchasing the pistols was attached to the bill. In addition, there were production problems. The company lost one large order because production did not start soon enough. By far, the biggest problem Colt had was the Militia Act of 1808, which stated that a small militia could purchase weapons only in current use by the United States military. Since Colt was unable to sell his guns to the United States military, he could not sell them to the numerous small militias either. After an economic crash and continuing problems with the Militia Act, the Patterson Manufacturing Company went out of business.

Colt went back to one of his original ideas—the underwater mine. He met Samuel Morse, whose invention, the telegraph, depended on the ability to carry electric current over long distances, including under lakes and rivers. Samuel Colt had developed a way to waterproof electric wire back when he was a teenager, and he had made some advances in the technique since. Morse and Colt seemed to be a perfect partnership. Colt concentrated on the manufacture of the waterproof cable, for which he was paid $50 per mile. Colt knew the business would boom right along with the expansion of telegraph services.

But Colt was not done making firearms yet.

During 1845, when units of the United States Dragoon forces and the Texas Rangers engaged in fighting the Indians in Texas, they credited their use of Colt firearms for their great success in defeating the native forces. United States War Department officials were impressed. When the Mexican War began in 1846, Captain Samuel H. Walker of the United States Army collaborated with Colt on the design of a new, more powerful revolver. Within a week, the United States Ordnance Department placed an order for one thousand of the new Walker model revolvers—named for Colt's collaborator on the project. Suddenly, Colt found himself back in the firearms business but without a factory. He turned to Eli Whitney, Jr., son of the famous inventor of the cotton gin, who was able to complete the order in his factory in Connecticut.

In 1855, the Colt Patent Fire Arms Manufacturing Company was formed with an initial issuance of 14,000 shares of stock, with Colt retaining ownership of the majority of shares. By 1856, the company was producing 150 weapons a day. The product's reputation for exceptional quality, workmanship, and design had spread around the world. Samuel Colt became one of the ten wealthiest businessmen in the United States.

As demand for his firearms grew, Colt expanded his engraving department to include exquisite gold and silver inlay on his show pieces, which consistently won prizes at international trade fairs. Many of these show guns were presented to heads of state, including King Frederick VII of Denmark, Czars

★ THE EQUALIZER ★

Nicholas I and Alexander II of Russia, and King Charles XV of Sweden.

As the country moved towards war in 1860, Samuel Colt's health began to fail. He continued to ship his product to customers in Southern states until the formal declaration of war was made. As soon as the war was official, Colt supplied only the Union Army. The Colt Armory was running at full capacity by the end of 1861 with more than one thousand employees.

Samuel Colt died January 10, 1862, at the age of forty-seven, having produced more than 400,000 weapons during his lifetime. His estate was reportedly worth $15 million, an enormous sum for the time.

The Colt revolver revolutionized weapon design and manufacturing techniques. Legendary as the gun that helped to tame the nation, it was praised by soldiers, ranchers, farmers, lawmen, outlaws, and cowboys as one of the finest guns ever made. The name Colt became synonymous with the revolver. To this day, Colt firearms are still linked to those rough-and-tumble years when our nation struggled to tame the wilds, settle our internal disputes, expand our national borders, defeat our enemies, and build a free nation. A popular post-Civil War slogan stated, "Abe Lincoln may have freed all men, but Sam Colt made them equal."

Brother Samuel Colt was a member of St. John Lodge in Harford, Connecticut.

TWENTY-SIX

The Empresario

"I make no more calculations except to spend my life here, rich or poor, here I expect to remain permanently."

The father's plan from the beginning was that one day his son would take over the family business and follow in his footsteps. The father began planning the boy's education and training very early in the boy's life. There were few details the father had not considered. When the boy was only four years old, his father, during a long voyage back home, wrote a thirty-eight page "Memorandum" for his son's later use. Though it was a memoir of his trip, it was not meant to be family memorabilia. Instead, the father intended for the document to have instructional benefits. It spoke volumes about his future expectations for his young son.

Years later, the eleven-year-old boy attended the Bacon Academy in New England, many miles from his father and the rest of his family in Missouri. The boy wrote to his family, but no reply came for months. The mail service between Connecticut and Missouri was unreliable. Then, finally, the homesick boy received a letter. He hoped for news from home about how his sister and younger brother were and whether or not his mother missed him. Instead, he found a letter from his father. The family news would have to wait. His father had more important issues to discuss and instructions to give.

His father wrote, "I hope and pray you will improve Every moment of time to the utmost advantage, and I shall have the satisfaction of seeing that my expectations are not Disappointed. Remember my Dear Son that the present is the moment to lay the foundation for your future greatness in life and that much money must be expended before your Education is finished and that time lost can never be recalled. Therefore be studious and attentive to obtain full information of all matters given to you to learn."

His father was already making plans for his son to succeed him as the patriarch of the family. He also wrote, "I hope to God I shall be spared until I see you arrive at an age to give protection to your Dear Mother, and Sister and little Brother Elijah Brown. Remember that to you they will look for protection should it so happen that my life should be shortened. Keep in minde that this may happen."

His father had additional advice about money and the kinds of friends the boy should make at the academy. "I do not expect you will expend money unwisely. Yet I do not wish you to render yourself Disagreeable to your young friends to avoid expending a few Dollars. When it appears necessary for you to form company pay readely your part of all expenses that may arise but Never lett yourself be imposed on by an improper Demand and if you finde a Disposition in any of your young friends to do such an Act, I charge you, have nothing more to Do with them, Keep not their Company and promptly tell them the Cause."

In the letter, there was no news of his family, other than his father's account of his own recent illness and a statement indicating that his mother and sister sent their blessings. Other family members surely wrote letters to the boy during the three years he spent at Bacon Academy. It is important to note, however, that the only letter he saved was the letter sent to him by his father. Obviously, he held his father's advice in high regard.

The boy would not disappoint his father. He became exactly what his father had wanted him to become. And he would carry out his father's last wish—a wish his father had wanted to complete himself.

In July, 1821, the twenty-seven-year-old with a party of fifteen men crossed the muddy waters of the Sabine River on horseback. To their backs lay Louisiana, the southwesternmost state in the United States of America, and before them lay the Spanish Empire. In his saddlebags was a document written in ornate Spanish, signed by the commandant general of the Eastern Interior Provinces. It gave the young man's father permission to settle three hundred American families in the Spanish Empire. But his father had died a month earlier, and the young man had inherited his father's dream and the document which made that dream possible. That document would play a central role in the young man's future and the future of the United States of America.

The young man was Stephen F. Austin, and the frontier province in which he had permission to settle was Texas. During the next fifteen years, Stephen Austin, the Empresario of Texas, would play a central role in settling Americans into Texas, in the events of the Texas Revolution, and in the establishment of the Lone Star Republic. Within a generation, because of events Austin helped to set in motion, the United States would achieve mastery over the part of the North American continent which is now the forty-eight states.

Stephen F. Austin was born on November 3, 1793, to Moses and Mary Brown Austin in the lead mining region of southwestern Virginia. When he was four years old, his family moved into the frontier west beyond the Mississippi River. His father bought a lead mining site called Mine á Breton in present-day Missouri forty miles west of the Mississippi River. When Stephen was ten years old, his family sent him to be educated at Bacon Academy in Connecticut. His father had originally planned for Stephen to attend Yale University after graduating from Bacon Academy, but due to problems with the family business and monetary concerns, Stephen attended Transylvania University in Lexington, Kentucky, instead. He graduated in 1810.

After graduation, Austin worked in the family's general store in Potosi, Missouri, and according to his father's plan, he took over the management of the family lead mining business. Austin was commissioned an ensign in the Missouri militia in May, 1813. Later, he enlisted as a private in the First Regiment of Mounted Militia commanded by Colonel Alexander McNair.

In 1818, Austin acquired a tract of land in Arkansas on the Red River called Long Prairie. After the family mining business failed in Missouri, Austin struck out on his own and moved to the Arkansas Territory in 1820. He earned a living in the mercantile business and in land speculation. While Austin was in Arkansas, the territorial governor, James Miller, appointed him as circuit judge of the first judicial district of the territory. He served as circuit judge before moving to New Orleans, Louisiana, later that same year. In Louisiana, he stayed with New Orleans lawyer and former Kentucky congressman Joseph H. Hawkins. Austin planned on studying law and becoming a lawyer.

After the failure of the family business, Moses Austin traveled to San Antonio where he gained a grant of land in the Spanish territory of Texas. It was Moses' intention to settle three hundred American Catholic families in Mexico as the grant allowed. At first, Stephen was reluctant to join his father's Texas venture, but due to pressure from his new friend, Joseph Hawkins, he decided to join his father in his quest to settle Texas.

When Moses Austin died on June 10, 1821, Stephen Austin was already aboard the steamer *Beaver* where he met with Spanish officials led by Erasmo Seguín. Stephen did not learn of his father's death until he was in Natchitoches, Louisiana, a month later. Stephen Austin wrote, "This news has effected [sic] me very much, he was one of the most feeling and affectionate Fathers that ever lived. His faults I now say, and always have, were not of the heart."

It was up to Stephen Austin to make his father's dream of settling Texas a reality. He took a party of men to San Antonio to reauthorize his father's grant. His party traveled the three hundred miles in three weeks, arriving in San Antonio August 12, 1821. After the grant was reauthorized by Governor Antonio María Martínez, Austin was allowed to explore the Gulf Coast between San Antonio and the Brazos River in order to find a suitable location for colonization.

In New Orleans, Austin began advertising the opportunity for free land for settlement with an exemption from taxes. The land was available along the Brazos and Colorado rivers. There was a great deal of interest in the offer. In December, 1821, the first colonists crossed into the new territory, by both land and sea, near present day Fort Bend County, Texas.

But Austin's plan for a colony was put on hold by the independence of Mexico from Spain that same year. The same governor who had reauthorized his father's land grant, Governor Martínez, later informed Austin that the *junta instituyente*, the new congress of Mexico, refused to recognize the land grant authorized by Spain. The Mexican congress created a new policy of using a general immigration law to regulate the settlement of Mexico, which included the province of Texas.

When Austin traveled to Mexico City, he was successful in persuading the *junta instituyente* to once again reauthorize the grant given to his father as well as the law signed by the Spanish emperor on January 3, 1823. The *junta* also provided for the employment of special agents, called empresarios, to promote settlement. Austin himself was made an empresario. He was to receive 67,000 acres of land for each two hundred families he settled into the Mexican province of Texas.

But the turmoil was not yet over for Austin. When the Emperor of Mexico, Agustín de Iturbide, abdicated in March,

★ THE EMPRESARIO ★

1823, the law was annulled once again. In April, 1823, Austin traveled to Mexico City for the second time and persuaded the congress to grant him a contract to bring three hundred families into Texas. In addition, in 1824, the congress passed a new immigration law and a constitution that allowed the individual states of Mexico to administer public lands and to open them to settlement under certain conditions. It was the law that when broken years later, caused so much conflict with the settlers of Texas, and led to the Texian rebellion.

Finally, however, the doorway to Texas was open for Austin. By late 1825, he had brought the first three hundred families to Texas—families now known in Texas history as the Old Three Hundred. Austin also obtained further contracts to settle an additional nine hundred families between 1825 and 1829. Austin established an effective civilian authority over the settlers and introduced a set of laws similar to American laws. The Constitution of Coahuila y Tejas was agreed on in November, 1827. Austin also organized a small, informal armed group to protect the colonists. This group would later evolve into the Texas Rangers.

But despite his successes, Austin was making little money himself for his efforts on the settlers' behalf. As empresario, he was allowed to charge the settlers 12½ cents per acre for his services. But because of conflicting Mexican laws, many of the colonists were unwilling to pay for Austin's services as empresario, seeing the fees as a tax that they were supposed to be exempt from according to their land grants. Most of the money that was made from the fees that were collected was spent on the processes of government and other public services.

By 1832, the colonists, now numbering over eleven thousand, were becoming less cooperative with Austin's cautious leadership. The Mexican government was also becoming less receptive to the continued growth in the colonies. Much of this concern was over the efforts of the United States government to buy the state.

The Mexican government began to introduce new tariff laws which led to several insurrections amongst the settlers, peaking in the Anahuac Disturbances. Seeing the possibility of rebellion, Austin felt compelled to involve himself in Mexican politics. He supported a new Mexican upstart in politics, Antonio López de Santa Anna. His support of Santa Anna, however, was misplaced. Following the success of Santa Anna, the colonists sought a compensatory reward for helping him to achieve his success, which they proclaimed at the Convention of 1832. The colonists' demands included the resumption of immigration, tariff exemptions, and a new independent state government for Texas. Austin, who did not favor the demands because he considered them ill-timed, tried to moderate them. When the demands of the colonists were repeated at the Convention of 1833, Austin traveled to Mexico City on July 18, 1833, to meet with Vice President Valentín Gomez Farías. Austin did gain certain important reforms—the immigration ban was lifted—but he did not gain a separate state government for Texas. Separate statehood required a population of eighty thousand before it could be granted, and Texas had only thirty thousand.

Austin returned, frustrated by the slow movement of the Mexican government. With the Mexican congress not scheduled to meet again until September, Austin wrote a letter urging Texas to unite to organize local governments independent of Mexico. On December 10, 1833, Austin was arrested and charged with insurrection for his letter. Austin was sent back to Mexico City and incarcerated in the Inquisition prison. For the next several months, he was held until the charges were dismissed, thanks to two Texas lawyers. After Austin was finally released, he returned to Texas with a different attitude toward Mexico and Santa Anna—he urged his people to prepare for revolution.

Santa Anna began sending forces into Texas with the intent of forcing the Texians, as Texans were called then, back into the United States. When the forces met with resistance,

★ THE EMPRESARIO ★

Santa Anna took charge of the forces personally. Following a string of victories, including the Alamo, he lost a major battle at San Jacinto on April 21, 1836. Santa Anna was captured by the forces led by Sam Houston. Texas became an independent republic, independent from both Mexico and the United States, and Sam Houston became the hero of Texas independence.

Austin was in New Orleans when he received word of Santa Anna's defeat by Sam Houston at San Jacinto. Returning to Texas, Austin announced his candidacy for president of Texas. He felt confident he could win the election. However, two weeks before the election, Sam Houston entered the Presidential race. Austin realized almost immediately that Sam Houston was the more popular candidate. Austin wrote, "Many of the old settlers who are too blind to see or understand their interest will vote for him." Houston swept the election to become the first President of the Republic of Texas.

On October 28, 1836, Houston appointed Austin as secretary of state. In December of 1836, Austin was in the new Texas capital city of Columbia when he caught a severe cold, which later worsened into pneumonia. Doctors could do little to help him. Austin's last words were "The independence of Texas is recognized! Don't you see it in the papers?" Austin died of pneumonia at noon on December 27, 1836.

Upon hearing of Austin's death, Houston proclaimed, "The Father of Texas is no more; the first pioneer of the wilderness has departed."

Each state in the Union is allowed two statues in the United States Capitol Building. Both of the statues from Texas date back to their independence from Mexico, years before they even gained admission into the Union. One statue is of Stephen Austin, and the other is of Sam Houston.

Brother Austin joined the Louisiana Lodge No. 109 in St. Genevieve, Missouri, in 1815. Louisiana Lodge No. 109 was the first Masonic lodge chartered west of the Mississippi River. He is often called the father of Texas Freemasonry. Austin sought to establish Freemasonry in the Mexican province of Texas in 1828. Freemasonry was well established among the educated classes of Mexican society, and there was a grand lodge in Mexico City.

On February 11, 1828, Austin called a meeting of Freemasons at San Felipe for the purpose of electing officers and petitioning the Masonic Grand Lodge in Mexico City for a charter to form a lodge in Texas. Austin was elected to be the Worshipful Master of the new lodge in Texas, but nothing more was heard of the petition after it was sent to Mexico City, and a charter was never granted. But by 1828, the ruling factions in Mexico were afraid that Texians might mount a rebellion to gain their independence. Fully aware of the philosophies of American Freemasonry—Santa Anna himself being a Mason—the Mexican government outlawed Freemasonry in Texas on October 25, 1828. Santa Anna was right. Texas did mount a rebellion. Whether that had anything to do with Texas Freemasonry is lost to history—although all three men who commanded the Alamo were Masons, as was the first President of the Independent Republic of Texas, Sam Houston.

TWENTY-SEVEN

The Old Scout

"Every Indian outbreak that I have ever known has resulted from broken promises and broken treaties by the government."

Within minutes of his death in Denver, Colorado, the news was being telegraphed from coast to coast and around the world. Western Union and the other telegraph services gave what was the biggest story of the day the highest possible status. "Clear the line" status meant that no other news was sent until news of his death was broadcast from coast to coast. The news of his departure even swept news of the war in Europe off the front pages of newspapers all over the United States. Within hours, telegraphs and messages from around the world flowed into his sister's home, where he had died. They came from the king of England, President Wilson, the kaiser of Germany, senators, governors, and friends from every corner of the globe.

Even before the funeral, a conflict arose between two states concerning where his remains were to be interred. It had long been known that his wish was to be buried on Cedar Mountain, Wyoming, "where the last rays of the sun touched the hills at night." But according to his widow, he had stated on his next to last day on earth that he wanted to be buried on Lookout Mountain near Golden, Colorado. "It's pretty up there . . . You can look down into four states," he had said. Many have come to doubt the story his widow told, but since the decision was ultimately up to her, he was buried on Lookout Mountain. That decision, which sparked a disagreement between two states, continues to be hotly contested ninety years later.

His funeral was an affair fit for a head of state. His body lay in state in the Colorado state capitol rotuda. An estimated twenty-five thousand people flowed between lines formed by Troopers from Fort Logan. Those giving their respects included the governors of Wyoming and Colorado, officers of the United States Army, members of fraternal organizations to which the deceased had belonged, delegations of legislators, veterans of the Grand Army of the Republic, and thousands of men, women, and children. Those that were closest to him were there as well, including a handful of old scouts and some Indians. The doors finally closed at noon even though there were still thousands waiting outside to pay respect to the great man.

The family then paid their respects to the great man, followed by a delegation of the Knights Templar from North Platte and a large group of old cowboys, saying to their friend, "Good-bye, old pard."

Five months later, he was buried. The burial once again proved to be a spectacular affair when nearly 25,000 people walked to the top of Lookout Mountain. Some 3,000 cars also made the journey. Since cars in that day were not designed for that kind of climb, the fact that they made it was a remarkable achievement in itself.

The funeral was described as having a circus atmosphere. It was claimed that six of the man's old sweethearts sat near the graveside. During the service, when the heat caused the inside of his glass-lidded coffin to fog up, one went over to the casket and held her parasol over his face to shelter him

★ THE OLD SCOUT ★

from the sun. "She stood there throughout the service, a fantastic superb figure. It was the gesture of a queen," wrote Gene Fowler of the *Post,* one of Denver's newspapers. Even though the casket was not scheduled to be reopened, his widow ordered it to be done. For two hours, mourners filed past two abreast for a final look at the old scout.

The ceremonies were conducted by Golden City Lodge No. 1 of the Ancient Free and Accepted Masons, acting on behalf of the North Platte Lodge to which the man belonged. The Masonic rites were given, and a lambskin Masonic apron was dropped into the open grave. "Taps" was sounded followed by a salute of eleven guns fired by Colorado's Battery B—the salute appropriate for a brigadier general.

The old scout was laid to rest in a grave which had been deeply carved into the solid granite of the mountain and then lined with cement. His coffin was encased in a steel vault to prevent those who wanted to take his body to Wyoming from stealing it. There were rumors of a bounty being put on the body by one of the Wyoming organizations to which the man had belonged.

A grand monument was planned. Even schoolchildren contributed, but they were limited to giving no more than a nickel each. The first contribution came the day after the funeral from schoolchildren at Maple Grove school—forty nickels. One grandiose plan included a 220-foot monument with an art museum. Another plan included a giant bronze sculpture of the man. But no monument was ever built. His grave is marked only by a tower of rough stones and a plaque.

The dearly departed man would likely have approved of all the hoopla that surrounded his death. He was, after all, one of America's greatest showmen and one of the most colorful figures in the Old West. He would have no doubt appreciated that the last show he was able to put on was one of his most memorable. The fact that schoolchildren had sent their nickels to build his monument probably would have pleased him as well. Children were among his greatest fans and their "buffalo nickels" were a great tribute to the man known the world over as—Buffalo Bill Cody.

William Frederick Cody was born in Scott County, Iowa, on February 26, 1846, to Isaac and Mary Cody. When Cody was seven, his older brother, Samuel, was killed when he fell off a horse. Because his death was such a shock to Mary Cody, the family decided to relocate. They staked a claim in Kansas and moved into a large log cabin.

But Kansas provided another difficulty for Isaac Cody, a staunch anti-slavery supporter. Believing Kansas should be a slavery free state, he spoke out frequently. During an anti-slavery speech at a local trading post, Isaac Cody so infuriated pro-slavery advocates that an angry mob formed. Isaac was stabbed twice in the chest. William was able to help drag his father to safety. Although his father survived the attack, he never fully recovered from the wounds he sustained. The anti-abolitionists began harassing the family on a regular basis, driving off their horses, threatening the family, and stealing their property. Isaac was instrumental in founding a new town called Grasshopper Falls, where both a sawmill and gristmill were built. In 1857, Isaac died of pneumonia and complications from his stab wounds. William Cody, at the age of eleven, was now the principal provider for his family of six.

It is very difficult to write a factual biography of William Cody because, as a larger-than-life showman, he and others embellished much of his life story. Even some of the events of his childhood are sometimes debated as being exaggerations or outright mistruths.

What is known for certain, however, is that Cody held a number of jobs in his life. One of the first was as a "boy extra" for a freight carrier. His job was to ride up and down the length of the wagon trains delivering messages. Later, he joined Johnson's Army as a scout assigned to guide the army to Utah, where there were false claims of a Mormon rebellion in Salt Lake City. When Cody was fourteen, he caught gold fever, but on his way to the gold fields, he met up with an agent of the

Pony Express who signed him up. After building several way stations and corrals for the Pony Express, he was given a job as a Pony Express rider. He kept that job until his mother fell ill, and he was called home.

After his mother recovered, Cody tried to enlist as a soldier, but he was denied because of his age. He began working with a freight caravan that supplied Fort Laramie. Shortly after his mother passed in 1863, he enlisted in the 7th Kansas Cavalry Regiment. He fought with them on the Union side for the duration of the Civil War.

While stationed in St. Louis, Cody met his future wife, Louisa Frederici. They were married after he was discharged from the army in 1866 and had four children. The marriage was an unhappy one. Cody's infidelities were numerous and legendary. He even attempted to divorce Louisa, but he was unsuccessful.

In 1868, Cody was employed once again as a scout by the United States Army. Part of the time, he scouted for Indians, and the rest of the time, he hunted buffalo for the army and for the Kansas Pacific railroad. He was an excellent shot, and his hunting skills were unmatched. He was able to feed both the army and the railroad workers.

That same year he earned his nickname—or rather he won it in a buffalo hunting contest. The nickname "Buffalo Bill" originally referred to Buffalo Bill Comstock, another famous scout and buffalo hunter, who was the favorite scout of George Armstrong Custer. The buffalo hunting contest was apparently conceived by the officers at Fort Hays, who backed their favorite, Bill Cody, and the officers at Fort Wallace, who backed Bill Comstock. The stakes were $500 per side with "the championship of the world" to be determined, according to posters advertising the event. Where the contest took place and if those posters were real—or forgeries made later—are two of the mysteries which surround just about every aspect of Bill Cody's life—mostly due to his own rewriting of his history.

What is not disputed is the outcome of the competition. When Cody and Comstock rode out into the massive buffalo herd, Cody's skill as a hunter was obvious. His strategy was to circle around to the front of the herd, shoot the lead bison, and then take down those that followed one at a time. He would then regroup the herd and repeat the pattern. He was much more successful than Comstock since he kept his herd tightly closed while Comstock, who hunted from behind the herds, scattered the animals over a distance of three miles. Cody won the contest 69-48 and the nickname "Buffalo Bill," which he used for the rest of his life.

After Buffalo Bill Cody left the army in 1873, he formed a touring company of performers called the *Buffalo Bill Combination*, which put on stage plays based loosely on his Western adventures. Cody was originally partnered with Texas Jack Omohundro. Later, he toured one season with Wild Bill Hickok.

But things were about to change. It was the age of great shows, such as vaudeville, and great showmen, such as P. T. Barnum. Buffalo Bill Cody expanded his show, which he renamed *Buffalo Bill's Wild West*. It was more like a circus show that toured annually with as many as twelve hundred performers. Hugely popular, it toured for twenty years. It had demonstrations and reenactments, the likes of which had never before been staged. It was as popular with parents as it was with children. In the age before television and movies, knowledge of the old Wild West was limited to what people might read in the dime-store novels of the time or in newspapers. *Buffalo Bill's Wild West* featured exhibitions of trick riding, racing, shooting, and roping—and, of course, the ever-popular reenactments of events like stage coach robberies and Indian attacks on wagon trains. The flamboyant, self-promoting Buffalo Bill became one of the most famous men in America—his show the most amazing thing most people at that time had ever seen.

★ THE OLD SCOUT ★

Buffalo Bill's Wild West was so celebrated in the United States that he decided to show it to the world. In 1887, he took it to Europe where he introduced Europeans to the rough-and-tumble world of the American Wild West. When he performed for Queen Victoria in London, she was particularly enamored with seeing the Cossacks perform.

But Buffalo Bill was not finished with the show yet. In 1893, he expanded the show again, renaming it *Buffalo Bill's Wild West and Congress of Rough Riders of the World*. His expanded show was even more spectacular than its predecessor. It included in its opening parade riders from all over the world, including Turks, Arabs, Mongols, Cossacks, and American Indians—all dressed in their colorful cultural attire and riding their native horses. Many famous Western characters performed in the show. Since the events of Custer's Last Stand at Little Bighorn were well known, imagine the reaction of the crowd when Sitting Bull himself, dressed in full regalia, and twenty of his braves on horseback thundered out onto the field in a cloud of dust, screaming war cries.

The performances included shooting exhibitions by Annie Oakley and her husband, Frank Butler. There were mock hunts with real buffalos and rodeo events like riding bucking broncos in the era before rodeos existed. The show changed every year, except for its ending which was usually a melodramatic reenactment of Custer's Last Stand with Buffalo Bill Cody portraying General Custer.

One of the best seasons *Buffalo Bill's Wild West and Congress of Rough Riders of the World* had was during the 1893 Chicago World's Fair. Buffalo Bill had requested that his show be a part of the fair, but his request was denied. He was not pleased with the decision. When he set up his popular show just west of the fairgrounds, he took many patrons away from the fair with two performances a day. Since he was not a part of the actual fair, he was not obligated to pay any royalties. Buffalo Bill entertained an average of 25,000 a day, seven days a week, and went home an extremely wealthy man.

★ GREAT AMERICAN FREEMASONS ★

Buffalo Bill toured with the show until 1915. It remained a great success through its entire run, but it was not only entertainment. Buffalo Bill intended for the show to be educational as well. For example, one celebrated part of the show was the villages set up to house the participants. Walking through these areas, customers could see that the Native Americans too had families and communities, and they could learn something about the native culture. The customers were also introduced to European and Arab cultures. On paydays, it was not uncommon for the show's participants to join the customers after the show to enjoy the rides and circus midway attractions.

Buffalo Bill had great respect for Native American Indians. He employed many of them in his shows. He was criticized at the time for how they were treated and portrayed in his shows. That criticism continues today. However, Buffalo Bill called the Native American Indians, "the former foe, present friend, the American." He knew the true culprit in the problems America had with its Native Americans was the government, which broke its promises and backed out of its treaties.

In the off-season, Buffalo Bill returned to his ranch, the Old Scout's Rest, in Cody, Wyoming—the town he founded. After his death, the people in that community in Wyoming believed they had the rights to the remains of Buffalo Bill. Although Colorado won the body, Cody, Wyoming, won the war. It is there that the spirit of Buffalo Bill seems to reside with its tacky museums and souvenir shops. Every year, thousands of tourists flock to the Old Scout's Rest, the place Buffalo Bill Cody called home.

Buffalo Bill has been treated by history as everything ranging from an elder statesmen to a showman to a flamboyant self-promoting charlatan. So much that is known about him was written by him that very little about the real man is undisputed. But there is no question that he left his footprint on American culture. He has an NFL team named for him. He has

★ THE OLD SCOUT ★

a town named for him. He has been portrayed more often in movies than any other real character in the American Wild West, including Wild Bill Hickok and Billy the Kid. Oddly enough, the first two times he was portrayed in a movie, he played himself— in 1898 and again in 1912. His persona has been portrayed dozens of times since in movies and on television by actors, such as Charlton Heston, Clayton Moore (The Lone Ranger), Brian Keith, William Fairbanks, Stephen Baldwin, Roy Rogers, Paul Newman, and Dennis Weaver, just to name a few. Buffalo Bill even met up with Ben Cartwright and his boys at the Ponderosa during the very successful Western series *Bonaza*.

History is starting to respect his legacy. Buffalo Bill received the Medal of Honor in 1872 as a civilian scout for "gallantry in action." Then, in 1917, less than a month after his death, the medal was revoked because he was a civilian and thus ineligible under the new guidelines for the award. However, the medal was restored to him seventy-two years later in 1989 by the United States Army.

Whoever Buffalo Bill was and whatever he might have been, it is unlikely there will ever be another like him.

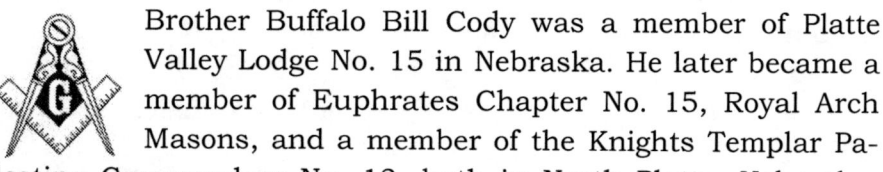

Brother Buffalo Bill Cody was a member of Platte Valley Lodge No. 15 in Nebraska. He later became a member of Euphrates Chapter No. 15, Royal Arch Masons, and a member of the Knights Templar Palestine Commandery No. 13, both in North Platte, Nebraska. He was also a Shriner at the Tangier Temple of the Ancient Arabic Order of the Nobles of the Mystic Shrine of Omaha, Nebraska.

TWENTY-EIGHT

The Aviator

"Is he alone who has courage on his right hand and faith on his left hand?"

The captain of the second boat in a small fishing fleet was up early, making coffee in the galley, when he heard the distant drone of an engine. He could not figure out what it could be so far out at sea, so he opened a porthole and looked out across the gray water of the northern Atlantic Ocean. Nothing was there, and he could no longer hear the sound.

But as he turned away from the porthole, he heard the drone again, this time sounding as if it were coming from above. Looking way up in the sky, he made out a tiny silver speck that got larger and louder, quickly changing from a tiny speck to a small aircraft as it plunged towards the water. The captain was certain the tiny plane was doomed. Then, at just over fifty feet above the ocean, it broke out of the dive and flew over the first ship, tilting its wing at just the right moment to avoid the mast as it passed over the deck. The pilot of the plane leaned out the cockpit window, looking for any signs of life on the ship below him. Seeing none, he turned the plane towards the second ship. The pilot did not see the captain of the ship peering at him from the porthole until he was just about over the ship. Perplexed, the captain watched as the silver-nosed plane banked and circled around for another pass.

This time, the pilot knew the captain was there. As the pilot approached the ship a second time, he banked his wing, casting the plane's shadow over the ship. Cutting back on the throttle, and gliding nearly silently, the pilot put the two men within fifty feet of one another. Of course, the captain had no way of knowing that the pilot had done this many times when he had found himself lost on mail runs in the Midwestern part of the United States.

"Which way to Ireland?" the pilot shouted out the window.

The unmoving captain stared in disbelief as the plane passed the porthole. Looking disappointed, the pilot revved up his throttle again and banked the tiny plane eastwards—towards what he hoped was Europe. The fishing captain watched the plane with the words "Spirit of St. Louis" painted on its nose until it disappeared.

At that moment, the fishing captain was one of only two men on Earth who knew the soon-to-be celebrated pilot and navigator was lost off the coast of Ireland and needing directions during the twenty-seventh hour of a long journey. The captain could not have known that in just over six hours, the pilot of that plane would be the most famous man in the world—the first to complete a non-stop transcontinental flight between New York and Paris.

The pilot was, of course, Midwestern barnstormer, airmail carrier, and daredevil pilot, Charles Augustus Lindbergh.

Charles A. Lindbergh was born in Detroit, Michigan, on February 4, 1904. His father, Charles Augustus Lindbergh, was a Swedish immigrant who practiced law. Later, as a United States congressman, he vehemently opposed America's entry into World War I. His mother, Evangeline Lodge Land Lindbergh, was of English, French, and Irish decent. She was a school teacher.

From a young age, Charles Lindbergh was interested in motors and machinery. His first interest was motorcycles. He had a Excelsior motorbike when he was young. As he got older, his interest switched to airplanes. He enrolled in a mechanical engineering program at the University of Wisconsin in Madison, but he quit in 1922, opting instead for a pilot and mechanics training program at Nebraska Aircraft.

Shortly after he bought his first airplane, a World War I surplus Curtiss JN-4 known as a "Jenny," the "Daredevil Lindbergh" began making appearances as a barnstormer. He trained as a pilot to qualify with the Army Air Service and later served as a mechanic at Logan International Airport in Billings, Montana. But he wanted to fly.

Later, after finishing a pilot training class, he took a job carrying airmail as chief air pilot. He flew routes out of Lambert Field in St. Louis, Missouri, carrying mail between Chicago, Springfield, and St. Louis. In his DH-4 biplane, he became renowned for sticking to the old post office creed "through rain, hail, sleet, snow. . . ." He delivered mail under any circumstance, including the most dangerous weather. Once, he even crashed his plane during a mail run. He parachuted to safety, escaping with just cuts and bruises. After finding a farmhouse and enlisting the help of the farmer, he managed to locate the downed plane in a cornfield where it had slid over eighty yards, barely missing a second farmhouse before coming to a stop. After retrieving the mailbags from the aircraft, he phoned the airport manager in Peoria to ask him to send a truck for the mail.

In 1919, New York restaurateur and hotel owner Raymond Ortieg had established the Ortieg Prize of $25,000 for the first non-stop flight between New York City and Paris, France. A successful flight either from Paris to New York or from New York to Paris would qualify. The prize generated a sensation worldwide and there were a number of takers. The trip, howev-

★ THE AVIATOR ★

er, would prove to be a deadly gamble. Eight years later, in 1927, French war hero Captain Charles Nungesser and his navigator Raymond Coli made the first attempt, taking off from Paris. Their last radio contact was made when they crossed the coast of Ireland. More deaths were to follow. Noel Davis and Stanton H. Wooster were killed when their New York to Paris entry crashed. Charles N. Clavier and Jacob Islaroff were burned to death at Roosevelt Field when Rene Fonck's Sikorsky aircraft, overloaded with fuel, crashed and burned at take off. There were also other notables in the race to be the first, including World War I flying ace Rene Fonck, Clarence Chamberlin, and Admiral Richard E. Byrd. All were unsuccessful.

Lindbergh was ready to make his attempt on May 20, 1927, from Roosevelt Field in Garden City, New York. He had selected a Ryan aircraft, loosely based on the M2 design. Because it was a modified version of an existing aircraft, the design time was greatly reduced. The wing span had to be increased by ten feet to lift the 445 gallons of fuel needed for the 3,600 mile journey, and the tanks had to be relocated to balance the plane. One critical change Lindbergh and the designers made was to load the largest tank in front of the pilot, thus eliminating the front windshield. There was no visibility forward of the cockpit, so a special periscope was mounted to provide the pilot with the ability to see ahead. It is uncertain, however, if Lindbergh actually used the periscope during the flight. Placing the tank in this position not only provided a better center of gravity for the aircraft but also put the pilot in a safer position in the event of a fiery crash. The plane was powered by a 223-horsepower air-cooled Wright Whirlwind engine. It was outfitted with a special mechanism that would keep it clean during the expected forty-hour flight between New York and Paris.

Weight was the biggest problem. Nothing nonessential was put in the aircraft, including a radio. Lindbergh's cockpit was so small because of the fuel tanks that he could not stretch out. He even had a special wicker seat made to reduce any added weight. Every ounce of weight they could eliminate was additional fuel that could be added to the tanks for the long flight. There were also fuel tanks in the wings and aft, requiring Lindbergh to switch the tanks periodically to keep the aircraft balanced.

The Spirit of St. Louis was still an unstable aircraft, prone to sudden dips and dives, but Lindbergh was a superior pilot. He felt that because of the length of the flight and the need for him to stay alert, it might actually be a good thing to be uncomfortable and to have to constantly struggle with the aircraft to keep it aloft.

The gamble paid off. Charles Lindbergh, exhausted and dazed, landed in Paris, France, thirty-three and a half hours after he took off from Roosevelt Field, New York. He was met by thousands of admirers. Honors were lavished upon him. The President of France awarded him the French Legion of Honor. He was escorted back to Washington, D.C., by a fleet of warships and aircraft. President Calvin Coolidge awarded him the Distinguished Flying Cross, and he was celebrated with a ticker tape parade down Fifth Avenue in New York. Later, he would receive the Congressional Medal of Honor.

Lindbergh became an important voice in aviation activities. His work included serving on the central committee of the National Advisory Committee for Aeronautics. But his politics were often called into question. He had traveled to Germany at the behest of the U.S. military to report on German aviation and the *Luftwaffe*. Lindbergh was impressed with the advances the Germans had made in new aviation developments. In 1938, he was invited to dinner at the U.S. Embassy in Berlin by the American ambassador to Germany. He dined with Hermann Göring, Ernst Heinkel, Adolf Baeumaker, and Dr. Willy Messerschmitt. He was presented with the Service Cross of the German Eagle by Göring. Not much was made of the award at the time, but later, when Lindbergh became a staunch isolationist and vocally objected to America's involvement in World

War II, he was criticized as being a Nazi sympathizer. There was a large outcry from American citizens that Lindbergh should return the honor, but Lindbergh refused, saying that returning the Service Cross would be an "unnecessary insult" to the German Nazi government.

Many allegations have been made about Lindbergh's politics of isolationism and his beliefs, but he spoke out against Germany's treatment of the Jews, supported a strong defense, and believed America should work to be alert and strong against attack. Many now credit Lindbergh for persuading the American public to also be isolationist. As a result, America delayed entering the war until Pearl Harbor was attacked in 1941. By that time, Stalin's military had been devastated which may have prevented war with Russia after the Germans were defeated. Lindbergh was right about a lot of things. For example, he had warned long before Pearl Harbor that America's weak policies in the Philippines would cause bloodshed there. He believed that the military should either fortify the islands of the Pacific adequately or pull out completely. He also predicted the "Iron Curtain" that would descend upon Europe.

In the 1960s, Lindbergh, as an older man, became concerned that the technological world and the natural world were becoming unbalanced. He became an advocate for environmental causes and the preservation of endangered species. He became instrumental in helping to protect the primitive Filipino group, the Tasaday. And in Africa, he assisted in protecting African tribes endangered by the encroachment of modern civilization and pushed for the establishment of a national park. His later writings still showed a love of technology, but they also showed a love of nature, stressing that "the human future depends on our ability to combine the knowledge of science with the wisdom of wildness."

Lindbergh's flight was perhaps the greatest accomplishment of his time. Very few accomplishments have lead to such a tremendous boon to industry and exploration. The flight proved without question that transcontinental flight was possible. It created a flurry of discovery and advances in aviation design, which made reliable air transportation between continents possible.

But it seems that when Lindbergh saw some of the things his accomplishment had created, his opinions began to change about his great love of flying. He made several remarks that indicated he was disappointed in what his beloved airplane had become. He said, "I have seen the science I worshiped, and the aircraft I loved, destroying the civilization I expected them to serve." The airplane had become not only a form of transportation linking all parts of the globe but also a great weapon of war. It was as if Lindbergh began to believe he had released a genie from the bottle, and it had gone from being an exciting new discovery to being a destroyer. He came to understand that because the airplane was able to go anywhere, taking civilization with it, the destruction of cultures and of the environment was a direct result.

Charles Lindbergh died on the Hawaiian island of Maui on August 26, 1974.

Brother Charles Lindbergh became a Master Mason at Keystone Lodge No. 243 in St. Louis, Missouri on December 15, 1926. He is also a member of St. Louis No. 33 of the National Sojourners. When he took his history-making flight, it is said that Brother Lindbergh wore a Masonic square and compass patch on his flight jacket.

CONCLUSION

As these men I have profiled in the book show, Masonry has always attracted capable and industrious people. Builders, doers, pioneers, and freethinkers tend to migrate towards Masonry for several reasons: to socialize with respectable men with similar ideals and values, to improve themselves, or to become involved in something worthwhile—or all of the above. Because Masonry builds from the strength of what the members share in common, together they have supported important causes, built grand buildings, made many good men better, and helped to forge the communities that make this nation so strong.

There are currently over two million Masons in the United States. Freemasonry in the United States spends approximately two million dollars per day on philanthropic causes. This amount is unparalleled by any other fraternal or social organization in existence. Some of the philanthropic enterprises are well know, but others take place at the community level. The vast majority of Masonic charities are children's charities since Masons believe that strong communities start with strong children.

Many people do not realize that Shriners are actually Masons as well. For more than eighty years, the well-known Shriners Hospitals have been treating children for severe burns, spinal cord rehabilitation, cleft palate, and orthopedic conditions—all free of charge.

Another noble philanthropic effort is the building of fifty-nine 32° Masonic Children's Learning Centers in fifteen states for dyslexic children, operated by the Scottish Rite of Freemasonry. More centers are planned. The 32° Masonic Children's Learning Centers have been actively engaged in helping thousands of children overcome dyslexia. These children receive free one-on-one reading and written language tutoring. Hundreds of school teachers and other individuals interested in becoming certified tutors have received training at no cost. Additionally, the Children's Learning Centers continue to support clinical research programs that focus on dyslexia.

There are many more charities supported by Masons, including local programs which vary from community to community. These local efforts often involve scouting, after-school programs, blood drives, community beautification, child-identification programs, sports, art and music programs, and student scholarships.

As based in tradition and rich in history as Freemasonry is, it probably is not surprising that Masons enthusiastically support efforts to preserve American heritage and history. The Museum of Our National Heritage in Lexington, Massachusetts, is an American history museum founded and supported by 32° Scottish Rite Freemasons. It was given as a gift by Freemasons to the people of the United States. The museum is open seven days a week. Admission is free. In addition to remarkable exhibits, there are lectures, workshops, family programs, concerts, and films presented throughout the year.

The George Washington National Masonic Memorial in Alexandria, Virginia, is another example of Masonry's efforts to preserve America's past. The memorial is the only Masonic building supported and maintained by all fifty-two Grand Lodges of the United States. The building houses the collection of the Alexandria Lodge, which includes the fraternal artifacts of George Washington—his Masonic apron, sash, past master portrait, and working tools as well as the trowel he used to lay the cornerstone at the United States Capitol building. The memorial is visited by more than fifty thousand guests every year.

★ CONCLUSION ★

But Masonry is not an organization solely composed of famous and illustrious men. Even though Masonry celebrates the accomplishments of many famous Masons, for every famous Mason, there are thousands of the more ordinary sort that the fraternity values even more—teachers, accountants, farmers, cashiers, bartenders, attorneys, musicians, and mechanics. These common men share the same ideals and principles as their more recognizable counterparts, and part of that ideal includes building men, building communities, and building institutions for the benefit of mankind.

It is not difficult to see what Freemasonry is today, but my first interest was in its origins. Some years ago—even before I became a Mason—I decided to find out what Freemasonry was, who those early Freemasons were, and where they originally had come from.

I had never studied a subject so easily researched. Hundreds of books about the subject are in print; libraries and bookstores are full of books about the "secret society." Early on, I filled most of a bookshelf with books about Freemasonry.

My first thought, as I began my research, was that for a "secret society," Masons sure have not been very successful at the "secret" part since the "secrets" have been out for several centuries. In fact, books about these Masonic secrets were in print shortly after the Grand Lodge of England formed in 1717.

The big question I had was when had the organization formed. It seemed to me to be a fairly simple question that should have had a fairly simple answer. In fact, I actually expected to find a date and a location as well. It seemed reasonable—we know when most things in history began and ended. We know when the dinosaurs lived and when they died. We know when the Bronze Age began. We know when Rome fell. We know what almost every general on both sides of the Civil War had for breakfast the morning of the last day at the Battle of Gettysburg. Going back three thousand years, archeologist even know when most of the pharaohs in Egypt were born and when they died, what they ate, how they lived, and what they accomplished during their lives.

But about the beginning of Freemasonry, there is no official text. There does not seem to be any clear consensus about where the organization actually came from nor when it was founded.

There is, however, agreement that originally Masonry was a guild of craftsmen—it was the world's first labor union. The question is when and how the builders' guild became something more. The original stonemasons, depending on which version is read, may have built the pyramids and the great temples, such as King Solomon's Temple in Jerusalem, along with the via-ducts, great roads, and castles of antiquity. As an operative mason entered the building guild, he was trained in the secrets of how to construct these monumental structures by a master craftsman. The Masons guarded their skills in mathematics and craftsmanship in secrecy. As a young stonemason learned the trade and honed his basic skills, he advanced through his apprenticeship, moving from one level of skills to the next in much the same way as apprentice plumbers and electricians are trained today. The operative masons were ranked from apprentice to master craftsman.

It was important that these building secrets were kept within the organization since the last thing the builders' guild wanted was for their employers to learn how they plied their craft—how they moved the stones, fitted the stones with such precision, and built strong arches and flying buttresses. If these mathematical and craftsmanship secrets were learned by the employers, they could build their own structures, and the stonemasons would be out of a job. To protect themselves and their craft, the stonemasons developed secret words and signs to identify other members of the craft as they traveled throughout Europe to different job sites. That way, the keys to their craft would remain with the craftsmen alone. Because they were so skilled and kept their secrets so well, the builders were in high demand throughout Europe.

★ CONCLUSION ★

Many of the craftsmen's secrets are still unknown, despite the work of modern archaeologists. Much of what they have learned is based on speculation rather than solid evidence as they try to understand how it was that ancient craftsmen built such amazing structures—many of which are still standing.

How the craftsmen built these amazing structures was never recorded—at least not in any records that have been discovered. We have put a man on the moon, but we still do not know how the giant obelisks still standing in Egypt were raised. We have built amazing structures in our own time, such as the Empire State Building and the Sears Tower, but it is still a mystery exactly how the great pyramids on the Giza Strip were constructed. We mastered flight, but it is still unknown how the ancient Romans managed to invent a rudimentary but very strong concrete—only to forget that skill for hundreds of years until mankind "rediscovered" the secret in more modern times. There is evidence all around us that our ancestors had some very impressive skills that we modern men still do not completely understand.

At some point in history, operative masons, a group with highly effective systems of maintaining important secrets, began admitting "speculative Masons." These new Masons were not stonemasons and did not ply their trade in building; but they were men who perhaps had secrets of their own worth hiding.

One theory is that it was in the Dark Ages when speculative Masons began to join the existing builders' guild. At the time, science, astronomy, philosophy, and mathematics were considered heresies because they sometimes disagreed with church doctrine and the teachings of the Holy Bible. Those discovered studying heretical subjects were often put to death. But there were those in the Dark Ages who continued to study these subjects, regardless of the risks. Scientists, astronomers, mathematicians, and philosophers were beginning to understand some of the basic laws of science and nature. These freethinkers may have hidden their activities from the church through the stonemasons' guild. According to this theory, Freemasonry became a secret society to help hide the emerging understanding of forbidden knowledge. It protected early thinkers from persecution by the church.

Another theory is that speculative Masons joined the organization to avoid their own destruction. Some theorists have tried to link Freemasonry and its many branches to the Knights Templar—a monastic order of monks charged with protecting pilgrims to the Holy Land after the crusades. The theory is that some of the remaining French Knights Templars fled to Scotland after the suppression of the Order by Pope Clements V. To avoid persecution by the church, they sought refuge in local Scottish stonemason's guilds, where they began to teach the virtues of chivalry and obedience, using the tools of stonemasons as metaphoric symbols for the principles they taught. Eventually, they began taking in other speculative masons in order to ensure the continuation of the Order of the Knights Templar and the principles they stood for. The Order of Knights Templar existed secretly in this form until the formation of the United Grand Lodge of England in 1717. Some evidence does exist to support this theory of a Knights Templar-Freemasonry connection. Both Templar and Masonic symbolism can be found carved in the Rosslyn Chapel in Scotland, which dates back to about one hundred years after the suppression of the Order of the Knights Templar. The chapel was owned by the first Earls of Rosslyn, the Sinclair family—a family with strong ties to Scottish Freemasonry.

What cannot be refuted is that Masonry is no longer a secret society. After the Grand Lodge of England was formed in 1717 and announced its existence to the world, the secret was out. Why the Masons decided to let their existence be known in 1717 is not fully understood. One prevailing theory is that since the world had changed, their reasons for maintaining a secret society were no longer valid. The world of 1717 was becoming "enlightened." New ideas and new theories were no

★ CONCLUSION ★

longer considered heresies. A great age of discovery was beginning, and Freemasonry, while still shrouded in secrecy, may have had a hand in bringing about that change in the world.

History may never reveal how Masonry began, what its original purpose was, or when it was founded. What we do know is that Masonry has cultivated some remarkable men during its long history. We also know that the history of Freemasonry is forever entwined with the beginnings of our nation. We may never know to what extent Freemasonry played a role in the founding of our country, but there is no question that some of its members played a critical part and continue to play important roles today.

It is important to know our history, not only to honor those who created it but also to become better Americans and citizens. We sometimes forget that we stand on the shoulders of giants. This country did not just happen. It evolved. America grew because of men who were willing to overcome tremendous odds, men who were willing to work hard, men who believed in American principles, and men who knew that in America anything is possible. Our challenges today are nothing more than ones we have already faced in our past. British Freemason Winston Churchill once said, "The farther backward you can look, the further forward you can see."

We are unique on the world stage. Every person in this book made an impact—whether in a big way or in a small way—that forever changed who we are as a country and how we see ourselves. Some were patriots who made our country free. Some were the military men who originally fought for our freedom against overwhelming odds and who have continued the fight for our freedoms generation after generation. Some were the Presidents in whom we placed our hopes—men who led us through dark and dangerous times and who shaped our nation through their vision of what America could be . . . and what American should be. Some were entertainers who helped to define our uniquely American culture through music, literature, and the performing arts. And some were larger-than-life figures who stirred our imagination about what is truly possible in the most powerful nation on earth. All of these men had one thing in common—they were all Freemasons, but, more importantly, they were all a part of the amazing story of America.

Selected Bibliography

Ammon, Harry. *James Monroe: The Quest for National Identity.* 1971. McGraw-Hill Book Company, New York, New York.

Bennett, William J. *America: The Last Best Hope (Volume I): From the Age of Discovery to a World at War.* 2006. Thomas Nelson, Inc., Nashville, Tennessee.

Bennett, William J. *America: The Last Best Hope (Volume II): From the World at War to the Triumph of Freedom* 2007. Thomas Nelson, Inc., Nashville, Tennessee.

Berg, A. Scott. *Lindbergh.* 1998. G.P. Putnum's Sons. New York, New York.

Bierley, Paul E. *John Philip Sousa: American Phenomenon.* 1973. Prentice-Hall, Inc. Englewood Cliffs, New Jersey.

Black, Conrad. *Franklin Delano Roosevelt: Champion of Freedom.* 2003. PublicAffairs a member of the Perseus Books Group, New York, New York.

Brands, H.W. *Andrew Jackson: His Life and Times*, 2005, Doubleday, New York.

Brands, H.W. *The First American: The Life and Times of Benjamin Franklin.* 2000. Doubleday a division of Random House, Inc., New York, New York.

Brinkley, Douglas. *Gerald R. Ford.* 2007. Times Books. Henry Holt and Company, New York, New York.

Buckman, Peter. *Lafayette: A Biography.* 1977. Paddington Press Ltd., New York & London.

Bullock, Steven C. *Revolutionary Brotherhood: Freemasonry and the Transformation of the American Social Order,*

1730-1840. 1998. University of North Carolina Press, Chapel Hill, North Carolina.

Burnstein, Andrew. *The Passions of Andrew Jackson.* 2006. Alfred A. Knopf, a division of Random House, Inc., New York, New York.

Campbell, Randolph B. *Gone to Texas: A History of the Lone Star State.* 2003. Oxford University Press, New York, New York.

Cantrell, Gregg. *Stephen F. Austin: Empresario of Texas.* 1999. R. R. Donnelley & Sons Company, Harrisonburg, Virginia

Carter, Robert A. *Buffalo Bill Cody: The Man Behind the Legend.* 2000. John Wiley & Sons, Inc. New York, Chichester, Weinheim, Brisbane, Singapore, Toronto.

Curtis, James. *W. C. Fields: A Biography.* 2003. Alfred A. Knopf, a division of Random House, Inc., New York, New York.

Davis, Ronald L., *Duke: The Life and Image of John Wayne.* 1998. University of Oklahoma Press, Norman, Oklahoma.

Davis, William C. *The Roads to the Alamo.* 1998. HarperCollins Publishers, New York, New York.

Day, Donald. *Roy Rogers: A Biography.* 1962. Davide McKay Company, Inc. New York, New York.

Dedopulos, Tim. *The Brotherhood: Inside the Secret World of the Freemasons.* 2006. Thunder's Mouth Press, New York, New York.

Denslow, William R.and Truman, Harry S. *10,000 Famous Freemasons.* 1957. Kessinger Publishing, LLC, Whitefish, Montana.

Donnelly, Matt. *Theodore Roosevelt: Larger Than Life.* 2003. Linnet Books, North Haven, Connecticut.

Doolittle, James and Glines, Caroll V. *I Could Never Be So Lucky Again.* 1991. Bantam Books, a division of Random House, Inc. New York, New York.

★ SELECTED BIBLIOGRAPHY ★

Duncan, Dayton, and Burns, Ken. *Lewis & Clark: The Journey of the Corps of Discovery.* 1997. Alfred A. Knopf, Inc., New York, New York.

Edge, Laura Bufano. *William McKinley.* 2007. Twenty-First Century Books, a division of Lerner Publishing Group, Minneapolis, Minnesota.

Ellis, Joseph J. *American Creation: Triumphs and Tragedies at the Founding of the Republic.* 2007. Alfred A. Knopf, a division of Random House, Inc., New York, New York.

Ellis, Joseph J. *His Excellency.* 2004, Random House, Inc. New York, New York.

Ferling, John. *Almost a Miracle: The American Victory in the War of Independence.* 2007. Oxford University Press, New York, New York.

Fields, Ronald J. *W. C. Fields: By Himself.* 1973. Prentice-Hall, Inc., Englewood Cliffs, New Jersey.

Fischer, David Hackett. *Paul Revere's Ride.* 1994. Oxford University Press, New York, New York.

Flexner, James Thomas. *The Indispensable Man,* 1969, 1973, 1974, Little, Brown and Company, Boston, Massachusetts.

Foote, Shelby. *The Civil War: A Narrative.* 1958. Published by Random House, Inc., New York, New York.

Forbes, Ester. *Paul Revere & The World He Lived In.* 1942. Printed by Houghton Mifflin Company, Boston, Massachusetts for The Riverside Press, Cambridge, Massachusetts.

Ford, Gerald R. *A Time To Heal: The Autobiography of Gerald R. Ford.* 1979. Harper & Row Publishers, Inc. New York, New York.

Foreman, Jonathan. *The Pocket Book of Patriotism.* 2005. Sterling Publishing Co. Inc., New York, New York.

Franklin, Benjamin edited by Rogers, George L. *Benjamin Franklin's the Art of Virtue: His Formula for Successful Living.* 1996. Acorn Publishing, Eden Prairie, Minnesota.

Gerson, Noel B. *Statue In Search of a Pedestal: A Biography of the Marquis De Lafayette.* 1976. Dodd, Mead & Company, New York, New York.

Gies, Joseph. *Harry S. Truman: A Pictorial Biography.* 1968. Doubleday & Company, Inc. Garden City, New York.

Glines, Carroll V. *The Doolittle Raid:America's Daring First Strike Against Japan.* 1988. Orion Books a division of Crown Publishers, Inc., New York, New York.

Goldman, Herbert G. *Jolson: The Legend Comes to Life.* 1988. Oxford University Press, New York, New York.

Gordon, Lesley J. *General George E. Pickett in Life and Legend.* 1998. University of North Carolina Press, Chapel Hill, North Carolina.

Graham, Don. *No Name on the Bullet: A Biography of Audie Murphy.* 1989. Viking Penguin, a division of Penguin books USA, Inc., New York, New York.

Grudens, Richard. *When Jolson Was King.* 2006. Celebrity Profiles Publishing Company Div. Edison & Kellogg, Stonybrook, New York.

Hodapp, Christopher. *Freemasons for Dummies.* 2005. Wiley Publishing, Inc., Indianapolis, Indiana.

Jeffers, H. Paul. *The Freemasons in America: Inside the Secret Society.* 2006. Citadel Publishing Company. Kensington Publishing Corp., New York, New York.

Jenkins, Roy. *Franklin Delano Roosevelt.* 2003. Times Books. Henry Holt and Company, LLC. New York, New York.

Keating, Bern. *The Flamboyant Mr. Colt and His Deadly Six Shooter.* 1978. Doubleday & Company, Inc., Garden City, New York.

Ketchum, Richard M. *Will Rogers: His Life and Times.* 1973. American Heritage Publishing Co., Inc. a subsidiary of McGraw-Hill. New York, New York.

Lavendar, David. *The Way to the Western Sea.* 1988. Harper & Row, New York, New York.

★ SELECTED BIBLIOGRAPHY ★

Levy, Debbie. *James Monroe.* 2005. Lerner Publications Company, Minneapolis, Minnesota.

Lindbergh, Charles A. *The Spirit of St. Louis.* 1953. Scribner Classics, New York, New York.

Lomas, Robert. *Freemasonry and the Birth of Modern Science.* 2004. Fair Winds Press, Gloucester, Massachusetts.

Longacre, Edward G. *Pickett: Leader of the Charge.* 1995. White Mane Publishing Company, Inc., Shippensburg, Pennsylvania.

MacNulty, W. Kirk. *Freemasonry: Symbols, Secrets, Significance.* 2006. Thames & Hudson, Inc., New York, New York.

McCullough, David. *Truman.* 1992. Simon & Schuster, Inc., New York, New York.

McDowell, R. Bruce. *A Study of Colt Conversions and Other Percussion Revolvers.* 1997. Krause Publications, Iola, Wisconsin.

Millar, Angel. *Freemasonry: A History.* 2005. Thunder Bay Press, London, United Kingdom.

Monroe, James. *The Writings of James Monroe.* Originally published 1899 by G. P. Putnam's Sons, New York, New York.

Morgan, Edmund S. *Benjamin Franklin.* 2002. R.R. Printed in U.S.A. by Donnelley & Sons, Inc. for Yale University Press, New Haven and London.

Morison, Samuel Eliot. *John Paul Jones: A Sailor's Biography.* 1959. Northeastern University Press, Boston, Massachusetts.

Morris, Edmund. *Theodore Rex.* 2001. The Modern Library, New York, New York.

Morris, Ph.D., 33rd Degree, S. Brent. *The Complete Idiot's Guide to Freemasonry.* 2006. Alpha Books. Published by Penguin Group, Inc., New York, New York.

Mosley, Leonard, *Lindbergh: A Biography.* 1976. Doubleday and Co., Inc., New York, New York.

Murphy, Audie. *To Hell and Back.* 1949. Henry Holt and Company, LLC, New York, New York.

Phillips, Kevin. *William McKinley.* 2003. Times Books. Henry Hold and Company, New York, New York.

Pike, Albert. *Morals and Dogma of the Ancient and Accepted Scottish Rite of Freemasonry.* Reprinted 2004 for the Supreme Council of Thirty-Third Degree for the Southern Jurisdiction of the United States. NuVision Publications, Inc.

Powers, Ron. *Mark Twain: A Life.* 2005. Simon & Schuster, Inc., New York, New York.

Prescott, Lawrence F. *Living Issues of the Campaign of 1900: Its Men and Principles.* 1899. Rochester Book Concern, Rochester, Indiana.

Remini, Robert V. *The Life of Andrew Jackson.* 1977. HarperCollins Publishers, New York, New York.

Ridley, Jasper. *The Freemasons: A History of the World's Most Powerful Secret Society.* 2001. Arcade Publishing, New York, New York.

Schmidt, Thomas and Schmidt, Jeremy. *The Saga of Lewis & Clark.* 1999. DK Publishing, Inc., New York, New York.

Schweikart, Larry and Allen, Michael. *A Patriot's History of the United States: From Columbus's Great Discovery to the War on Terror.* 2004. Published by the Penguin Group, New York, New York.

Shaara, Michael. *The Killer Angels.* 1974. David McKay Company, Inc., a division of Random House, Inc., New York, New York.

Sousa, John Philip. *Marching Along.* 1928. Hale, Cushman & Flint, Boston, Massachusetts.

Thomas, Evan. *John Paul Jones: Sailor, Hero, Father of the American Navy.* 2003. Simon & Schuster, Inc. New York, New York.

Thompson, Frank. *The Alamo: A Cultural History.* 2001. Taylor Trade Publishing, Dallas, Texas.

★ SELECTED BIBLIOGRAPHY ★

Tucker, Glenn. *Hancock The Superb.* 1960. The Bobbs-Merrill Company, Inc., a subsidiary of Howard W. Sams & Co., Inc., Indianapolis, Indiana.

Twain, Mark. *The Autobiography of Mark Twain.* 1917, 1940, 1958, 1959 by The Mark Twain Company. Copyright 1924, 1945, 1952 by Clara Clements Samossoud. Copyright 1959 by Charles Neider. Harper & Row, New York, New York.

Warden III, Herbert W. *American Courage.* 2005. HarperCollins Publishers Inc., New York, New York.

Warren, Louis S. *Buffalo Bill's America: William Cody and the Wild West Show.* 2005. Alfred A. Knopf Publishing. New York, New York.

Wills, Garry. *John Wayne's America: The Politics of Celebrity.* 1997. Simon & Schuster, New York, New York.

Zall, P.M. *Mark Twain: Laughing.* 1985. The University of Tennessee Press, Knoxville, Tennessee.

About the Author

Todd E. Creason is the father of two daughters, and lives with his wife, Valerie, near the family farm where he grew up. He works as a business manager at the University of Illinois. He is an active member of his local Masonic lodge, and also enjoys reading and music. *Famous American Freemasons* is his first book.

Visit the Author Online!

For current news, reviews, and information on future books visit Todd E. Creason at

www.toddcreason.org